Praise for *Downshifting*

'Genuinely inspiring . . . Every home should have a copy'
Christina Hardyment, *Independent*

'An entertaining, evangelising read' Paul Heiney, *The Times*

'Full of sound advice about the things you should
consider before you make the leap'
Maureen Freely, *Guardian*

'The Downshifter's Bible . . .' *She*

Downshifting

The Guide to Happier, Simpler Living

POLLY GHAZI
AND JUDY JONES

HODDER
MOBIUS

Hodder & Stoughton

Typeset in Minion by Palimpsest Book Production Limited,
Polmont, Stirlingshire
Printed and bound by Mackays of Chatham Ltd, Chatham, Kent

Hodder and Stoughton
A division of Hodder Headline
338 Euston Road
London NW1 3BH

This book is dedicated to our parents

Acknowledgements

We extend our grateful thanks to the following: Ian Christie for his great support and insights from the very beginnings of our research, back in 1996 when he was Associate Director at the Henley Centre for Forecasting; and Allan Thornton and Jessie for their unstinting support and enthusiasm.

During our research we spoke to many experts at think tanks, academic institutions and non profit-making groups. It is not possible to name them all here, but special thanks for help and encouragement go to: Ray Pahl, Research Professor of Sociology at the Institute for Social and Economic Research, University of Essex; in the US, simple living guru Duane Elgin, Professor Juliet Schor of Harvard University and Vicki Robin of the New Road Map Foundation. We are also grateful to Better Business (formerly Home Run), the magazine for the self-employed, whose material we drew on in Part Four and to New Ways to Work whose flexible working guides were a great resource.

We are also indebted to our editors Rowena Webb and Emma Heyworth-Dunn at Hodder & Stoughton, and to Caradoc King and Martha Lishawa at A.P. Watt for their support and encouragement.

Last but not least, we thank all the downshifters we have interviewed for the honest accounts they have given us of the ups and downs of their transformed lives. We hope that their stories will inspire, inform and encourage readers, and provide food for thought.

A Tale of Two Downshifters:
About the Authors

Judy Jones

Leaning on the stone wall at the end of my garden, I'm looking out at the island of water meadow encircled by the various tributaries of the Avon that thread their way through north Wiltshire, my recently adopted home patch. There are people who have lived round here for 20 years or more and still hesitate – or respond somewhat apologetically – when asked if they are local. Despite having spent most of my life in cities, I have taken to life on the edge of a small rural town like a duck to water. Never felt more at home anywhere, in just six years. It wouldn't suit everyone of course, but it suits me fine.

When Polly and I sat at adjoining desks as staff journalists on the *Observer* newspaper back in the mid-1990s, we used to chat about whatever we were writing about, and all sorts of other things besides. It was good for our morale. There weren't many women on the paper. We were a sort of mutual support system.

It was about this time that I first heard the word 'downshifting'. Duane Elgin, the American author of a book called *Voluntary Simplicity*, was visiting Oxford to take part in a debate about the downshifting movement that was sweeping America. He forecast that it was likely to become an important trend in Britain too. Polly was writing an article about it for the paper. Approaching my fortieth birthday, feeling stressed and overloaded by work as usual, and a headless chicken management culture, I remember saying to her: 'That's it, that's what I want to do. Now, Polly, how do I do it exactly?'

We mused upon the subject at some length. Meanwhile, fate intervened as our employers at the paper announced that they were offering voluntary redundancy packages. The timing could not have been better. Polly and I made early calls on the company's head of human resources. I think both of us thought that we would never get a better opportunity to downshift. I had toyed with the idea of going freelance before, but had never done anything about it. It looked like one of those 'now or never' moments.

The morning I found out that my application for voluntary redundancy had succeeded, my emotions vacillated between two extremes. I set off at lunchtime at a brisk pace, head down against the light drizzle, for the Ironmonger Row Baths, in Finsbury, London, my pillar-box-red swimming bag slung over my shoulder. As usual, I was in two minds. On one level, I felt piqued, almost shocked, that I should be considered so dispensable by my employers. After all, I was a vital cog in an extremely important wheel, the health correspondent of a national Sunday newspaper, respected if not admired in my field (wasn't I?). How on earth would they manage without me? Did they realise what they were doing, letting me go? Redundancy, I felt, means no one needs you any more. Middle age was suddenly hitting me like a fist from the dark.

Why had I done it? Well, it was gradually dawning on me that time appears to shrink as you get older. One minute you feel young and your life is before you. The next you are staring into the mirror and wondering who this baggy-eyed, worried-looking stranger is. I thought of all the things that I never quite got round to because I was too busy establishing myself in my career and getting on with it: things like getting married, having children, becoming an Olympic standard horse-rider, or even just horse-owner or, in fact, dog-owner. Progressively and without realising it, I had become a one-dimensional person. When I wasn't working, I was more than likely travelling to or from work, worrying about work, or planning work; journalists often find it hard to 'switch off' because they are always looking for new ideas for articles, weeding them out and bouncing them off others.

So how has downshifting been for me? Touch wood, it's been going pretty well. Mostly, I've been having the time of my life.

A year after leaving the paper, I had sold up in Ealing, west London, separated from my partner of 15 years, and headed for the wild wide skies and undulating downland of Wiltshire, whose glorious landscape I had enjoyed as a visitor for many years. I fell in love with the first cottage I saw on the market on a Saturday in June 1997, and put in an offer (rejected) on the Monday. I moved in a month later and have never regretted my decision.

Is my life happier and simpler? Well, yes, it is on the whole. Living in Malmesbury, and working largely from home is great – but that is partly because I have kept in touch with close friends from my old life, as well as finding delight in new ones. And I can just about take the restricted budget, and variable (usually months late) freelance earnings. Revisiting London for work or pleasure is positively exciting. I am like a kid in a sweet shop. But when I leap on to the train at Paddington, clutching my return ticket to Chippenham station, joy is pretty well unconfined.

True, I took great care to have my cake and eat it. I live about three minutes' walk from the services, shops and nattering opportunities I need for most purposes each day; and a slightly shorter walk to the fields and rivers. Regular walking has become a necessity as well as a joy since the arrival of Fly, a neurotic Border collie and redundant farm worker, who shares my home with me and is the apple of my eye.

I was recently co-opted on to the town council, and find my new duties interesting to say the least. My appointment diary has rarely been so gripping or elliptical: 'Visit cemetery. Joint Burial Committee. Take string', and 'Sunday Market extraordinary council'. But don't believe all you read about rural idylls, because they don't exist. If anyone tells you that downshifting is only about moving out to the country, don't believe a word of it. It's a state of mind, a change of attitude and perspective that may or may not cause you to move house, down the road, to another part of the country or overseas. Or stay put.

Life is what you do with where you are, and the resources and strength you can call on. Don't chase rainbows, for you will not find them and never underestimate the power of Sod's Law.

Shortly after moving to Malmesbury, my brother and I (he lives in Herefordshire) persuaded our parents to move from Winchester in Hampshire to my new stamping ground, as we thought we could better look after them, being closer by. Soon after they settled into their new home, my mother fell and broke her hip, and could no longer look after Dad, whose health was deteriorating steadily. We were fortunate in getting him moved into a care home in Malmesbury, where the staff have looked after him better than we could have hoped.

At the time of writing, my dear dad is getting frailer, fading away by the day. Seeing his rapid decline makes me all the more determined to lead the best life I can with the resources and wit I have, go hold his hand and ramble on about nothing in particular, as often as possible, while I have the chance still to see him smiling back at me.

Polly Ghazi

When I first joined the *Observer* full-time in October 1989, aged 27, it was the fulfilment of every young, ambitious journalist's dream. Getting to Fleet Street, as it was then still known, and working on my favourite paper, was hugely exciting. For the first four and a half years or so, I loved every minute of it. The buzz of front-page stories; the travel opportunities that came with my environmental brief; even the pressure of constant deadlines. I thrived on it all.

Slowly, however, I began to be ground down by the high-pressure, high-stress lifestyle. I had begun by working very hard to prove that I deserved a permanent place on the paper and found it hard to step back once my position was assured. At the same time the *Observer*, its sales declining, was coming under increasing financial pressure. When the offer of voluntary redundancy came up, I decided to apply.

Why did I choose to go? For many reasons, personal and professional. First, my health was suffering from work-related stress. Second, I was a year into my marriage and beginning to resent working every Friday night and all day Saturday. Third, I felt ready for a change of direction in my career. I wanted to switch from being a news reporter to concentrating more on comment and longer analytical articles. This was a role I thought I could more easily carve out for myself by writing for a range of publications. Fourth, the voluntary redundancy scheme was generous and I felt that such an opportunity might not arise again.

All these arguments won the day. But it was a very tough decision. Seven years later, my life transformed for the better, I look back and wonder how I could have agonised so long and hard.

The first few weeks after leaving my job were an emotional roller-coaster. I left only six weeks after applying for redundancy, which seemed a tremendously abrupt parting. Nevertheless, the first week I was euphoric. Sleeping late in the morning was wonderful and ordinary chores like cooking or going round the supermarket became much more enjoyable because they weren't done at a breakneck pace. I realised how much I had been living in 'absent' time when at home, my mind constantly on something else (work!) when I should have been enjoying the present moment.

After a fortnight or so, however, I suddenly found myself rushing around like a mad thing looking for work. Suffering from the terminal insecurity that most journalists feel as soon as their name is not in print for a while, I rang up various newspapers and magazines and fixed up and wrote a few articles. After these appeared, I calmed down a little. But then came an attack of the blues. For a month or so, I felt dislocated, claustrophobic at home in our two-bedroom flat, and often tearful.

Thankfully, some six weeks after starting my new life, this feeling lifted. I became used to working at home and began to appreciate the benefits. When I needed to sleep in, I did and then worked occasional evenings. If I had a few busy weeks, I would take it easy for a few days once the project was over. I began to see my family and friends more often, exercise more often and eat more healthily. My quality of life began to improve daily.

During my last 11 months on the paper, my husband Allan and I had tried unsuccessfully to conceive, a state of affairs I blamed at least in part on work-related stress. Six weeks after I left my job, to our delight, I became pregnant. My daughter Jessie is now six and downshifting has enabled me not only to take control of how and when I work but to find a good, healthy balance between work and family life.

I still work from home, combining journalism, book-writing and consultancies and putting in around 30 hours a week, ten months a year. I work the hours of the day (or night) that suit me and often take my laptop into the garden on sunny days and the coffee bar on rainy ones. When Jessie is sick, I simply have to ask the boss if I can take the day off and, funnily enough, she says yes every time! During half terms and summer holidays I have none of the sinking feelings that afflict other working parents desperate to find childcare for their school kids – and often paying through the nose for it. Jessie has afterschool care twice a week and the other three days I pick her up at 3.15 p.m. and can enjoy quality mummy–daughter time.

Allan is Canadian and in late 1999 we moved to Washington DC. Although we both fly back to London quite often, for work meetings, the move has helped facilitate our shift to a slower, simpler way of life. Despite being the world's most powerful capital city, DC only has 600,000 residents (compared with London's 8 million) and has a small town feel and – at least in our neighbourhood – a strong community spirit. Commuting to the office for Allan is now a 15-minute bus ride rather than a one-hour trial by London Underground. There is much less traffic and pollution than London and people are less harassed and have more time for each other. We rent a small three-bedroom house which takes much less cleaning and upkeep than our London home (which we partially rent out) and I have the time to get closely involved in Jessie's school, writing a regular PTA newsletter.

Of course it has not all been plain sailing. While I work fewer hours and with much less stress than on the newspaper, sitting alone at a desk in your bedroom can be isolating. And my annual income is only two-thirds of my former salary. On the other hand, Allan and I have cut our spending by about a third from my high-earning days with very little pain.

How? Well, first, we now have the time and energy to cook and eat in instead of out five times a week. Second, I no longer speed around in taxis because my life is so busy I don't want to waste time walking or waiting for a bus. Third, my formerly deep need for retail therapy has abated. I used to buy a new piece of clothing once a fortnight or so. I also indulged in frequent massages to relieve tension and stress. Now I don't feel or look so tired, the necessity – and the excuse – has vanished. Nowadays I get a lot of pleasure out of my work – writing books and for a range of papers and magazines is pretty stimulating – but, on the whole, very little stress.

Is there anything I miss? Of course. I still sometimes miss the buzz and comradeship of a busy newsroom. I occasionally have pangs for the high-level networking which goes with a cor-respondent's job on a national paper. But the compensations are enormous. Yes, I have lost income, but also the eye bags and irritable bowel syndrome that plagued me when work dominated my waking moments. Above all I feel in control of my working life whereas in the past I felt swept along by an uncontrollable tide of events. Not a bad trade-off.

Will I jump back on the treadmill and take another full-time office-based job? I am only 41, so the honest answer is maybe. But one of the main lessons of this book is that it is just as possible to influence people and even events from outside the traditional career structure as within it. For me, downshifting is categorically not about opting out. It is about creating the circumstances for a happy, rewarding and balanced life which enables us as individuals to give the best of ourselves – at home, at work and in the wider world.

Contents

Preface: If Life Is So Good, Why Do We Feel So Bad?   1

Part One: Overworked, Overloaded, Over Here

1. Our Consuming Passion   7
2. Happiness – The Missing Link   14
3. Mission Impossible: Living Against the Clock   21
4. A New World View   26

Part Two: Downshifting: A Renaissance of Simpler Living

5. Simple Living Through the Ages   37
6. The New American Dreamers   47
7. The British Way of Downshifting   59
8. Real Lives – Downshifters Tell Their Stories   70

Part Three: Preparing for Change

9. Could It Be You?   113
10. The Gender Agenda   123

Part Four: From Here to Simplicity: Putting Ideas Into Practice

11. You and Your Money   137
12. New Ways To Work   152
13. Home Front   173

Part Five: Living Better on Less

14. Food and Drink   189
15. Transport   199
16. Household Management   209
17. Growing Your Own   217
18. Leisure and Pleasure   228
19. Holidays   236
20. Making a Better Community   245

Part Six: Simplify and Save – 50 Life-Changing Tips   251

Part Seven: The Downshifter's Directory

Information on 50 organisations that can
help you build a simpler, better life.   263
Bibliography and References   289
Index   293

Preface: If Life Is So Good, Why Do We Feel So Bad?

No longer simply a dreamy aspiration to pursue in the distant future, quitting the rat race has now become a practical proposition for millions in the UK and throughout Europe. Stressed-out men and women are voting with their feet, swapping one-dimensional work-driven lives for a more balanced and sane existence. Subversive and liberating, downshifting has moved steadily from the margins to the mainstream of lifestyle choices. While the same old problems remain in Britain – long working hours, job insecurity, epidemic levels of stress-related illness, gridlocked roads and creaking railways – the continuing climate of dissatisfaction has new, more sinister elements. Fear of random terrorism, fuelled by the fallout of the World Trade Centre atrocity in New York in September 2001, and the war in Iraq in 2003, appears to have prompted many more people to take stock of their lives. Growing numbers are seizing opportunities to pursue what really matters to them, rather than continue being buffeted along by events, bosses and jobs they loathe.

It's hardly surprising. Not only are the sources of people's dissatisfaction with conventional lifestyles apparently on the increase, but, more positively, it is gradually becoming easier for individuals to strike out in a new direction.

Increasingly, employers and financial institutions are responding to changing aspirations: the former by offering a growing range of flexible and reduced working hours practices; the latter

1

by offering more flexible mortgages and pensions to help people change course in mid-life. Computer technology too is becoming ever cheaper and more portable, enabling many more of us to work from or closer to home, and thereby giving us more control over our lives.

While the culture is changing, progress in this direction often remains painfully slow. We Brits still work longer hours than our counterparts anywhere else in Europe: 47 hours a week for men in full-time employment and 43 for women. But it is not just the length of the working week that matters. The *quality* of the work experience and the level of *control* we can exert over the way we work probably has a greater impact on our health and sense of well-being.

Research seems to bear this out. A long-term study of 10,000 Whitehall civil servants has found that staff can tolerate a high-pressure working environment if they have a good measure of control over their working lives, and feel well supported. It's a big 'if'. More than 13 million days are lost each year because of stress, according to the government's health and safety watchdogs. Around a quarter of the UK population are estimated to be depressed or anxious at any given time. We are all brought up to believe that if we work hard and apply ourselves diligently, life will be good, or at least better than it otherwise would be. But for many, the Protestant work ethic, evolved over 500 years, is beginning to look like a hollow credo, shattered by contemporary market forces. We can get thrown on the scrapheap of unemployment, having played by the rules of all our established institutions, just as easily as those who never chose to or who never had the chance. All bets are off. Rarely since the Industrial Revolution has a generation of children left school or college so uncertain about their own prospects, and those of our damaged planet. Rarely have their parents' generation felt so insecure about their jobs and careers, and so confused about how they – and their own parents – will live out the rest of their lives. For our insecurity is boundless. We now live in an increasingly self-help society, where not only the boundaries of government, but also our much-cherished Welfare State, are fast retreating.

Britain and the world face unprecedented uncertainty and bewildering choices. Overpopulation and overconsumption are threatening the planet. Many of us feel our lives are truly on the edge.

How did we end up in this predicament? In the euphoria of post-World War II economic and technological advance, we came to despise almost anything that was from an earlier era, whether it was a piece of furniture or a set of values. We wanted to throw it out, and replace it with something a bit more modern. Consumption became the thing: a refrigerator, a front-loading washing machine, a TV set for the sitting-room, a nice car for trips out at the weekend. All mod cons: that's what we wanted. We aren't so sure now whether the twin gods of capitalism and rampant consumerism have landed us quite where we want to be. The welter of political spin and propaganda surrounding the aftermath of the conflict in Iraq has made it hard to be sure of anything, least of all whether it had made the world a safer place. Perhaps more than ever before, we are wondering what life is all about, what it's for. We are searching for meaning and balance. Many are turning to alternative ways of living, and downshifting is one of them.

In this updated and revised version of our book, we explore fully the whys and hows of downshifting. Why are so many people stepping back from conventionally successful modern lives and why do so many more want to join them? What kind of people are downshifters? How are they making it work? How do people's attitudes about the kind of world they want to live in and the kind of lives they want to lead translate into personal lifestyle changes? We've updated the experiences of seven of our initial interviewees for the Real Lives section, seven years on, providing (we think) a fascinating insight into long-term downshifting. There are also new real lives stories, featuring two couples – one British, one American – who have swapped countries in search of a more balanced, fulfilled life.

Happy reading!

PART ONE

Overworked, Overloaded, Over Here

Life is about more than just maintaining oneself, it is about extending oneself. Otherwise living is only not dying.

SIMONE DE BEAUVOIR (1908–1986), FRENCH SOCIALIST, FEMINIST AND WRITER

1

Our Consuming Passion

Oh Lord, won't you buy me a Mercedes-Benz? My friends all have Porsches, I must make amends.

JANIS JOPLIN, 1971

As you move around your home take a good hard look at its contents. It's likely that your living-room will feature a TV set, video recorder and DVD player and your kitchen a microwave oven and dishwasher. If you are a typical British householder, your bedroom drawers and wardrobes will be stuffed with almost three times as many clothes as your parents wore in the 1950s. You almost certainly own a car and quite likely a home computer; probably holiday abroad and eat out at least once a week. If you could see the volume of rubbish your dustbin accumulates over a year, you would be truly horrified.

The typical British household now enjoys a luxury of lifestyle beyond the grasp and perhaps the imagination of any previous generation. And we are not alone. The lucky seven in ten Britons who live above the poverty line are members of a global consumer society which embraces most North Americans, Japanese and Australasians, together with the inhabitants of the

7

Middle East oil sheikhdoms and the city-states of Hong Kong and Singapore. The consumer class is on the rise, too, in Eastern Europe, Latin America and South and East Asia. In Chinese cities, two-thirds of households now own washing machines.

So powerful is this worldwide urge to buy and consume that it is easy to forget how recent a phenomenon it is. In his book *How Much is Enough?*, Alan Durning of the Washington-based Worldwatch Institute traces the birth of the consumer age to 1920s America. It was then that brand names first became household words, that packaged foods became widely available on shop shelves and that the motor car, consumerism's ultimate symbol, began to take its place at the heart of modern American culture.

But the consumer society really came of age after World War II. With the basic survival needs of most of the population catered for, American politicians and business leaders needed a new formula to drive the engine of economic progress. Their answer was to aggressively promote mass consumption. One prominent American retailing analyst of the post-World War II era, Victor Lebow, summed up the new credo: 'Our enormously productive economy . . . demands that we make consumption our way of life, that we convert the buying and the use of goods into rituals, that we seek our spiritual satisfaction, our ego satisfaction, in consumption. We need things consumed, burned up, worn out, replaced, discarded at an ever increasing rate.'

The formula succeeded beyond Lebow's wildest expectations. Almost half a century after the end of the Second World War, the American consumer society provides the model to which ordinary citizens in every corner of the globe aspire. In America itself, the average couple owns twice as many cars, covers 25 times as much distance by air, and uses 21 times as much plastic as their parents did in 1950. Shopping mall mania and fast-food frenzy are the order of the day. Some 60 per cent of the food Americans eat is bought ready-made in supermarkets, at take-away outlets or in restaurants. Everything is bigger, from the supersized portions in fast-food joints to the vast homes, nicknamed 'McMansions', which fill the affluent suburbs of every major city.

Japan, Western Europe and Australasia are not far behind. In the last half a century, we British, the French and the Germans have all tripled the amount of paper we use. Consumption of processed and packaged 'convenience' foods, soft drinks and toiletries has also skyrocketed. In Sweden, packaged meals and products now make up an astonishing 87 per cent of all food eaten. In 2002 bottled water sales reached 39.8 billion litres across Europe – 101.5 litres per person – and 20 new sports and energy drinks were launched in the UK alone. Meanwhile the choices laid before us have proliferated to a bewildering and tyrannical extent. Take something as simple as buying a toothbrush. It used to be simply hard brush versus soft. Now Boots pharmacies stock 75 varieties. Even doing the weekly food shop is no longer a simple matter. The average Tesco supermarket – believe it or not – now boasts more than 40,000 products compared with 5,000 in 1983.

In Asia, one of the most striking expressions of growing affluence has been in foreign travel. The number of Japanese tourists flocking abroad rose from 4 million in 1984 to 18 million in 2000, while more than 10 million Chinese now travel overseas every year.

Luxury fever

The global spending spree triggered by the rapid growth in affluence has encountered little resistance in either America or Europe. Rather the opposite. Egged on by a celebrity-driven culture which encourages us to desire and ape the lifestyles of the rich and famous, consumers the world over are eagerly embracing a 'shop till you drop' mentality. This in turn has given rise to a new malady – luxury fever – in which people feel 'poor' while earning incomes their grandparents would have considered a small fortune. Here in Britain almost 50 per cent of people earning £35,000 a year and 40 per cent of those earning £50,000 believe they 'do not have enough money to buy essentials', according to a Cambridge University study. Yet average incomes are nearly three times higher, in real terms, than in 1950. 'The real concerns of yesterday's poor have become the imagined concerns of today's rich,' the study's author, Clive Hamilton, told the *Guardian*. It is, he added, 'hard to avoid the conclusion that the political system actively foments dissatisfaction amongst the middle classes'.

He has a point. Consumption strategies now underpin the entire global economy. Money and the goods and services it buys have become the shallow yardstick by which we in Western nations judge each other's social worth. Governments the world over now live by the narrow mantra: 'It's the economy, stupid.' First coined by American political strategist James Carville, who used it to help Bill Clinton turn George Bush senior out of office in 1992, the phrase has become synonymous with a world obsessed with material wealth.

Advertising: the dream machine

By the age of 18 the typical British teenager will have already been bombarded with about 150,000 television advertisements. Nor is he or she alone. From Moscow to Seoul to Dhaka, Western-style billboards and television commercials provide the raw fuel that drives the relentless expansion of mass consumption.

The world of advertising well understands human nature, and ruthlessly exploits human frailty. It generates new needs, so that it may endlessly sell us new products. Advertising fuels our wants and desires. For it to succeed, it must persuade large numbers of people that enough can never be enough. It works by making us feel unhappy or insecure about our diet, appearance and possessions, in other words, every aspect of our lives. Nine times out of ten it is selling us something we don't really need. British children, for example, are eating far too much sugary, salty and fatty food in their school lunchboxes, says the Food Commission, because of the malign influence of TV advertising. Companies also go to enormous lengths and expense to sell us their products. According to Euromonitor, in 2002 Coca-Cola spent £50 million on UK advertising alone, including the sponsorship of England's World Cup team.

Some sociologists have argued that clever advertising exploits our vulnerability and our uncertainty about life's most fundamental dilemmas; that it has come to eclipse religion in shaping people's ideas of what they expect and want out of life. Nevertheless, there are limits to the advertisers' powers. The huge gap between the images and desires which agencies conjure up to sell their products and the reality that consumers experience is becoming harder to reconcile.

When less is more

We don't want more anything any more. What we want now is less. More and more less.

Faith Popcorn, American trendcaster

In the new millennium, there are signs of a small, but growing backlash against the stranglehold of mass consumption. The spend-spend-spend culture has plunged many Britons into debt, with credit card debt trebling between 1996 and 2003. Insecurity over jobs and pensions has made us more cautious in our approach to spending. For some of us possessions are becoming less a pleasure than a burden. And a new uncomfortable feeling is also beginning to emerge: that society is paying a high price for the benefits of ever-increasing spending power for the majority.

In Britain the gap between rich and poor remains uncomfortably wide, especially among children. Across the world, fuelled by the devastating impact of HIV/AIDS, it is a deepening chasm.

One-fifth of the world's population now takes home 64 per cent of world income. This amounts to 32 times as much as that earned by the world's poorest fifth. The world's 358 billionaires now own as much wealth as the poorest 2.3 billion people – almost half the global population.

Greater spending power has brought Westerners previously undreamed-of lifestyles and travel opportunities. We have become understandably wedded to our comfortable houses, foreign holidays and cars. But many people are beginning to sense that indefinitely expanding the boundaries of our lifestyles is likely to take a heavy toll on ourselves, our society and the environment in which we live. Polls suggest that as many as 87 per cent of Britons believe our society has become too materialistic. Alternative economist David Boyle argues in his book *Authenticity: Brands, Fakes, Spin and the Lust for Real Life* that a genuine 'No Logo' movement is emerging here and elsewhere with 40 of the world's best-selling 75 brands losing value in 2002. 'The rise of local brands, slow food, real ale, reading groups . . . are all symptoms of the same thing – a demand for human-scale, face-to-face institutions and authentic experience,' he argues. As we grow increasingly uncertain about the future, so our values and attitudes are starting to shift.

We are, of course, still a long way from renouncing a culture of 'more' for one of 'enough'. But the simple truth is that debt and overwork are making us miserable while retail therapy is failing to cheer us up. In response, a growing minority of people are tuning out mall culture and switching gear to simpler, more self-sufficient and affordable lifestyles.

Values for the Future

From 'Global Consumer'	To 'World Citizen'
Global Consumer	**World Citizen**
Me	We
More	Enough
Materialism	Holism
Quantity	Quality
Greed	Need
Short-term	Longer-term
Rights	Responsibilities

Source: *'Who Needs It?'* SustainAbility

Happiness –
The Missing Link

Unless a person learns to enjoy it, much of life will be spent desperately trying to avoid its ill-effects.
MIHALY CSIKSZENTMIHALYI, 1992

One of the most powerful reasons why we are losing faith in consumerism as a guiding light is the realisation that money does not buy happiness. The truth of this maxim, which we are fond of quoting, is borne out by rigorous academic research. Trying to answer the question 'What is Happiness?' has become a growth industry for think-tanks and psychologists. The more they delve into our psyches, the more evidence they uncover that the link between money and contentment is a tenuous one for all except the poorest in society.

People achieve happiness when they have eliminated inner conflicts between their achievements and aspirations. The contemporary political and economic debate assumes that there is a strong correlation between income and contentment, that extends beyond the basic need for survival. This assumption is applied to individuals and societies. Politicians, economists and media commentators extrapolate from these assumptions to conclude that the 'feel-good factor', of which we hear so much, consists of making money, and being secure in the knowledge that one will go on making money, in ever larger proportions.

The economic and social policies of Britain's main political parties are constructed around these assumptions. Yet happiness has little to do with economics, unless you are unfortunate enough not to have the money you need to buy the essentials of life: food, clothing, adequate shelter, heat and light. But when basic material or survival needs have been met, what then?

We need meaning and purpose in life to feel good about it. Oxford psychologist Professor Michael Argyle, who has spent more than a decade researching what makes people happy, argues, in his seminal work The Psychology of Happiness, that many influences can trigger this feel-good factor. A fulfilling job or leisure activity, gardening, sport, a loving relationship, a close network of friends or bringing up children can all do the trick. Extra spending money comes way down the list of factors that people actually find important. As we focus relentlessly on working and earning, Argyle's book suggests, so two of these three crucial spheres, social relations and leisure, have begun to suffer and our happiness levels to wane.

The Pursuit of Happiness

While you can aim at pleasure, you cannot aim at happiness. You must have other aims – ambitions, goals, values and ideals – with which your personal life is entwined, if you are to be happy.

Roger Scruton, philosopher and writer

Happiness is a condition that must be prepared for, cultivated and defended privately by each person. People who learn to control inner experience will be able to determine

---

> the quality of their lives, which is as close as anyone can come to being happy.
> Mihaly Csikszentmihalyi, psychologist
>
> In order that people may be happy in their work, these things are needed: they must be fit for it; they must not do too much of it; and they must have a sense of success in it.
> John Ruskin, Victorian social reformer
>
> People are happy when they are 'in control' that is, when they feel competent to satisfy their needs and reach their goals.
> Francis Heylighen, Belgian academic
>
> Life, liberty and the pursuit of happiness –
> American Declaration of Independence

Research from around the world supports the evidence from Britain that the direct link between money and personal happiness is a weak one. Ruut Veenhoven, a psychology professor at Erasmus University, Rotterdam, has established an on-line World Database of Happiness. It lists around 3,500 academic studies and 1,900 international surveys on the topic, carried out between 1946 and 2000. This summarises happiness as a 'person's subjective appreciation of life as a whole'.

Veenhoven has concluded that beyond a certain prosperity level rising incomes no longer affect reported well-being. In the poorer countries, which cannot afford welfare safety nets, income remains a life and death issue. But in the richer consumer nations, Veenhoven found that money no longer plays a central role in individual well-being. He discovered that the more affluent the nation, the smaller the correlation between people's bank balances and their personal happiness.

Even in the poorest countries, it is a mistake for economists or anyone else to assume that people measure their quality of life merely by the income they can scrape together. In 1988 the Indian academic N.S. Jodha asked farmers and villagers in two villages in Rajasthan to list their own criteria for being well-off. They produced 38 examples, including quality of housing, wearing shoes, eating a third meal a day and sleeping in a different room from the family animals. Jodha found that 36 households which ranked themselves as better off on their own terms had actually suffered more than a 5 per cent drop in hard cash income over the previous year!

Rising economic growth and consumption levels have been the twin mantras of Western politicians for decades. But if growth doesn't deliver extra well-being to the citizens these politicians serve, then what is the point of it? And what message does all this hold for us as individuals?

When people are asked about what makes life rewarding and enjoyable for them, they often recall events that enabled them to achieve more than was expected of them. It can be something as simple as expressing views during a conversation that you never realised you had, playing tennis, or finishing a particularly challenging task well and on time. 'After an enjoyable event, we know that we have changed, that our self has grown; in some respect we have become more complex as a result,' writes Mihaly Csikszentmihalyi in his book *Flow: The Psychology of Happiness*.

While the sensation of pleasure requires no psychological effort, the enjoyment of an experience comes from concentration and total absorption in an activity. This is a state of 'flow'. It can be achieved by taking control of your own consciousness, and in doing so taking control of the quality of your experience. 'Flow doesn't require education, income, high intelligence, good health or a spouse. It requires a mind,' says Csikszentmihalyi.

His argument is essentially this: sooner or later in life, you are likely to ask yourself: 'Is this it? Is this all there is to life?' As

17

disillusionment sinks in, some respond by renewing their efforts to acquire more of the things that they believed would make them happy, such as a bigger car or house, more power and status at work. But, as we have seen, all the evidence suggests that acquiring and accumulating ever more stuff is unlikely to bring long-term satisfaction and contentment. Many of us need to find a meaning in life that transcends our own everyday material existence. Of course there is absolutely no consensus about what that meaning is, a point underlined in an intriguing study by psychologists at Arizona State University.

They assembled and analysed some 238 quotations by 195 eminent people, mostly twentieth-century figures, indicating their views about the meaning of life. These were then distilled into themes or categories of meaning. The top ten themes, and examples of those whose quotations were studied, can be seen in the box:

The Meaning of Life?

Top ten purposes and themes ranked in a study of quotations by 195 eminent people:

1 Enjoy or experience life. Enjoy the moment/ journey (17 per cent)

Ralph Waldo Emmerson, Janis Joplin, Cary Grant, Thomas Jefferson, Eleanor Roosevelt

2 Love, help, or serve others. Show or experience compassion (13 per cent)

Albert Einstein, the Dalai Lama, Albert Schweitzer, Jean Jacques Rousseau, Gandhi

3 Life is a mystery (13 per cent)

Albert Camus, Bob Dylan, Napoleon, Stephen Hawking

---

4 Life is meaningless (11 per cent)

Jean-Paul Sartre, Bertrand Russell, George Bernard Shaw, Sigmund Freud, Franz Kafka

5 Serve or worship God and prepare for the next life (11 per cent)

Martin Luther King, Billy Graham, Mother Teresa, Muhammad Ali

6 Life is a struggle (8 per cent)

Charles Dickens, Benjamin Disraeli, Jonathan Swift

7 Develop or evolve as a person or species, pursue truth, wisdom, higher level of being (6 per cent)

Plato, Frederick Nietzsche, Robert Louis Stevenson, Henry David Thoreau

8 Contribute to something that is greater than ourselves (6 per cent)

Margaret Mead, Richard Dixon, Benjamin Franklin

9 Create your own meaning (5 per cent)

Carl Jung, Simone de Beauvoir, Carl Sagan, Viktor Frankl

10 Life is absurd or a joke (4 per cent)

Albert Camus, Charlie Chaplin, Bob Dylan, Lou Reed, Oscar Wilde

Source: 'What Eminent People Have Said About the Meaning of Life', *Journal of Humanistic Psychology,* winter 2003, Richard Kinnier et al.

'Most individuals seek meaning in their lives,' comments the study's lead researcher Richard Kinnier. 'The search typically involves introspection, and consultation – with friends, family members, and mentors, as well as with literature, poetry and song lyrics. We view the results of this study as just another source of amalgamated wisdom . . . a stimulus for thought and discussion.'

Mission Impossible:
Living Against the Clock

It was going to be one of Rabbit's busy days. As soon as he woke up he felt
important, as if everything depended on him. It was just the day for
Organising Something, or for Writing a Notice Signed Rabbit . . .
A.A. MILNE, THE HOUSE AT POOH CORNER, 1928

Modern man suffers from a 'hurry sickness' induced by a 'time
famine', wrote the late Michael Young in his book *The
Metronomic Society*. The advent of electric lighting enabled and
encouraged people to work longer and longer hours round the
clock, upsetting the natural rhythmic cycles that were a feature of
our evolution. Industrialisation also made us more reliant on the
clock as a regulator of daily lives. Young wrote: 'We are continu-
ally having to start this or stop that at the appointed moment.
Life is strung between a whole series of precisely-timed beginnings and ends which have a lot to do with man and little with
nature.'

Moderate amounts of stress are essential to motivate us and
make us feel challenged, but above a certain threshold they make
us feel anxious and unable to cope. Thresholds will vary from one
person to the next. When we encounter more challenges than we

can cope with, or else too few to stimulate us, stress is the result.

Too much stress raises blood pressure, which increases the risk of blood clots forming. Over time that makes you more vulnerable to strokes and heart attacks. It interferes with the immune system, the body's natural defence mechanism that protects you from bugs and viruses. Most doctors now accept that stress can be a major contributory factor to the development of some forms of cancer. We are remarkably resilient in keeping going under stress for short stretches. But eventually we pay the price. How often have you gone on holiday only to be laid low on the first day by a cold or flu or worse? It's because the pressure is suddenly off. There's no adrenalin surging around keeping the show on the road, and your brain on red alert.

Stress and overwork don't just make us ill by undermining our natural defence systems. They make us behave differently, unnaturally and unhealthily. We drink too much coffee to wind ourselves up, and too much alcohol to wind down. We rush our food instead of savouring every mouthful. We graze on junk food and pre-packaged convenience food instead of sitting down to proper meals, made with fresh and nutritious ingredients. Then we're more likely to flop in front of the television (or carry on working) with a bottle of wine or a six-pack of beer rather than engage in some active pursuit.

Stress-related illness has become one of the most rampant epidemics of the modern age. Rates have doubled since 1990, according to the government's Health and Safety Executive (HSE). Teachers and health professionals, under the ever-tightening screw of performance monitoring, targets, league tables and star-rating systems, are the hardest hit. Surveys of doctors over the past decade have regularly found large majorities planning to quit before reaching retirement age because of rising workloads.

Lack of control over work, long hours, unreasonable demands by managers, and bullying or other unacceptable behaviour by colleagues are the most frequently cited causes of stress and anxiety. More than a third of people surveyed recently for the Samaritans emotional support charity said that work was one of the most stressful aspects of their lives. Yet employers and successive UK governments have been reluctant to take the problem seriously, until fairly recently.

The Costs of Burn-Out

Former social worker John Walker was the first person to argue successfully in court that his employers were liable for his nervous breakdown. In a landmark judgement in 1996, the High Court ruled that his 'impossible workload' had triggered the breakdown, and ordered Northumberland County Council to pay him £175,000 for the personal injury he had suffered. 'More and more was being squeezed out of the same pint pot,' said Mr Walker. 'I tried to do my best. I was told to get on with it.' His union Unison urged employers to take heed – or face similar pay-outs. 'It's no longer acceptable for employers to leave staff to struggle on, trying to provide under-resourced services on the cheap, or risk their health in doing so,' said Unison health and safety officer Sarah Copsey. Sickness absence through stress lands the UK with an annual bill of £7 billion in lost production and treatment costs to the NHS.

While the public sector appears particularly susceptible to ill-health through over-work, a worrying one in five workers across all sectors exhibit 'extremely high' stress levels, a recent Home Office study indicated.

It seems that information overload, poor line management, and toppling in-trays overwhelm a large portion of the corporate world. How else do these problems impact on our lives? A rather chastening survey by ICM Research for the *Observer* found that most workers in full-time employment were regularly too exhausted to enjoy themselves in their free time and even to make love. Nearly half of those sampled said they regularly worked more than 48 hours a week. Given an extra hour in bed each day, most workers reported that they would rather sleep than have sex.

We are richer than ever before, through our hard labour (and for the lucky, rising house prices), but too weary to reap the benefits of our affluence.

Although the Labour government of the late 1990s and early 'noughties' embraced the rhetoric of 'work-life balance' and more flexible working, working hours have continued to rise in the UK, while declining elsewhere in the European Union. Our average working week is now longer than anywhere else in the EU. This is partly because the UK, alone among its European partners, allows its workers to opt out of the 48 hours maximum working week limit laid down by the EU in the late 1990s. But is this opt-out a genuine individual choice – or are people coerced by their employers?

Research by the TUC suggests that two-thirds of employees working more than 48 hours a week have not signed an opt-out agreement with their bosses, as is required under the EU legislation. The unions, detecting a sea-change in public opinion, are once again flexing their muscles, with some success.

The empty promise

The main activities carried out by people in the UK are sleeping, working in their main job and watching TV.
UK 2000 Time Use Survey, Office of National Statistics

All around us we can see evidence of the fragmentation of work, community and personal relationships. The UK's rates for divorce and teenage pregnancy have been hovering at or near the top of EU rankings for more than a decade. The Brits are more likely to 'binge drink' than most of our European counterparts, and the suicide rate among 15–24-year-olds has more than doubled since 1971.

The massive redundancies of the early to mid-1990s, mainly in manufacturing, have abated, but some 650 people a day in the UK are still being told that their jobs no longer exist.

Yet although it's generally agreed that the 'job for life' is fast disappearing, apocalyptic predictions of an automated 'workless economy' appear wide of the mark.

At the time of writing, the number of jobs in the UK (29.7 million) and the number of hours worked each week (901.6 million) are the highest since records began in the late 1950s. People need to work not just to pay their weekly bills, but to service their growing debts, currently totalling an average of £3,400 per person, excluding mortgages.

While the economy booms, society busts, it would seem. When we are not sleeping or working, we're just too busy watching TV to bother helping out our neighbours or contributing to community life.

According to time use surveys by the Office of National Statistics, adults typically have about five and a half hours of 'free time' a day. Of this, four minutes are spent volunteering, eight minutes helping others, and 44 minutes socialising. TV watching absorbs the biggest chunk of our leisure time – around three hours a day.

Truly, the couch potato reigns supreme. Most of us prefer to watch sport on television than take part in it, and passively to consume 'reality TV shows' than the real thing – actively engaging the life and opportunities around us.

4

A New World View

And there is no greatness where there is not goodness, simplicity and truth.
LEO TOLSTOY, WAR AND PEACE, 1865

It is not only time and happiness that elude us, but peace of mind. Over-worked and stressed, we see many grey clouds on the horizon. Close to home we are anxious about our plunging pensions, our children's schools, traffic-choked, fume-filled streets and the state of the National Health Service; further afield our fears expand to include climate change and the random threat of global terrorism.

Many of us are confronted daily by polluted air, neighbours who are strangers and exhausted, brittle friends and colleagues. Most of us now earn more than enough for our basic needs, yet yearn for more from life than employment and money. While few of us still attend church, millions are turning to spiritual alternatives including meditation, self-enlightenment and Buddhism in search of reassurance and a deeper meaning in life.

We worry about the path down which society is leading us. We fear that over-work is making us ill and damaging our relationships. We are anxious about crime levels and the decline of neighbourliness. We have trouble believing that our children will inherit a better, more stable world.

A nation of worriers

Job insecurity and the effects on our health of gruelling working hours feed into this malaise. One poll of managers in 24 countries, funded by BUPA, found – yes, you guessed it – the British to be the most stressed and least healthy, ranking below those in Hong Kong and Bulgaria. In our information-saturated world, reports another survey by the Future Foundation, people's worries stretch 'from the minutely personal to the global'. One in three men, their polling revealed, fret that their stomachs are too large, while four in ten women worry about protecting the environment. Paranoid parenting abounds with three in four mothers and fathers saying they would like their children to wear an electronic tag bracelet and four in ten admitting they would like a video link to their child's classroom. About eight in ten people think Britain has become a more dangerous place in the past ten years and half of all 18–35-year-olds worry about money and work. Astonishingly, one 19-year-old even told the researchers: 'I've chopped and changed too much . . . I must decide my career soon, I'm getting quite old.'

Why are so many of us beset with worry when we are so much better off than previous generations? 'It's the paradox of progress,' says the Future Foundation's Michael Willmott. 'Today's generation is richer, healthier, safer and enjoys more freedom than any in the past, yet life seems more pressured because it is more complex.'

Yet the fast pace and bewildering choice of today's world is not solely to blame. Perhaps a greater source of our unhappiness lies in the growing gap between economic well-being on the one hand and social and environmental well-being on the other.

Britain's Gross Domestic Product (GDP), the traditional barometer of a country's wealth, remains one of the world's highest. But an influential alternative measurement, the Index of Sustainable Economic Welfare (ISEW), suggests that our rising incomes are being cancelled out by a deteriorating quality of life.

Applied to Britain by the New Economics Foundation, a London-based think-tank, the ISEW builds into its calculations the quality of health and education services, the loss of natural resources such as woods and wildlife and the costs of pollution clean-up. It estimates that air, water and noise pollution alone are costing the country over £22 billion a year. And its gloomy prognosis is mirrored, to some extent, by the government's own figures. The environment department's 'quality of life barometer', published in June 2003, revealed that traffic on streets and motorways is growing, farmland birds are disappearing and violent crime is on the rise.

Of course everybody has different views about what makes life worth living. Many Britons are no doubt more than happy with their lifestyles and it is clearly dangerous to make too many assumptions about how 60 million individuals view the world. Nevertheless, it is fair to say that as a nation we are both more affluent than ever before and yet fearful for the future. Our anxieties embrace the future of our jobs, our relationships and the environment we live in.

Costing the Earth

Our environmental concerns are hardly surprising given the mounting damage inflicted on the natural world, both nationally and globally. Most of us cannot fail to notice, for example, that our local beauty spots are being bulldozed or neglected and there is not as much wildlife as there used to be. Nor can we shut out the headlines warning that a world without tigers, orang-utans and pandas is probably only decades away. As childhood asthma rates climb and streets remain traffic-choked and fume-filled, a significant minority have even begun to question our love affair with the car.

We are increasingly sceptical and even fearful about what we eat. Widespread distrust of genetically modified foods is only the latest in a string of food safety scares. Others include CJD, the human form of 'mad cow disease' linked to eating beef, salmonella in factory-farmed eggs, listeria in soft cheese, pesticide-tainted vegetables and the presence of dioxins, a suspected carcinogen, in milk from farms located near incinerators. Meanwhile chemical oestrogens, found in common household cleaning products and transmitted in tap water, are suspected of playing a role in the falling sperm counts of British men.

We are also uneasy about our diet for ethical reasons. When we take the time to think about it, we recoil against the conditions in which livestock and poultry are kept on intensive factory farms. The message is coming home that farm animals are paying a high price for cheap supermarket food. Likewise, while we believe in science and technological progress and some of us may be prepared to eat the genetically engineered tomatoes already available in our stores, public hostility to cloning and cross-breeding animals and foodstuffs has been overwhelming.

Nor are our concerns confined to Britain's borders. The searing summer of 2003 brought home across Europe the reality of climate change, triggered as carbon dioxide emissions released from cars, planes, factories and energy plants heat up the atmosphere. Across Western Europe, too, fishing catches are declining, car and lorry travel is rising, wildlife havens are diminishing and chemical production is soaring. By 2100, says the European Environment Agency, the waves lapping the continent's shores could rise by as much as nearly a metre.

As individuals, we are contributing to this ecological disaster through the impact of our daily lives, sometimes known as our 'ecological footprint'. An American citizen's footprint – the amount of food, energy and other resources that he or she consumes – is about 16 times heavier than that of the average African, while a West European's is five times heavier.

The ethical citizen

Of course it doesn't have to be this way.

The fact that most of us still drive cars and that vegetarians remain greatly outnumbered by meat-eaters is interpreted by politicians as evidence that worries about food safety, pollution, waste and climate change are confined to a small minority. Nothing could be further from the truth. Polls consistently show that worries about environmental pollution rank high in voters' concerns. The strength of feeling, while it may not bring protesters out on the streets, is reflected in the size and influence of the green lobby. Excluding the National Trust, British environmental and conservation groups boast a paying membership of around 4 million, several times more than the three major political parties combined.

People are also using their buying power to register unease with mall culture and display changing values. Ethics man and woman have come of age. All the major supermarkets now stock organic and fair trade foods and farmers' markets are hugely popular. According to the Social Market Foundation, a whopping 82 per cent of shoppers would prefer to buy from companies that are environmentally and socially responsible and 23 per cent do so even when it costs them more money. In 2001 we spent £7 billion on ethical products, and ethical investment funds are also booming in the wake of corporate scandals such as the Enron débâcle.

Rebellion in the workplace

This emerging rebellion against the consumer work-spend culture extends beyond the high street and into the workplace.

As we pointed out in our preface, people across Europe are quitting the rat race in droves. There were an estimated 12 million downshifters across Europe in 2002 and 2.6 million in Britain.

Among the majority still slogging it out in full-time, conventional jobs, attitudes are also shifting. In December 2002 the Department of Trade and Industry published the startling results of a poll of 4,000 active jobseekers. Almost half said flexible working was the top benefit they were seeking, while only 10 per cent wanted a company car. A third even claimed they would rather have flexible hours than an extra £1,000 pay.

All these findings appear to underline a real shift in attitudes from 1990s workaholism and the money-driven mentality of recent decades. Employees, it seems, are showing increasing reluctance to give everything to their work to try and hold on to their job and/or achieve promotion. Instead, for many, achieving a better division of time and energy between work and home lives has become the new Holy Grail.

Why is this so? For each individual and family, of course, the dynamic is different, but we can hazard some educated guesses. On the one hand, Britain's workaholic culture shows no sign of abating. The Department of Trade and Industry's own figures, for example, show overtime is higher than ever, with one in six employees working 60-plus hours a week in 2002, up from one in eight in 2000. While most of the public sector and many large companies now offer flexible working options such as term time working and job shares, others remain firmly embedded in a time warp. Take BA's costly dispute with its Heathrow ground staff about clocking in swipe cards in 2003. The company was accused of ignoring the childcare-juggling needs of its mainly female shift staff and paid the penalty in a wildcat strike.

On the other hand, new technology has made it easier to break away from the conventional workplace. Teleworking for an employer from home or starting a freelance career has now become a realistic and affordable proposition for millions. For others, the growth of flexitime and 24-hour shift patterns has meant they can keep the security of a staff job while working at times that suit children's needs or fit in with their hobbies. Downshifting, in short, is becoming an acceptable career path; an increasingly mainstream route to re-ordering our priorities between work and the rest of our lives.

A sustainable future?

The workplace rebellion is being accompanied by another citizens' movement, dubbed 'anti-politics' by the think-tank Demos. One symptom is the growing disenchantment with mainstream politics and politicians. According to Mori, 75 per cent of us expect politicians 'not to tell the truth', while 51 per cent were dissatisfied with their performance in 2003, up from 39 per cent in 1999. The inquiry into Dr David Kelly's suicide, apparently triggered by the government's public outing of the weapons expert after he told journalists of his misgivings over the Iraq war, has only deepened this sense of distrust and alienation. Polls suggest that only half of us may bother to vote at the next election.

On the upside, we are finding our own alternatives to Westminster, Whitehall and town hall politics. One example is the flourishing at local level of alternative economies, such as bartering and shoestring community enterprises. Another is growing support for environmental politics and the anti-globalisation movement, with on-line protests and petitions a new weapon in the citizen's armoury. Another is the level of involvement in community and residents groups – for example the spread of reading circles – up and down the country.

Of course there is nothing new about mass campaigns or protest movements. What is different today is the depth and vitality of the new anti-Establishment backlash and the influential allies it is beginning to foster. This new alchemy is represented at a national level by the Real World Coalition, founded in 1996. Friends of the Earth, Save the Children, Church Action on Poverty and 30 other environmental, social justice and development groups signed up to a common political platform and urged the three main political parties to sign up too. Britain was paying too high a price, they argued, for economic growth and rising consumption. New priorities of alleviating poverty, rebuilding communities and conserving natural resources must be set.

These very ideas have now been adopted by the Government-appointed UK Sustainable Development Commission, headed by environmentalist Jonathon Porritt. In June 2003 they threw down the gauntlet to No 10 Downing Street and the Treasury, urging them to 'redefine prosperity'. Britain would be better off, they argued, if ministers started focusing on 'improving true quality of life for all citizens' and 'rethinking economic growth as the driving force in modern politics'.

Clearly, these are radical ideas, but they chime with the views and the unease shared by millions. 'If people are not getting happier, why is our economic strategy still dedicated to delivering more of the same kind of growth?' asks Jonathan Porritt. Why indeed?

PART TWO

Downshifting: A Renaissance of Simpler Living

Downshifters Through History And Literature

Jesus

Buddha

St Francis of Assisi

The Quakers

Henry Thoreau

Gandhi

William Morris

The Wombles

Robin Hood

Robinson Crusoe

The Horse Whisperer

Robert Blatchford

Don Quixote

Tom and Barbara Good

John Ruskin

The Amish

Mother Teresa

Aristotle

Plato

Winnie-the-Pooh

Hugh Fearnley-Whittingstall

Desert Orchid

Alistair Campbell

Alan Milburn

Rupert Bear

John Noakes

Alfred Wainwright

Three Men in a Boat

Simple Living Through the Ages

We agree that we are overworked, and need rest – A week on the rolling deep? George suggests the river – Montmorency lodges an objection – Original motion carried by a majority of three to one.

JEROME K. JEROME, THREE MEN IN A BOAT, 1889

Although downshifting can be described as a reaction against the frantic consumerism of modern urban life in the overdeveloped West, its historical roots run deep. The yearning for a simpler, more balanced life can be traced through countless civilisations and religions.

The great philosophers of early Greek civilisation, Socrates, Plato and Aristotle, all emphasised the importance of a 'golden mean' through life. This they described as a middle way between wealth and poverty which involved disdaining material possessions in favour of a more spiritual, intellectual life.

People have been bemoaning the pace of urban life and withdrawing into quieter, gentler worlds at least since Roman times, possibly longer. As well as building Britain's first urban cities, the Roman legionaries and administrators who ran the country also built fine villas in the countryside as retreats from the pressures of ruling Britannia.

Life was far more hectic of course at the very heart of the Roman empire. Many authors in ancient Rome wrote about how they recoiled from the noise, the traffic and the crowds. Horace complained of 'that bit of Hell/ Known as big city life'.

The Protestant work ethic, which flourished in northern Europe in the Middle Ages also emphasised simple living virtues. It crossed the Atlantic with the Pilgrim Fathers. The culture of colonised North America in the seventeenth century was strongly influenced by the frugal, spiritual and community-centred ethics of the Puritan and Quaker settlers.

All the world's great religions embrace the simple living ideal. The need to balance the spiritual and the material underpins most of the Bible's teachings: 'Give me neither poverty or wealth' (*Proverbs* 30:8). In an increasingly atheistic or agnostic West, the message continues to have resonance. In 1973, a coalition of American Christian groups developed the 'Shakertown Pledge' through which believers committed themselves to 'lead a life of creative simplicity, and to share my personal wealth with the world's poor'. The Eastern religions, Hinduism, Buddhism and Taoism reflect the same emphasis on spiritual rather than material wealth. 'He who knows he has enough is rich,' goes an ancient Taoist saying, while simplicity, balance and frugality are at the heart of the Buddhist way of life.

In Britain

Both the dream and the practice of escaping busy, noisy, polluted towns for the countryside go back centuries. The yuppies of Medieval England, the rising merchant class, began buying country properties in the twelfth or thirteenth century, often as a way of establishing rural dynasties, based on agriculture. Many failed and were replaced by endless waves of *nouveaux riches*.

There was a growing awareness that the countryside was not only a pleasant place to live, but a healthy one, away from the epidemics that would periodically sweep through the towns and cities.

In the wake of the Industrial Revolution that began in the late eighteenth century, towns and cities grew rapidly as thousands of people migrated from the countryside into the urban areas in search of work. The physical conditions in which the ordinary family lived were often appalling.

The Industrial Revolution provoked fears among many intellectuals and social reformers that the great rush to mechanisation would bring wealth to the very few and misery to the masses, spread inequality and injustice and diminish the soul of all mankind. Throughout the nineteenth century the voices raised in alarm at the impact of new production systems and the urban way of life they generated and depended on were as notable as those that greeted the new order as 'progress'.

John Ruskin (1819–1900) was one of the very first to warn that untrammelled industrialisation would prove to be morally and aesthetically harmful. Born in London, he was a man of letters, an outstanding artist and art critic and an influential thinker, whose writings inspired Gandhi and the British socialist movement. He harked back to the Middle Ages as a Utopia and his romantic attachment to an age long gone expressed itself in much of his writing: 'When men are rightly occupied, their amusement grows out of their work as the colour-petals out of a fruitful flower – when they are faithfully helpful and compassionate, all their emotions become steady, deep, perpetual and vivifying to the soul as the natural pulse of the body. But now having no true business, we pour our whole masculine energy into the false business of money-making,' he wrote in *Of King's Treasures*, a lecture published in 1865.

William Morris (1834–96) was another whose 'passion for the past' was matched by his reaction against the values of the industrialising present. He wrote a romance called *A Dream of John Ball* (1888), in which the narrator abandons the 'hurried and discontented humanity' of Morris's times for the slower, smaller scale, more humane fourteenth-century England. *His News from Nowhere* (1891) conjured up a future pastoral England where the machinery worked itself, freeing men and women to work on what they enjoyed doing and at their own pace.

One of the Victorian thinkers who best harnessed ideas about ecological sustainability with healthy living and community values was Robert Blatchford (1851–1943). In his book, *Merrie England*, he wrote that England had to make a choice between the quality of men's lives and the quantity of production. His abhorrence of the factory system was uncompromising: 'It's evil in its origin, its progress, in its methods, in its motives, and in its effects. No nation can be sound whose motive power is greed.' More than a million copies of Blatchford's tome were sold within a few years of publication.

The people's revolt: the rise of the garden cities and the plotlanders

Doubts about the direction of capitalism and materialism continued unabated between World Wars I and II. The economist John Maynard Keynes (1883–1944) warned that the pursuit of money as an end in itself was the moral problem of the age. In *Essays in Persuasion*, 1932, he wrote: 'The love of money as a possession . . . will be recognised for what it is, a somewhat disgusting morbidity, one of those semi-criminal, semi-pathological propensities which one hands over with a shudder to the specialist in mental disease.'

It was all very well for middle-class intellectuals to analyse the ills of the world. But how were ordinary people, and their champions, responding to the spread of urban sprawl and its impact on well-being and spiritual health? The social reformer and visionary of the early twentieth century, Ebenezer Howard (1850–1928), embarked on one of the most ambitious experiments in town planning by trying to blend aspects of the country into new urban areas. He pioneered the concept of the Garden City, an urban environment that incorporates large areas of green space, tree-lined streets and pleasant vistas. The Hertfordshire villages of Letchworth and Welwyn were the first to be expanded into garden cities using Howard's blueprints.

But some communities did not wait to be organised in such a 'top-down' fashion. The little Sussex town of Peacehaven, later dubbed 'the garden city by the sea', was envisaged in the early 1900s as a holiday resort. In fact it became a frontier settlement for working people from city and urban areas in search of a quieter, healthier place to live. In a bungalow and a little green plot, that one could buy for as little as £25, lay paradise.

In their book *Arcadia for All*, Dennis Hardy and Colin Ward chart the social history of Peacehaven and the quest of thousands of working-class people who became known to local authorities as 'plotlanders'. They were mainly poor Londoners in search of fresh air, peace and a sea view. Over the first half of the twentieth century, they abandoned the urban sprawl to find their own patch of paradise along the coastline of south-east England. Old railway carriages, army surplus huts from World War I, trams and garden sheds were given a new lease of life to form makeshift landscapes. The trouble was that this early and ramshackle form of ribbon development tended to horrify their neighbours living in more conventional dwellings, and ruined what had hitherto been *their* Arcadia.

So Peacehaven came to symbolise both the passionate desire of ordinary workers and their families for a simpler, cleaner life, and the horror of the better-off at the blots on the coastal landscape created by these ramshackle, makeshift Arcadian dreams.

Looking at just a few historical snapshots makes one thing clear. People from all walks of life, even those on the lowest incomes, have managed to find ways to satisfy their yearning for a simpler existence. In particular, the plotlanders' odyssey is mirrored today in the leisure habits of millions of ordinary Britons who flee the towns and cities whenever they can.

While the plotlanders' makeshift settlements were largely shattered by the bulldozer, the planners and the middle-class preservation societies, their aspirations, values and dreams live on.

How small became beautiful

The level of 'green consciousness' aroused in Victorian Britain by Morris and Ruskin, but popularised by Blatchford's *Merrie England* was not matched until about 75 years later. It was E.F. Schumacher's resonant and much-discussed attack on the economic structures of the Western world, *Small Is Beautiful* (1973) that helped to revive modern popular concern about the environmental and human price of technological and industrial progress.

He depicted this 'progress' as a kind of Frankenstein's monster, out of control, lacking any moral framework, all-powerful yet increasingly remote from basic human needs. We had become enslaved by the logic of materialism, he argued, not liberated by it. But what was far worse than this social malaise was the reckless depletion of natural resources and the environmental pollution caused not only by large corporations in pursuit of profit, but by implication ourselves – their customers.

Schumacher concluded that the only release from this self-induced slavery could come from establishing systems of smaller working units, with local accountability, and using local labour and resources. He cited a report commissioned in 1972 by the Secretary of State for the Environment which explored the profound moral choices facing humanity on an industrialised planet. It acknowledged the need to bring pollution under control, and to steer the human population and its consumption of resources towards a sustainable equilibrium. The report warned: 'Unless this is done, sooner or later – and some believe there is little time left – the downfall of civilisation will not be a matter of science fiction. It will be the experience of our children and grandchildren.' (From: *Pollution: Nuisance or Nemesis,* HMSO, 1972.)

Flower-power and 'The Good Life'

'Tune in, turn on and drop out,' the late Timothy Leary exhorted us all, and indeed millions did to a greater or lesser extent in the West through the 1960s and 1970s. They grew their hair long, and ambled around in purple loons and psychedelic tie-dye T-shirts. Fuelled by flower-power, and high on all sorts of chemical, romantic and intellectual stimulants, many found the perfect focus for their rebellious energies in America's military involvement in Vietnam. They earnestly told the world to *'Make love, not war.'* As slogans go, it wasn't a bad one.

Dropping out, or opting out, was a defining feature of the 1970s, but Vietnam was not the only focus for the cultural revolt against the direction taken since World War II by consumerist capitalism. Increasingly, opting out became associated with the modern back-to-the-land movement, pioneered by environmentalists such as John Seymour, whose self-sufficiency manuals became bibles for thousands who wanted not so much to stop the world and get off, but rather to slow it down and do their bit to make it a healthier place.

Its philosophy filtered through into mainstream popular culture. It was the theme of BBC Television's *The Good Life*, one of the funniest and most successful comedy series of that decade. Its heroes, Tom and Barbara Good, were no hippies. But their attempts to create Arcadia in suburbia, self-sufficiency through smallholding, certainly made them early, albeit fictional, radical downshifters.

The Good household's homespun Green romanticism and 'downward mobility' was a constant source of embarrassment and irritation for their snobbish, social-climbing, acquisitive neighbours Jerry and Margot.

The series captured not only superb social comedy but also a sense of unease. The back-to-the-land suburbanites were eccentric, but not as absurd as the well-heeled Jerry and Margot, forever keeping up with consumer ambitions. What if the Goods were right to be looking for another path to follow? What if, fundamentally, the joke was on those who saw them as hopeless idealists whose outlook would always be marginal?

The Goods are a caricature, but an endearing and enduring image also of a search for a more balanced life. That search has been renewed 20 years on as fresh generations become all too aware of the downside of the consumer dream. The search has become a quest not necessarily for the 'good life' of a hippy Arcadia but rather for more *balance* between work and leisure, and for consumption that fulfils *needs* rather than generating endless new *wants*.

The simpler solution

Growing numbers of people are now finding ways of breaking free from the 'work-spend-consume' straitjacket that binds so many lives. Quietly, but quite radically in some cases, they are loosening the chains, casting them aside and downshifting their lives. People are already doing it in their thousands, by opting to switch to lower-paid but more satisfying jobs, working part-time or from home, or negotiating new working arrangements with current bosses. They see downshifting as a way of striking a better balance between work on the one hand, and family, friends and leisure on the other.

Worlds Apart

Rat racer	Downshifter
Consumer	Citizen
Stock markets	Farmers' markets
Fashion	Style
Soldiering on	Getting a life
Celebrity culture	Horticulture
Bankability	Sustainability
Fast bucks	Social capital
Retail therapy	Aromatherapy
Going to the gym	Going for a walk
Essex man	Ethics, man!
Live to work	Work to live
Corporate branding	No logo

Put simply, downshifting means freely trading part of your income for more time – to strike out in a new direction perhaps or to enjoy a fuller, more rounded life. To us, it's about kicking over the traces, and seizing control over your life (as far as you can), without waiting for someone to give you permission. 'Change one's lifestyle to one that is less stressful', is the *Concise Oxford Dictionary's* more succinct definition of the verb to downshift.

The origins of this modern manifestation of the simpler living ideal can be traced back at least as far as the 1980s, a backlash perhaps against the 'greed is good' era of conspicuous consumption, high-octane living fuelled by Reaganomics and stock market booms. In the US, downshifting and its forerunner voluntary simplicity were well established by the time these lifestyle trends crossed the Atlantic to the UK and continental Europe in the mid-1990s. What has been the American experience, and what does it reveal about how the phenomenon might develop further in the UK?

The New American Dreamers

Voluntary simplicity. I call it downshifting out of the rat race and upshifting into the human race.

DUANE ELGIN, US DOWNSHIFTING GURU, 1996

In the US, the word downshifting is already common parlance. Between in 20 and one in four Americans are believed to have opted for a simpler, more balanced lifestyle in the past ten years or so. Dozens of downshifting guidebooks and simple living news-letters with titles such as *The Penny Pincher* and *The Tightwad Gazette* cater to converts. Glossy magazines with titles such as *Real Simple* adorn the shelves of Borders bookstores and the CBS downshifting drama *Sea Change* has become a hit. Oprah Winfrey regularly features downshifting gurus on her television show. And the movement has even been the subject of adverse commentary in the *Wall Street Journal*, which warned that the frugal behavior of downshifters could potentially undermine the great American economy.

In the US business world, people are talking of the 'exit strategies' deployed by those stressed-out workers who are preparing to downshift, or are in an early phase of the process.

Employers are looking on with growing concern as huge numbers of talented and successful professionals, many of them in secure jobs, are seeking their own personal exit from the rat race. According to Inferential Focus, a respected New York trends analysis company, 'the desire to take flight from current employment predicaments has become pandemic'. Lately, it has been fuelled by reactions to the 9/11 terrorist attacks and to collapsing stock markets and personal pension funds, as people with marketable skills seek to take control of their own futures.

The word downshifting first surfaced in an article in the *Arkansas Democrat-Gazette* in October 1986 which told the story of a former high-flying PR executive who cut her working week from 50 to 30 hours after going freelance. The term was popularised in the mid-1990s by Gerald Celente, director of the Trends Research Institute in Rheinbeck, New York, who marked downshifting down as a 'significant and growing trend'.

'Western societies right now are very miserable places,' he says. 'People are very empty and they are looking for much deeper passions in life than those provided by material accumulation or through vicarious association with status symbols and people who represent them.'

America, of course, has had a strong simple living tradition from the days when the Puritans first landed in the New World. Its thread is traceable through the frugal-living Quakers to the nineteenth century Transcendentalists Henry Thoreau and Ralph Waldo Emerson who preached that a simple lifestyle could bring people closer to both Nature and God. Today it lives on, in its most extreme form, in the plain, self-reliant lifestyles of the Amish communities of Pennsylvania, who spurn even the motor car.

But the peculiar circumstances of the past two decades are driving unprecedented numbers out of the traditional work-place and making simple living converts out of millions. Many, of course, have been involuntarily downshifted by losing their jobs. More than 3 million workers employed by America's top 500 companies lost their jobs between 1980 and 1990 alone. The boom years under President Clinton saw a return to near full employment, although many new posts were contract-based or part-time, far from the jobs for life enjoyed by previous generations. Then the pendulum swung back again, with almost 3 million jobs lost between November 2001 and September 2003.

Over-work: an American epidemic

At the same time, those still in work are being asked to slave away harder than ever. The average American only takes two weeks off every 12 months and, incredibly, works 350 more hours a year than the average West European, according to the International Labour Organisation. Almost 40 per cent of Americans, often fearful of redundancy or of losing promotion prospects, now work more than 50 hours a week.

One study of 1,000 adults chronicled the despair and helplessness many feel at their work-driven lives. Questioned by the New York-based Families and Work Institute, nine out of ten agreed that their job required them to work 'very hard' or 'very fast' and/or was so demanding that they 'never had enough time to get everything done'.

'Our findings strongly suggest that every employee reaches a point when increasingly work demands simply become too much – a point at which personal and family relations, personal health and the quality of work itself are seriously threatened,' says the institute's Ellen Galinksy. 'Today's 24/7 economy appears to be pushing many employees up to and beyond that point.'

The result, predictably enough, is unhealthy, sedentary lifestyles, epidemic levels of work-related stress and enormous strain on personal health and relationships. Most affected is the

Baby Boomer generation: 36–54-year-olds frantically trying to juggle their prime career years with the demands of young families and ageing parents. So serious and institutionalised has America's overwork culture become that the US Senate passed a resolution in October 2003 pledging to seek to reduce work-home conflict as a national priority.

But the embattled worker is also fighting back. Surveys show that up to half of adult Americans are now prepared to sacrifice some of their earnings and possessions in return for more time with family and friends and to themselves. Many young and middle-aged employees, over-worked and chronically insecure, are choosing to jump before being pushed. Home-working and part-time employment is booming, as is the number of professionals hedging their bets by offering consultancy services to several employers at once.

James Portwood, Professor of Human Resource Administration at Temple University, Philadelphia, has coined his own term for the droves of downshifting professionals. 'I call them MUMPS, Mature Under-Motivated Professionals,' he says. 'Most of these people would say they have done it by choice. But I don't think they would have done it *unless* the world of work had changed so substantially. Work used to be partly entertainment and to have a tremendous social value for people. It used to be like going down to the club to meet friends. Now it's more like being in a war. You don't want to get too close to somebody in the office because tomorrow they might be dead. The world of work has shifted so far in favour of the "hire 'em, fire 'em" style of employer that the risks to many workers of staying with a company have soared while the benefits have plummeted.'

His analysis is shared by many American economists and political commentators. Professor Juliet Schor, a Harvard University economist and author of the best-selling book *The Overworked American* believes slaving away at work in pursuit of more money and possessions has become a social disease. 'It is not surprising that downshifting has taken root in America because America was the first consumerist nation and, along with Japan, remains the foremost consumerist society today,' she says.

The simple living pioneers

The exact scale of downshifting in the US remains unclear. But it is almost certainly there to stay. A growing mass of polling data provides an unequivocal picture of deep nationwide discontent with stressful, money-driven lifestyles. Half of all Americans, for example, would trade a day's pay for a four-day week – if they could still afford to pay the bills – according to a 2003 poll for the Centre for a New American Dream.

So what about those who have gone ahead and made the change? What kind of jobs did they leave behind? What kind of people are they?

Still the most comprehensive picture to date of the simple living movement in America was provided by a 1995 survey commissioned by the Maryland-based Merck Family Fund, and overseen by Professor Juliet Schor. Of the 800 people interviewed by telephone, 28 per cent said they had consciously made changes in their lives – other than normal retirement – which meant making less money. A third of these were in their thirties and they included more women (32 per cent) than men (23.5 per cent). The most common changes were cutting work hours, taking a lower-paid job, or giving up work to stay at home.

The survey suggests that tens of millions of Americans are swapping some of their money for more quality time. The typical American downshifter identified by the poll is well-educated and both younger and more likely to have children than the general population. In the Merck focus groups, downshifters described their new lifestyles in glowing terms:

- 'I left a job making three times the money I'm making now; but by the same token, I've got more time with my family, less stress. I've just had a little boy, I want to watch him grow up.' Indianapolis man.

- 'It's been a sacrifice . . . our pay was cut in half . . . but I think it's the best choice because you're with your children and they're in a loving environment.' Dallas woman who left her job.

- 'As I started climbing the corporate ladder, I really decided that I was hating it more and more and I was bringing more and more work home . . . I was already hiring people to clean my clothes, watch my kid and clean my house. I changed careers and got paid less. I sold the car and bought a '65 Falcon – and I'm much happier. I'm working two blocks from home and doing something I really enjoy.' Los Angeles woman.

An overwhelming 81 per cent of the downshifters interviewed said they now led happier lives. But there were some sacrifices involved. Fifty-one per cent admitted to missing the extra money they had given up and a further 9 per cent were unhappy with their new circumstances.

Professor Schor herself confirms that downshifters such as those her survey identified are no 'drop-outs' in the ordinary sense of the word. More often than not, she says, they are high-achieving, high-salaried professionals such as doctors, lawyers, teachers and administrators. 'What is so interesting is that this is a very mainstream trend. It isn't just about people who are dropping out of society. It often involves highly-skilled people who still want very much to contribute, but from outside the rat race.'

The US government has not yet analysed the stampede to simpler lifestyles and there are no official statistics breaking down those involved by gender, age and class. What does emerge clearly from information such as the Merck survey and from personal testimonies in simple living newsletters and mainstream media articles is that American downshifters:

- come from all classes and ages although the most popular age groups are the thirties and forties

- are more likely to be women than men, but only by a 6–4 margin

- tend to be highly educated and liberal in their politics. Teachers, doctors, lawyers and administrators are all prime candidates

- come from all income brackets. The Merck research revealed downshifters right across the income spectrum, from $100,000 a year to $10,000

- tend in their previous lives to have worked long hours and suffered high stress levels

- tend to continue working, although often supplement or substitute paid employment with voluntary or community activities

- tend to have strong support networks. Community halls, churches, cafés and living rooms are providing the setting for thousands of voluntary simplicity study and self-help groups

- live across the USA. The Pacific Northwest, especially Seattle, probably boasts the highest concentration. But every state has its converts. Alaska and, surprisingly, Washington DC, seat of the US government, come out top of one national mailing list of 25,000 downshifters

Drawing a new road map

People closely involved with the American simple living move-ment have differing theories about what is motivating converts and whether the majority will stick with simpler lifestyles or find it impossible not to jump back on to the treadmill.

For Professor Schor it all boils down to time versus money. Most downshifters, she argues, are economic refugees who may want to upshift in the future given half a chance. Her views are shared by the American establishment which hopes and believes that downshifting will prove to be a transient phenomenon, easily snuffed out by economic upturn. Other trendsetters and watchers believe motivations for choosing a simpler life run much deeper, often because it has proved true for themselves.

In Seattle, which has evolved into the epicentre of the national downshifters' network, you will find many adherents of the latter view. Foremost among them is Vicki Robin, whose personal finance bestseller *Your Money or Your Life,* co-authored with the late Jo Dominguez, is credited with transforming the lives of tens of thousands of grateful fellow citizens. She now runs the New Road Map Foundation, a resource centre for downshifters and environmentalists, with a 25,000-strong supporters list, through which they tap into the movement's zeitgeist.

They regularly broadcast their message on America's prime-time TV and radio chatshows and agree with Juliet Schor that down-shifters come from all backgrounds and income groups. They disagree, however, that most are temporary rat race refugees who will jump back on the treadmill when the opportunity arises. They point out that many people on low incomes or middle-class couples who have overstretched themselves have used their book purely to get themselves out of debt, but then find themselves becoming simple ˑ converts. 'They start out without any plans for a simpler life-ˑ ˑut then they get hooked,' says Vicki. 'They love it, they ˑhe maw of materialism and they never go back.'

Still in Seattle, former college administrator Cecile Andrews, another downshifter-turned-guru, has as much first-hand knowledge of what makes people turn to simple living as any other living American. Highly educated, with a doctorate from Stanford University, she followed a traditional teaching career path before ditching her job in 1993, aged 51. She now spends her time running simplicity workshops and study circles, where small groups of people discuss practical ways to make their lives simpler, then go home and act on it. Since she opened her first group in 1992, 300 have started up in Seattle alone, with another 3,000 flourishing across America using her how-to-do-it booklet as inspiration.

In her personal experience, a remarkable 95–98 per cent of downshifters have college degrees and a majority are aged 35 to 55. They are also widely read, more than averagely concerned about the environment, generally liberal in their politics and are what she calls 'high and middle achievers' – doctors, lawyers, teachers, junior administrators and clerks, downsized company managers, and so on. These people, she says, are so busy working they are achingly lonely and they worry deeply about community break-up and growing inequality in American society.

'The people who come to the workshops are people who have had a certain philosophy all their lives. They have been supposed to be getting ahead, having a good career and making money and all that is supposed to have made them happy, but it hasn't. It is once they've been through all that that people start to make changes. It's a mind-changing movement.' In her booklet she describes how many attendees come gradually to reject mass consumerism. 'A lot of people discover they never liked shopping or consuming much anyway. It was like being hypnotised, following the directions of some evil genie. We're like kids in a candy store, eating everything we can until not only does nothing taste good, but we get sick and begin a search for something more nourishing.'

Are downshifters opting out of mainstream society? Yes and no, she says. 'These are high-achieving people who want to live their lives fully and make a difference, but they also want to simplify their lives and maybe grow their own vegetables and so on.' She adds the important point that many downshifters, by pursuing portfolio lifestyles, are actually more secure financially than many mainstream workers. 'I have all these friends who used to have traditional careers and are now earning a living from two or three jobs. They may work part-time in a traditional job and then help run a newsletter and maybe make some extra money from a hobby like knitting or weaving and these people are actually much more secure than those in permanent, full-time jobs.'

Voluntary simplicity: a way of life

Whatever the majority's motives, a small sub-set of American downshifters are driven first and foremost by ecological concerns. Adherents of voluntary simplicity in its purest sense, they choose to spend and consume less in order to conserve the Earth's natural resources. For them, living frugally is not the means to an end, but the end itself.

The slightly unwieldy term 'voluntary simplicity' was coined in 1936 by Richard Gregg, a British disciple of Mahatma Gandhi. He defined it as 'singleness of purpose, sincerity and honesty within, as well as avoidance of exterior clutter, of many possessions irrelevant to the chief purpose of life'. Duane Elgin's seminal book *Voluntary Simplicity* expands the concept further. 'The objective is not dogmatically to live with less,' he writes, 'but is a more demanding intention of living with balance in order to find a life of greater purpose, fulfilment and satisfaction.'

America's voluntary simplicity disciples take Elgin's words at face value. They are community-minded green consumers who earn just enough to meet their needs. According to Elgin, they tend to be very self-reliant – teaching themselves basic carpentry and plumbing skills and so on. They also tend to work with only a small number of other people, to eat a mainly vegetarian diet, to have few clothes and possessions, to recycle religiously and to be political consumers – boycotting companies they believe are unethical. Many are also highly spiritual, although not necessarily religious. In 1977 Elgin conducted a national survey of simplicity adherents to which 620 people responded. Of these, 88 per cent were involved in 'inner growth' activities, with meditation top of the list.

Elgin, a former business consultant, is no woolly-headed idealist. He is anxious to lay to rest several 'myths' about the voluntary simplicity movement, which he believes now embraces several million people. Firstly, it is categorically not another 'back to the land' movement like that of the late 1960s and early 1970s, but is 'about making the most of wherever you are'. Secondly it does not mean living in poverty. And thirdly it is not a movement which has great ideals but will inevitably run out of steam for lack of skilled leadership because, he argues, there are many talented people among its ranks.

It's here to stay

Academics and trendwatchers disagree over how many downshifters fit into the voluntary simplicity category. At present it is clearly a small minority. Many people who practise it say they feel like isolated islands amid the huge sea of American consumerism. Yet as Vicki Robin and Cecile Andrews point out, many Americans driven to downshift by rat race pressures are finding they also enjoy simpler, green living for its own sake. America's rediscovery of its simple living roots is beginning to foster a new ecological awareness in the world's most profligate nation.

Of those tens of millions of Americans who fit the downshifting category, some will have lived the simple life for decades; many others will have been forced into it by losing their jobs;

more still have been encouraged to join in as the snowball effect takes hold, encouraged by the vast array of inspirational DIY books on offer. Nearly every American family now has a story of someone they know who has moved from city to town or town to country, who has cut back their hours or switched to a less stressful job. City couples are starting again running bed and breakfast businesses in the country. Successful lawyers are learning to farm. Tens of thousands of professionals, especially women, are setting up as home-based consultants. All are jumping on to a rolling band-wagon. Quite where this new American odyssey will lead is uncertain, but one thing's for sure. Coca-Cola and McDonald's, Bloomingdales and Macy's should all be looking nervously over their shoulders.

The British Way of Downshifting

We headed the procession when it took what we see now to be the wrong turning, down into the deep bog of greedy industrialism, where money and machines are of more importance than men and women. It is for us to find the way out again into the sunlight.

J.B. PRIESTLEY, ENGLISH JOURNEY, 1934

The first hard evidence about the prevalence of downshifting practice and aspirations in the UK came with a study in 1996 by the Henley Centre for Forecasting, in London. A survey of 2,000 adults found that 6 per cent of those in work said they had voluntarily taken steps to reduce their income in the previous two years. When asked whether they planned to take such steps in the following year, again 6 per cent replied 'yes'. Much higher proportions said they were cutting back on their spending and actively seeking more balance in their lives.

Four in ten full-timers said they would choose to work part-time if they felt they could afford to do so, and some 28 per cent said they would prefer more time off than a pay rise. Half the sample agreed with the contention that 'dedicating yourself to your job is not worth the sacrifices you have to make'.

The Henley Centre research confirmed emerging anecdotal evidence: while there was huge enthusiasm for the idea of downshifting, many people still clearly found it hard to bite the bullet and follow their hearts.

Nevertheless, Ian Christie, who co-ordinated the research, detected in the responses the seeds of a 'reaction against unfettered business-as-usual industrialisation that could become a major movement'.

Through the late nineties and the early years of the new millennium, that reaction steadily spread. The Labour government, elected in 1997, had promised to turn around failing public sector services, notably the NHS, and get gridlocked Britain moving again, with more investment in rail services. The economy ticked along in reasonable health, but the nation's social ills and rising workloads appeared to continue unabated. Ministers made encouraging noises about the importance of 'work-life balance', and urged employers to recognise that having happier staff was generally good for business and productivity.

Seven years after the Henley Centre report, market research analysts Datamonitor published a study suggesting that more people were abandoning the rat race than ever before. It showed that the numbers downshifting in the UK had risen to 2.6 million in 2002 (up from 1.7 million in 1997) and were projected to rise to 3.7 million by 2007. Across Europe, some 12 million were estimated to be opting out of conventional career paths in search of simpler, more satisfying lives.

The main drivers of this shift were identified as:

Work overload:
increasing fragmentation of European families and housholds meant that more people had to manage their social, domestic and professional lives on their own or in smaller family units

Knowledge overload:
the Internet, e-mails and mobile phones brought greater contact with work, while quickening the pace of life

Hype overload:
exposure to more marketing messages than ever before, an estimated 1,600 a day per person in the UK

While over-work was central to the trend, other aspects of modern life were crowding in on people, making them more reflective about their lives, according to Dominic Nosalik, the report's author. 'The catalysts for simplicity are well established and increasing, and are not related to the terrorist attacks of September 11th,' he said. 'However, the attacks have brought greater focus to what people truly value in their lives.'

'Sustainable' simplicity

Those at the 'greener' end of the downshifting spectrum, the voluntary simplifiers, would emphasise that the pursuit of simplicity alone is a fairly meaningless and pointless exercise. Making a conscious decision to adopt a more environmentally sustainable lifestyle must also be part of the deal – what the government's own Sustainable Development Commission summarises as 'low-maintenance, low-throughput, low-stress' patterns of work, recreation and home life:

> The clearest manifestation of this has been described as 'downshifting', detected in a growing number of people quietly reconfiguring their work to spend more time at home with their children, doing other things – entailing a lower income but a higher quality of life. The fact that this is a predominantly middle class phenomenon does not invalidate its significance, but it inevitably raises questions

about its usefulness in policy-making. With levels of poverty as high as they still are in the UK (and indeed in many developed nations, let alone in the developing world) alternatives to economic growth are non-starters unless underpinned by an equally strong commitment to poverty . . .

Source: *Re-defining Prosperity*, UK Sustainable Development
Commission, June 2003

Far from fitting neatly into any mainstream political or economic models of society's needs and wants, and what constitutes a better life for average citizens, downshifting remains a largely taboo subject for politicians. This may be partly because downshifters aren't interested in conventional definitions and trappings of success. Indeed they are quietly redefining success on their own terms, whether their behaviour and values meet with others' approval or not. It's also true that although the numbers practising this form of lifestyle change are undoubtedly growing in the UK, as we've seen, the debate around downshifting has yet to engage the public as widely and passionately as it has in the USA and, more recently, in Australia. One survey by the Australia Institute found that nearly a quarter of 30–59-year-olds were downshifting, and that the trend cut across income groups, not just highly paid professionals and business people.

Downshifting and the over-fifties

However, the UK government *has* demonstrated awareness of the need to encourage more flexible retirement options for older workers, so that people can cut their hours gradually over a period of years without severely jeopardising their final pension. In April 2000 the Performance and Innovation Unit of the Cabinet Office highlighted the problem: 'Where individual schemes allow such flexibility, it is often not well known or promoted . . . The Government should disseminate good practice about downshifting. DSS [now the Department of Work and Pensions (DWP)] should ensure that their Best Practice Guidance for pension schemes includes the flexibilities allowed by Inland Revenue rules for downshifting without damaging pension entitlement, and information to employees that such flexibilities are available.'

In a speech at the Oxford Institute of Ageing in September 2002 Andrew Smith, the work and pensions minister, pointed out that the number of over-fifties in work had increased by 900,000 since 1997. There were growing opportunities for second or third careers in later life, and it was important to promote best practice in pensions policy to 'avoid disincentives to downshifting'.

Home and away?

Many people downshift their lives successfully without feeling the need or inclination to move house. Those lucky enough to live in friendly neighbourhoods with good schools, parks, plenty of community and leisure facilities may conclude that the good life is already within their grasp – they just need more time and energy to tap into what's already around them. We suspect they may make up the silent majority of downshifters. Staying put might well be the best plan, provided that the alternative employment options that you're looking for to improve the quality of life are available or negotiable.

On the other hand, where you live may be part of the problem, rather than part of the solution. Londoners appear to be the least satisfied geographical group in the UK, ground down by high housing costs, poor transport services and unsociable neighbours, according to a survey by the National Housing Federation. People living in the north-east of England emerged as the most satisfied, and the friendliest, and the West Country was judged to be the best place to bring up children.

Moving from town to country – or to another country – is one way of downshifting. TV programme-makers, and viewers, apparently cannot get enough of relocation dramas and documentaries that track people's progress as they seek better lives elsewhere. There are subtler shifts going on too, however, that enable people to change down a gear and live simply at a slower pace.

Moving abroad

An estimated 2 million Britons live abroad permanently, and many more dream of heading overseas for a life of sun, olive groves and cheaper living costs. Renting a home in continental Europe is far more common than in the UK, and property prices in more rural, spacious countries such as France, Spain and Italy can be much lower for those who prefer to buy.

And you don't have to live cheek by jowl with other Brits on the Costa del Sol, whiling away your evening playing bridge or Monopoly, to get a slice of this new gold-rush. Increasingly the smart money is being laid on the rural inland areas of Mediterranean countries, particularly Spain. The British are now, by a long chalk, the largest incoming group of Europeans settling permanently in Spain, whether on the coast or inland.

Best-selling books such as Peter Mayle's *A Year in Provence*, *Driving Over Lemons* by Chris Stewart and *Under the Tuscan Sun* by Frances Mayes, the last recently made into a Hollywood movie, help fuel the public imagination and fascination for the idea of living better amid glorious surroundings, and stunning scenery – on less money. Cheaper air travel and easier all-round access to the Mediterranean countries mean that more of us can experience them too before we even contemplate making a bigger commitment than the occasional holiday.

Abbey (National Plc), a major provider of overseas mortgages, believes that around 1.2 million properties in France and Spain are now owned by British people. It's not clear how many of these are second or retirement homes, and how many represent permanent moves by people of working age. Research was commissioned by the bank (in 2003) to find out what sort of home people would buy – and where – if they hit the National Lottery jackpot. Nearly one-third (32 per cent) said they would leave the UK for mainland Europe, mostly citing the better weather and quality of life available there.

Buying abroad can be a sound business proposition in any event however, provided you do your homework, as the barriers to trans-national property dealing gradually come down.

Shrewd investment in the overseas property market, investment that will enhance your quality of life over the long term rather than the next couple of years, requires serious research. Blagging a free holiday at your mate's converted pigsty or swanky villa in Tuscany will only get you so far. You need to sample ordinary working life as well as leisure in foreign lands if you are to get it right. House-swapping and exchanges, through local town twinning associations perhaps, can open doors when you are thinking of downshifting abroad. Specialist magazines and websites can also open your eyes to the realities of life abroad, as can information and links via UK estate agents who are increasingly diversifying into overseas markets.

Homes Overseas magazine recently published their Top Ten emerging property markets for those considering investing overseas to live or to let:

Top Ten Emerging Overseas Property Markets

1 **Hungary:** Budapest has excellent public transport and the River Danube is a World Heritage Site, plus there's all that fabulous architecture and art. Handy for Vienna.

2 **Auckland, New Zealand:** Undergoing big surge in popularity with tourists and house-buyers, as a result of the country's big screen exposure in the *Lord of the Rings* films.

3 **Turkish Riviera:** Beaches, culture, but Turkey's human rights record may deter some.

4 **Bulgaria:** Black Sea coast, and good skiing. You may still be able to buy a house for the price of a (new) car in the UK – if you get your skates on.

5 **Crete:** Reasonable autumn/winter climate. A short hop from Athens airport.

6 **Almeria, Spain:** Hottest and driest area of mainland Europe but up-and-coming investment hot spot.

7 **Andorra:** Tax haven. Good skiing.

8 **Le Marche, Italy:** Country houses, towers and castles are the order of the day. A beach is never far away, and the stunning countryside is comparatively untouched.

9 **Croatia:** War-ravaged only relatively recently, now the new Tuscany according to some property-watchers.

10 **North-east France:** Like Kent, glorious weather cannot be guaranteed. Highspeed Channel Tunnel rail link, promising a ride from Calais to King's Cross in under an hour, is however due for completion in 2007. May compensate for grey cloudy days.

Source: *Homes Overseas*, October 2003

Simply holidaying overseas is unlikely to give you the perspective you really need to consider moving to a country. Spending some time working and living in a foreign country is a good way of researching your suitability for moving to one permanently. One route that's both instructive and worthwhile is via Voluntary Service Overseas. In 2000 VSO published research indicating a surge in the number of applications for overseas postings from UK business and management professionals, dissatisfied with stressful workloads and drifting lives. The findings pointed to one common motivating factor: 'a rejection of materialism', a VSO spokeswoman said.

Another trend that's helping people to reassess their lives and maybe change direction is the growing popularity of the gap year across all age groups. No longer confined to youngsters between school and college or university, gap year travellers are increasingly in their thirties, forties and fifties, taking a career break from stressful jobs.

Moving to the country

More than a quarter of the UK population (28 per cent) now live in rural areas, an increase of 12 per cent since 1981, according to the latest census. This amounts to a significant migration out of cities and large towns into the countryside. A study commissioned by Sainsbury's Bank showed that between April and September 2003 alone, some 6 per cent of all home-owners on the move – some 61,000 people – were downshifting to rural areas.

Lucy Hunter, the bank's Mortgage Product Manager, said that a rising property market was making home-owners in towns and cities feel wealthier, but not necessarily happier: 'Many are considering cashing in on this wealth and moving to the countryside where properties and the cost of living are less expensive and there is the opportunity to leave the rat race.' However, in September, the bank released further research indicating a rather muddier picture: that the downshifters on the move to the country, and people 'upshifting' in the other direction to towns and cities were evenly balanced at 4 per cent in each case.

A country cottage, preferably in the south-west of England, remains most people's dream home however, according to the Abbey research mentioned earlier. But how often does the reality of country life match expectations for the average city dweller and townie whose hearts are set on rural relocation?

The answer seems to depend on several factors: your sociability and general outlook on life, for example, the area you choose and which surveys you believe. In its 2003 State of the Countryside Report, the government's Countryside Agency cited evidence that rural dwellers are much more likely to be involved with local organisations, and interact with their neighbours than those living in urban areas. They may be more entrepreneurial too: business start-up rates and levels of self-employment tend to be higher in the countryside than in towns and cities, partly because of a dearth of alternative employment in many areas. Although three-quarters of the land area of the UK is rural or agricultural, under 5 per cent of the rural population is now employed in farming.

Tensions between incomers and born-and-bred locals can of course turn the countryside into a battleground of conflicting interests and mutual suspicion. Where youngsters on low to average earnings find themselves priced out of the housing market by affluent refugees from the cities and large conurbations, the resentment can be acute. Stress and depression can be as common in some rural areas as they are in urban areas, as the decline of traditional farming takes its toll on local communities and livelihoods.

The rise of the bi-locals

The growing number of properties bought as holiday or weekend retreats demonstrates opportunities for serial downshifting, as opposed to the full-blown version. The Countryside Agency estimates that there are some 100,000 holiday homes dotted around rural England, although in some popular holiday areas such as the Lake District and the New Forest the proportion of residential properties used as holiday homes can be as high as 60 per cent or more. Again, the lack of affordable housing for local people in these places is forcing many to move to the towns and cities in order to get on to the property ladder – sometimes commuting back to their rural roots for work.

In response, some councils in Devon have already raised the council tax on second homes from 50% to 90% of the full rate. This tension between local populations and affluent incomers buying up homes that are empty for much of the year shows no sign of abating. We would suggest that low-impact second home-owning – on mobile home 'leisure parks' (caravans that stay put), beach huts or canal boats – are better bets within the UK for those with the cash and the inclination for the bi-local life. We discuss some of these issues further in later chapters (Home Front, p. 173 and Holidays, p. 236).

8

Real Lives
– Downshifters Tell Their Stories

You see things and say: 'Why?'; but I dream things that never were and say: 'Why not?'

GEORGE BERNARD SHAW (1856–1950)

1: The post-modern romantics

Daniel Butler, 40, and Bel Crewe, 39. He was a business magazine journalist, she a charity fundraiser. They quit London to run a 13-acre smallholding on a remote hillside in mid-Wales. Daniel now writes about environmental issues and Bel has recently taken on two part-time jobs working for her local community. Their son Jack, nine, and daughter Molly, six, go to the local village school.

From their sixteenth-century farmhouse a few miles south of Rhayader, Dan Butler and his partner Bel have the most glorious panoramic views south towards the foothills of the Cambrian mountains, uninterrupted by buildings or roads. It's one of the few places in Britain where the only background sounds come from the birds and the elements. What they see from the windows at the front of the house has barely changed in thousands of years. Outside the great glens of Scotland, this is the most isolated and under-populated part of Britain.

This is home for two rat race refugees who left London back in December 1993 in search of a simpler, more rational and more enjoyable life. They bought the four-bedroom house, high above the Wye valley, along with 13 acres of pasture, woodland, duck pond, pigsties and stone barns. It set them back £100,000, the same price that Dan got for his two-bedroomed flat in Islington, north London. For him, it was a childhood dream coming true. 'I always wanted to be self-sufficient, and read all the John Seymour books about it when I was growing up,' recalls Dan. The son of eminent Oxford academics David and Marilyn Butler, Dan spent his twenties working as a lobbyist and as a journalist for the Haymarket stable of business magazines after graduating from Cambridge University in history.

In May 1991, amid a prolonged staff dispute with the management over union recognition, Dan was offered redundancy. He accepted without hesitation. 'It was the best thing I ever did,' he recalls, as he prepares a delicious lunch of home-made pasta and salad from the garden. He met Bel in his late twenties just three days after he left London to stay in a borrowed cottage in Oxfordshire, to raise ferrets, to freelance and to work out what on earth he would do next. Not so long afterwards, Bel became pregnant. Dan decided this was the perfect opportunity to make his dream come true – to yield to the twin temptations of cheap property and romantic visions of rural life. In short, to head for the Welsh hills. Bel had yet to be 100 per cent convinced.

A former charity fundraiser with a degree in art history, Bel was in the early stages of pregnancy and feeling pretty awful when they began scouring Wales for a smallholding. Estate agents eyed the couple warily and routinely questioned them about their intentions: 'What are you going to do to make a living? There's not much round here apart from forestry and agriculture, you know.'

What Bel remembers more than anything about this time was the misery of being sick out of the car window as they inspected properties for sale or bursting into floods of tears at the sheer disappointment of what they encountered at the end of various fruitless searches. 'There was one place we saw in the middle of nowhere. It had no phone, electricity, or kitchen. The nearest shop was ten miles away. Dan thought it was romantic, but it was actually hideous and I cried for an hour. What I'd had in mind was Exmoor or Somerset, or somewhere by the sea.'

Eventually, they rolled up at Tan-y-Cefn. Each of them was seduced by the spectacular views from the house, and the sheer peacefulness of the place. They decided their search was over, bought it and moved in. It rained solidly for the next three months.

Undeterred, they began to make themselves a new life, quite unlike the old one. Bel took charge of fruit and vegetable growing, using whatever books, magazines and newspaper articles came to hand to find out what, where and how to plant. 'I knew nothing. It was all trial and error,' she says. 'I find the vegetable and fruit growing absorbing – especially if it works and they come up.' Now her staple produce includes seven different types of potato. More exotic delicacies such as asparagus, sugar snap peas, mangetout, chillies, melons and lettuce-leaf basil have also cropped successfully. She grows everything from seed. It's virtually all organic. The experience has changed her outlook, especially as it has meant their children are getting a far more nutritious diet than they would have got in London. 'I've become more aware of environmental and conservation issues through growing our food. It makes you more respectful of what's around you, more thoughtful. It just makes such a difference, knowing exactly where it's come from and what it contains. It's so much healthier, and that's important to both of us.'

Dan reared two Tamworth pigs, and bought in turkeys, ducks, geese and chickens. The pigs were slaughtered and the bacon eaten over the course of the first two years. The couple reckon they are about 50 per cent self-sufficient in the summer months, less so during winter even though they freeze what they don't eat fresh from the soil. They don't even have to grow some of their free foods – like wild mushrooms – they just walk up the hill and pick them. Such is their accumulated expertise on this front that Dan now runs regular 'funghi forays', short weekend courses for mushroom-lovers who want tips on picking their own, and where to find them. The first one they did was not entirely successful. 'The weather was terrible, the mushrooms didn't come up, we charged too little and the group was too big,' says Dan, opening a huge jar of cep mushrooms, also known as *porcini*. 'But you learn from experience how to pitch it right. We are about to have an Italian ex-restaurateur coming back with his entire extended family, which should be interesting.' Dan also leads 'raptor rambles', walks devised for birds-of-prey-spotting.

But Bel and Dan don't simply exploit the land for themselves. They're careful to improve it and put something back too. They now have red kites nesting on the smallholding: 'We inherited an acre or two of conifers, which we've been replacing with some deciduous native hardwoods,' says Dan. 'I have to plant 800 trees myself this winter. We're laying and planting new hedgerows as well, using hazel, hawthorn and dog rose which will attract more birds and other wildlife.'

Neither was earning much in London, and their joint income was lower still during their early years in Wales, but so too were their monthly outgoings, including mortgage payments. Instead of supporting a combined £70,000 loan on their respective flats, their new mortgage was £50,000. Self-sufficiency for much of the year means they don't need as much money as they did in London. Instead of automatically buying something they need, as they used to do, they will probably have a go at making it. Dan has acquired a cordless drill and has already made an outdoor table and cold frames for the vegetables. Bel had trouble finding fresh pasta locally, so she makes her own.

As a business and economics journalist, Dan used to spend hours every day on all sorts of activities *associated* with work, but not actually working – like commuting, business lunches, chatting to colleagues by the photocopier. It took up several hours a day, all of them non-productive. Now, he writes articles and books about environmental issues and wildlife. The difference is that he does it when he wants and needs to, not necessarily every day. 'You don't have all the time-consuming distractions from the business of working here, so when I'm working to earn money, that's *precisely* what I'm doing.'

Inside the house, the tools of their transformed lifestyle are the computer and the fax-modem, the most high-tech possessions they own. These plug them into the outside world, and are essential for Dan's writing. For Bel, in particular, the technology is a lifeline to family and friends. 'It only costs a few pence to e-mail people, so I use that more than the phone these days – it's so much cheaper,' says Bel. 'I even persuaded my sister to go on e-mail so we can keep in touch better. It is isolated here. When we first came, I felt like we'd retired. It would be nice to have more people to visit locally.' Like Dan, Bel writes, but for her own satisfaction, not for money. 'I write to get my brain cells moving. I keep three diaries: a gardening one, one for mushrooming and for observing nature and one for everyday stuff. I would love to write stories too. I feel the need to do something else, to have another project, another skill.'

Dan thought he had earned about £25,000 and spent £26,000 during their first year on the smallholding. In fact he was earning £9,000 and spending £10,000. In 1995 his earnings rose to about £15,000. As the children have got older, Bel has taken on two part-time jobs with local charities. By 2003 their joint income had grown to £35,000. 'For us, the important thing is that our quality of life has risen immeasurably. You cannot put a price on the view across the hills that we have here, being able to see rare birds of prey like red kites, peregrine falcons and goshawks wheeling around the sky.'

They have been fortunate in having loans and moral support from their parents in the early days to help ends meet. Some friends from their London days have not been so enthusiastic. 'The general reaction was that we must have been barking mad,' recalls Dan. 'My brother has made some very sniffy comments, and there are some friends for whom the life we lead would be hell on earth.' Bel adds: 'My friends in London are extremely reluctant to come out here for a weekend. For most, the journey is too long. At first it was all a bit too wild when people came here and they sometimes sat in embarrassed giggles, shivering. But we're a bit more organised now, we've got the guest room painted and decorated.'

There is a downside of course. It's called winter, and in this part of Wales it can stretch to almost half the year round. 'The days are so short, and the weather so bad you can't get out and do very much. We tend to watch a lot of TV,' says Dan. 'We've been snowed in a few times, but I rather liked that. I was rather lonely in London, but here I've been happier than I ever dared to hope. It's been much harder for Bel, she's had quite a tough time.'

Her lowest point came when she developed complications during her labour with Jack. She endured an agonising one-hour ambulance journey from the cottage hospital at Llandrindod Wells to the general hospital at Hereford where she underwent an even more agonising forceps delivery. It took her over a year to recover. She remains philosophical about the experience: 'I could have had just as bad a time had I been living in Muswell Hill. Who knows?'

Their lives are dictated by the seasons, the weather and local culture, now, rather than the clock, as they once were. Dan explains: 'If you go into a local shop here, then chances are you have to wait while the old lady in front of you has her chat with the assistant, and then tries to find the right change to pay. If that happened in London, she'd probably get stabbed or something. Here, it just doesn't matter – it's normal.'

Although Bel feels more settled now she would not rule out moving to somewhere less remote: 'I was the reluctant partner coming here. I can imagine moving slightly closer to London perhaps, and living somewhere with a nicer climate.

'I'd never want to give up the gardening and the growing. Dan would stay here or somewhere like it, for ever, whereas I feel more ambiguous about the future. You have to have a lot of energy to do what we have done. I am not sure whether the life we lead is sustainable, indefinitely.'

Dan, however, can imagine living somewhere even wilder, where the skies are even wider for indulging his passion of flying his hawks Freya and Tache. 'I am obsessional about flying hawks. It's what I love doing.' His partner draws the line at the idea of going somewhere even more remote. 'Dan knows that if he goes to Scotland, it's going to be a very lonely drive,' she says, firmly.

Dan's downshifting tip

'If you are thinking of moving somewhere isolated and doing self-sufficiency to a greater or lesser degree, get to know your neighbours before you buy a property, however far away they are. You can save yourself a lot of trouble that way by establishing where the local rights of way are, finding out the history of planning applications that might affect you and so on.'

Bel's downshifting tip

'If you plan to move to a new area, I would say rent a property there for a while, maybe a year, so you can really get to know the place and the people, before buying.'

2: The liberated mandarin

Petra Laidlaw dedicated her life to a 'fast-track' career in the Civil Service, in classic textbook style. She ran the private offices of three Cabinet ministers, co-ordinating all the work that a busy government department does for its ministers. At the age of 45 and earning £60,000 a year, she had gone far and looked as though she would go further, but opted to take voluntary redundancy. What she discovered was a life beyond Whitehall more liberating, exhilarating and delightful than she ever dared to expect.

It took Petra Laidlaw only a short while to conceive and plan an early exit from a high-powered career in the Civil Service, but a full decade to implement it. As far as most colleagues were concerned, here was an independent and capable career woman who had the talent and the application to make it pretty well to the top of her profession, and make a success of it until she retired. They were right. She had those qualities in abundance, and indeed rose to the ranks of senior management, still an uncommon achievement for women in the Civil Service. But by her mid-thirties, Petra was questioning whether she really wanted to give up all the best years of her life to hard graft, however exciting and rewarding. 'I thought about the 15 years I had already done, and then reflected that I still had another 25 years to go. It seemed an awful lot. It occurred to me that I could get to the age of 60 and not have done anything else with my life.'

She resolved privately to set herself a new goal and drew up a strategy to achieve it: to save and invest enough money to leave work at 50 and to start exploring the rich potential of life beyond the office. Her goal was simple enough, but one that few consider achievable, if they consider the idea at all – namely to secure for herself a life of leisure while still young and healthy enough to enjoy it.

'I always enjoyed my work right up to the end,' recalls Petra, relaxing in summer sunshine in the garden of her elegant Victorian semi-detached house in north London. 'It was fascinating work. I always got a buzz from sorting out political crises, or achieving impossible tasks against impossible deadlines!' For most of her career she was working 60 to 70 hours a week, and by the end was running a division of over 70 staff. 'I don't think I would have been regarded as particularly workaholic. The Civil Service I joined was notorious for its long hours culture, and for many years I was happy enough to go along with it. But, probably around the time I was deciding not to work past 50, I saw the light about working smarter instead of harder, and tried hard to keep my own hours and those of people working for me within reasonable bounds. I was no longer prepared to take work home with me or work at weekends. I tried to do my bit about spreading the word that long hours are bad for everyone's health – including the organisation's – and that shorter hours are a sign of efficiency and virtue.

'But even then I had precious little time to myself. All my weekends were spent doing the weekly shopping, seeing to domestic correspondence and trying to keep up with my closest friends. Even then it was hard to get round all my closest friends more than once or twice a year. Once I had done all that, there was no time to relax and do anything else I wanted to do.'

So, she sat down to work out the minimum sum of money she needed to save if she was going to be able to live on the income from it. 'For a minimum income of, say, £10,000 a year, I needed to save up a capital sum of £200,000. I reckoned that if I set aside a fair part of my salary every month and invested it in a way that would produce growth, I could build up that sort of sum over 10 to 15 years. So I made that my target and stuck to it. And saving a high part of my salary made me used to living all along on a lower income than the salary suggests – a good preparation for when I stopped work.'

Petra did all this with very little advice from others. 'I spoke once or twice to financial advisers, but in the end did my own financial planning. I prefer to make my own mistakes rather than have others making them for me. It's also cheaper. You can pay out an awful lot to all the intermediaries wanting to take a cut along the line.' And she kept the plan away from her managers at work: 'It would have been very unwise to reveal anything other than 100 per cent commitment.'

So how was it that such an eminently bright, capable and independent woman decided to cut short at her prime such a fascinating career at the heart of British politics and government with plenty of money and status?

Well, to understand that you need to know a little more about her personality and about the changing culture of Britain's Civil Service. Petra graduated from Reading University in the early 1970s in Italian and Linguistics. Her first job was teaching at a special school for severely mentally handicapped children. She decided to do a Post-Graduate Certificate in Education, part-time at the South Bank Polytechnic in London. After a year, she and her fellow students were told that their qualification would not, after all, be recognised by the Department of Education. 'So I thought: to hell with this, I'll do something else, and if I can't beat them I'll join them.'

She applied for the 'fast stream' of the Civil Service training, got accepted and 'drifted in'. Petra felt at ease with her new colleagues, the surprising informality of the Whitehall environment and its co-operative ethos. 'I would never have wanted to work in an environment where backstabbing for personal advancement was the rule. People do not generally tend to go into the Civil Service for personal glory – there is little to be had. The pleasure comes from contributing something, however anonymously, to our national life and doing the job honestly and well.' At the Department of Education and Science (now called the Department for Education and Employment) in her early career, she helped to develop policy on bullying and truancy and

79

worked on a major survey of the nation's school building stock.

She was closely involved in the original thinking on the radical school reforms of the late 1980s and early 1990s, the development of the national curriculum and the creation of OFSTED. She was private secretary to Norman St John Stevas (now Lord St John of Fawsley), when he was Leader of the House of Commons. Later she was principal private secretary to two education secretaries: John Patten and Gillian Shepherd.

Petra looks back wistfully at the job she had in the mid to late 1970s, dealing with medium- to long-term expenditure plans. 'With the discovery of North Sea oil, all the talk was about educating people for all the leisure we would be enjoying by the 1990s. It seems hopelessly naïve now. But at the time, everyone was envisaging that with our new-found national wealth and computers to take away all the drudgery, we would all be working something like a 30-hour week, and enjoying an egalitarian affluence.'

Although she likes to think that by opting for redundancy at 45 she opened up opportunities for other people, Petra would be the last to say she was acting altruistically. When the offer came, she was still some way off her target of £200,000 by age 50, but the redundancy money would make it up. She calculated that she could square the circle financially, and went for it. 'I was just lucky that my circumstances fitted. I was not bringing up children and my mortgage was much lower than someone who had bought their house later on would have been.' A lot of people she worked with wanted to take redundancy, but it was not so easy for those who had not made financial plans well in advance.

Petra will never forget the day she left Whitehall for the last time: 'It was a glorious sunny day. I walked home and my soul was singing. For several days afterwards I just walked around London – a city I am probably unusual in loving. Everything looked so good, buildings that I had not seen, old details that I had never noticed, old alleyways into little gardens I did not know existed. I just went where my feet took me – no maps – all round the East End, the West End, north London and Docklands. I just wanted to go where my fancy took me. It was a metaphor for what was happening in my life. The sense of freedom was phenomenal.'

Eight years on, Petra has not regretted 'even for a nano-second' her decision to quit the Civil Service in mid-career. In the early years of her new-found freedom, she did occasional consultancy work, researched her family history and relished spending more time with friends and her partner John.

She's since branched out into freelance photography, had her work published in specialist journals and plans to convert the basement flat under her house into a darkroom and studio.

'Photography is great fun – something I always wanted to do,' she says. 'I found myself in the position of having the capital to buy the flat, but not the income to do it up. So in the last year or so I have been doing consultancy work full-time to help pay for that. But I am hoping to free myself from that soon and get back to photography.'

Another bonus of changing tack when she did is that Petra, now 53, had the time and energy to help look after her late mother and step-father in their declining years. 'They both developed dementia unfortunately, and it was a relief for me not to be tied to a demanding job while also trying to look after them. I was glad that I could be there for them. I think this is becoming quite an issue for people in their forties and fifties, as their parents live longer and dementia affects more families.'

Petra lives modestly, but comfortably. She paid her mortgage off out of her redundancy money and reckons that simply no longer having a high-flying career is saving her considerable sums each year. 'I used to spend well over £100 a month on home-to-work transport, and another £100 on my cleaning lady, who was anyway due to return to Sweden when I gave up work. On top of that I must have spent something like £500 a year on clothes for work and several hundred on entertainment at work for my staff, the occasional business lunch, and so on.'

In addition, she finds that being able to do things in her own time comes cheaper. 'Instead of madly stocking up on everything in sight when I go to the supermarket, I just buy what I need when I need it. Going to the theatre, the cinema or the gym at the times they call off-peak – which is when I want to go anyway – is much cheaper. And I don't feel the same need to splash out and crash out on exotic holiday destinations. All in all I need much less money now than when I was working.'

Petra Laidlaw's story illuminates several truths about our attitudes to paid work, the huge and sometimes excessive sacrifices the work culture extracts from us, and about the imbalance work has wrought upon our lives. In particular, it helps to nail one popular canard: namely that women are keener than men to opt out of the rat race simply because they want to spend more quality time with their children. Petra has no children. She has struck out simply so as to get more out of life. She had no particular project or alternative career in mind when she left her job. 'Certainly, I was taking a great leap in the dark, but for me that feeling, that very uncertainty was one of the attractions, part of the great pleasure of it all.'

Petra's downshifting tip

'Know yourself! And know the environment you work in. If you don't see yourself working there until you are 60 or more, plan ahead. But keep it to yourself. Even in these days when people are expected to switch occupations several times, employers want to think they have your undying loyalty. If they think otherwise of you, you may be out before you're ready. Work smart, think smart and you'll be in command of your own destiny.'

3: The woodlander

Cornishman Bill Robinson, 57, a former British Telecom manager, now earns his living cutting logs and making charcoal from the woodland opposite his village home near Truro. Both he and his wife Kay, 53, are registered childminders. They have two children, Rachel, 26, a post office worker and Chester, 22, who recently completed a degree in photography at Exeter University.

Beneath the billowing green canopies of oak trees in Idless Wood, a mile or two north of Truro, Cornwall, lies a hidden world of foxes and badgers, wrens and chiff-chaffs. Go walking in these ancient woods on a dry day and you might spot wisps of pungent smoke drifting up from a clearing off the main track, near an Iron Age hill-fort. When it's wet, you're more likely to hear the whirring of a chainsaw and the muffled thud of logs encrusted with moss and lichen being hurled into a trailer. For as well as being a haven for wildlife and country walkers, this woodland is also Bill Robinson's workshop.

Bill joined British Telecom straight from school as an engineer and over three decades worked his way up the organisation. He ended up running the company's business line installation and maintenance operation for Cornwall. Privatisation in the 1980s had triggered wave after wave of cost-cutting, streamlining and job-shedding, as BT faced growing competition in a global market. So by the time Bill was at the peak of his managerial responsibility, in charge of about 30 employees across the country, the pressure on him to perform was relentless.

'I enjoyed it all, but by the end it had become a rat race,' he recalls over breakfast at his home one wet May morning. 'We had to keep the head count down, but this proved increasingly difficult. Cornwall is a long thin county with a scattered population. It often takes a long time to get anywhere. When there were thunderstorms, for example, and the lines came down somewhere, then

we had to bring in staff from Wales to fix them. Your performance figures for that month were terrible, although from the
customer's point of view that was all part of providing a good
service.

'Budgets were being reduced, but all the time you were
expected to make improvements.' Bill had to travel a great deal
for business meetings, to Plymouth, Exeter, Bristol. This was fine
while BT put him up overnight in a comfortable hotel, with a
good dinner and a drink with his colleagues at the end of a hard
day. But these perks were cut and soon he was having to travel
to these meetings and back in a day. 'I was getting up at 6 a.m.,
and driving maybe 100 to 200 miles on a day trip. I was getting
home later and later, after the children had gone to bed, so it
wasn't good for family life.' In the late 1980s he was asked to train
to be a customer care tutor. He had to go away on courses more
and more. 'I enjoyed it, but it was taking me away from my basic
job, which caused a bit of friction.'

One day in 1994, with another round of job losses in the
offing, Bill's senior manager took him aside on one of his regular
trips to Plymouth and asked: 'Bill, have you thought about redundancy?' He had. BT's redundancy packages had become more
attractive with every round. At the same time, Bill's enthusiasm
for the corporate life was waning fast, and he yearned for a new
and less stressful life. He began to wonder whether the woodland
on his doorstep which he had loved to roam from childhood
might provide him with a more interesting source of income.

'I was listening to an item about charcoal burning on the BBC
radio farming programme early one morning and thought maybe
I could try that. I found a charcoal burner called Mark Ventham
near Plymouth and he showed me how to make charcoal. I
bought my first kiln from him.'

As we bumped along the rutted track heading up to the wood
in Bill's battered Land-Rover, he went on: 'I had always had a
good rapport with the Forestry Commission, which owns this

wood, so I went to see Ben Jones, the local beat forester. I told him I was thinking of taking redundancy, and about what I had in mind. He said, "Well, I've got some trees on the old Iron Age fort site that need some sympathetic thinning." That was it. I decided I would leave BT.'

Within a few days, Bill was the proud owner of 3,000 standing oak, birch, beech, hazel and holly. He swopped his briefcase for a chainsaw, and spent two days soaking wet from the rain learning how to use it. A grant of £1,400 from the Devon and Cornwall Training and Enterprise Council helped pay for courses and new machinery. He paid over £400 to the Forestry Commission for the right to cut down the selected trees on the neglected, over-grown ancient site. They got the woodland thinned out, so the remaining wood grew more vigorously, and attracted more wildlife and plants: he kept the timber he had felled to turn into logs for firewood and charcoal, in his kiln set up a few hundred yards away from the fort site.

The proprietor of the newly formed Cornish Coppice Company struck his first deal at Mallet's hardware store in Truro. It was selling imported charcoal. Bill went in one day and persuaded the owner to take a bag of his. 'When I went back the following week the bag had sold and he asked me for more. Luckily my first summer's trading coincided with some wonderful weather, which meant that people were having plenty of barbecues. I sold virtually everything I made.'

More than a decade on, Bill has no regrets about his decision to change tack. He was earning £28,000 a year, and working 50–60 hours a week when he left BT. 'There, I was just another manager, whereas now people are more interested in me and what I am doing, and I enjoy work more. I've visited Poland several times through the new skills I have learned, and my son and I have done a lot of long-distance walks together, which has been great.' He has cleared the overgrown woods on the Iron Age site. Now the sunlight can penetrate, there's an abundance of new life among the remaining younger trees, and the rowan and birch saplings that have appeared: honeysuckle and bilberry, wrens, jays and butterflies. He has since bought a second kiln, and built a good client base for selling his logs and charcoal, but he is still earning less than during his BT days. Working much closer to home – in the area where he grew up – however, has enabled him to devote more time to his family and community life.

When he burns charcoal, the process takes 24–30 hours. For safety reasons, Bill has to watch over it the whole time. 'I have to stick a tent up, the family brings a meal up to me and it's actually quite pleasant all sitting round the kiln. If I was at home, I'd probably be sat in front of the TV.

'What I like is the flexibility. If I don't have a customer to supply that day, I can go off walking. I've got more time for the community – I'm a school governor and I'm on the parish council.' But how has the switch affected his family? Do they enjoy having a woodland entrepreneur among them, where once they had a besuited manager? 'My daughter Rachel is an outdoor type, very practical and has always been interested and supportive.'

In his teens, the couple's son Chester was the least happy family member about his father's change of direction. Missing the family holidays abroad, the regular salary and status he associated with other dads, Chester initially remained unimpressed when Bill pointed out that he was now the managing director of his own company. 'Yes, and you're the only employee too,' Chester would cuttingly retort. As he has got older, Chester has not only become more comfortable with the new family order, he's also been working in the wood recently, clearing scrub between newly planted trees, on a temporary contract.

It was lucky that Bill's wife Kay switched jobs at about the same time as he did. She swopped her working life as a school lunches supervisor to become a home-based registered childminder, and is now much in demand among the working parents of nearby

Truro. They like to bring their children out to a countryside home, replete with ducks and geese marching around their large hillside garden and maybe the chance to explore the woods with Bill.

'I did have some doubts at the start,' says Kay. 'If Bill hadn't got something lined up when he left BT, I don't think it would have worked out so well as it has. If I want to get away for a break, to visit my sister in Cheshire, or I have a dental appointment, then Bill can arrange to look after the children as he is a registered childminder too now. I like being my own boss, as Bill does. It suits us well.'

For the Robinsons, opting for a simpler lifestyle wasn't the financial gamble it has been for some. They don't have a mortgage, for instance. Perhaps because they have always been careful with money, they are hard pushed to think of material sacrifices they have had to make. Bill says: 'For the first few years, we didn't go to the pub much and we cancelled our daily newspaper. Now I cycle to get a Sunday paper, and we sometimes walk to the pub for lunch or a drink. We find we don't need to spend like we used to.'

What about the downside? 'I sometimes miss the company of work colleagues at BT, and talking over the everyday work decisions that I now have to make on my own. But overall, I'm happier now.'

Bill's downshifting tip

'Make sure you have something to do after you leave your current job, and enough money to live on. Don't take on too many things at the start, as I did; I was looking to do hurdle-making and supplying bark for tanning at the beginning, as well as the charcoal-burning and the logs – ridiculous, too much. Lastly, don't get blinkered. Keep your mind open to change, be flexible. You may enjoy your new work, but who knows? Something else might crop up in a couple of years that might suit you better, and you might like more. It hasn't happened to me yet – but I don't rule it out.'

4: Downshifting entrepreneurs

Andrew James, aged 55, and Sophie Chalmers, aged 40. He lost his job as a marketing manager in 1991 and her television research contract ended soon afterwards. They ploughed their life savings into a new business providing advice and support for professionals working from home, and nearly lost everything. They sold their comfortable London home and bought an old mill set in a secluded and lush green valley in south Wales. Their joint income fell by more than half to £30,000 during the first five years, but has steadily recovered since turning the business round. They have three children, Caspian, 12, Saskia, ten and Emlyn, six.

'Men are such boring old farts,' exclaims Andrew James over lunch at the family home near Chepstow. He is musing on the psychology of plunging into self-employment from the relative security of mainstream jobs, and pointing out that women are often the more adventurous sex. 'Women tend to be so much more creative and imaginative in selecting new business ventures, whether it's cake-making or marketing organic meat. But men tend to carry so much baggage with them when they leave their old jobs and often just go on doing what they did before, but as consultants, working for themselves using their old contacts.'

Andrew should know. He speaks from bitter experience after losing his job in 1991 as a marketing manager. It soon dawned on him that he was not only ill-prepared but completely unsuited for work as an independent consultant.

Now he and his wife Sophie make their living helping others

steer their way through the minefields of running a small business from home or elsewhere. They are downshifting entrepreneurs, for want of a better description, and so are many of their customers. It sounds like a contradiction in terms, but let's examine what this couple has done, where they are now and where they hope they are going.

They have opted out of traditional ways of working and established a socially useful business that chimes with the changing shape of a service-led economy and the new corps of independent 'knowledge' workers. They work together as a team, blurring the edges between home, work and family life that help provide definition and structure to most people's lives.

Like most good ideas, their subscription-only magazine *Better Business*, edited by Sophie, published by Andrew, was conceived out of personal experience and a gut feeling that it would plug a gap in the market. Along with countless others trying to launch themselves into self-employment, Andrew had come unstuck at a pretty early stage. 'I hadn't had any training or experience of how to charge for my time, for instance, and quickly became disillusioned. I realised I was too much of a perfectionist to be any good as a consultant.'

At this time Sophie, whose contract as a television researcher had ended soon after her husband's redundancy, was combining freelance typing at their home in London with caring for their baby son Caspian. Change was very much in the air: 'A cousin set up a business marketing ski pole stop-watches, but he hadn't a clue at the start,' recalls Sophie. To find someone to make the product for him, he looked in the *Yellow Pages*, and went to the first person he found. He launched at the wrong time of year. At each stage something went wrong, in the great tradition of British amateurism.' The experience led them to resurrect an idea Andrew had had some months earlier, to launch a newsletter for home workers. 'Suddenly, here was the person I could envisage reading the magazine, picking up tips about how to make your new business work and avoid some of the pitfalls,' says Sophie.

On a wing and a prayer in July 1992 they sent out a mailshot to 15,000 potential clients, using £8,000 of their savings. Only 50 took out subscriptions and sent cheques. 'We should have written off the £8,000 and returned the cheques, but we were too stupid. We sent out the newsletter and had two very tough years when it was just haemorrhaging money like mad.'

The business was on the brink of collapse, having absorbed all £22,000 of their savings, and there was nothing to pay their mortgage. By happy coincidence, an article about *Home Run* (the forerunner of *Better Business*) appeared in the *Daily Telegraph* in 1994. The piece renewed interest and brought more subscriptions in the nick of time. Soon the business moved into profit for the first time. Their daughter Saskia was born. They sold their London house, put everything into storage and started house-hunting in rural south Wales, close to a cottage they used to rent for short breaks near Chepstow. They took out a reduced mortgage and bought Cribau Mill together with 20 acres of pasture, grazed by neighbouring farmers' cows and sheep.

Andrew takes charge of the computer technology and the technical side of the business. Sophie edits and shares the administrative responsibilities. 'We work as a team. I do the first run of the magazine and then he pulls to pieces what I've written,' says Sophie. 'As editor, I have the last word.' They recently took on an assistant for the business so that Sophie no longer had to work a seven-day week, and there is a nanny to care for the three children during the day.

Long gone are the 'perks' of their old lifestyle, the company car, the BUPA health cover, the monthly salary cheque, the sick pay. Their joint income has fallen to £30,000 compared to about £65,000 before Andrew's redundancy. The perks of their downshifted life are less tangible, but worth a great deal more – at least to them. Andrew got on the phone one day to a public relations contact in London, who asked him: 'What are you up to? What's going on in the country, then?' Andrew replied: 'Well, the sheep are bleating.' 'Yes.' 'The hunt's just gone past.' 'Hmm, uhuh . . .' 'And I'm looking at the flowers in the garden.' 'Oh, shut up, that's enough,' replied the jaded PR man.

Sophie adds: 'I wouldn't go back to a town to live if you paid me. It's safe for the children to run around and play. They're happy at their school in the village. We have a much more relaxing time with our friends, when they visit for a weekend, than in London when we would gabble our news over dinner.'

Andrew and Sophie were never ones for flashy clothes or fast cars in London. Travelling was their luxury – to Nepal, Africa, Australia, France. 'We used to have two expensive holidays a year, now we have one short inexpensive holiday every two years. We don't need holidays now because we are where we want to be.' They work hard and play hard. Instead of watching TV, she relaxes by doing tapestry and writing a novel: 'My outlook has changed. Our work and income begins and ends with us. If we don't get the money we don't pay the mortgage. There are no perks, no BUPA, no sick leave, no company car. On the other hand, we are in control. We are NOT going to be made redundant. The hard work we have put in is finally being rewarded.

'It is idyllic. Emotionally, I am happier in the country. I am a real country bumpkin. I love going out running and falling over badgers going out for their evening snout around. It's so fresh, clean and quiet here. When I go to London I feel so sorry for my friends living with all that congestion and filth. The nearest thing I have seen to a traffic jam here is three cars at a junction on Remembrance Sunday. It wouldn't suit everyone of course, perhaps if you're used to having a corner shop handy or nipping out to Peter Jones. Having children is a bonus out here, because you meet other people through your children and their playgroups. We've stopped eating out at restaurants – we go for dinner to other people's houses.'

It wouldn't suit every couple to work and live together 24

hours a day. These two manage it by being extremely good friends and giving each other time off. 'We're equals, although when we started it was very much Andrew running the show and I was the unpaid secretary. I learned my editing skills as we went along, and Andrew was generous in giving me space to grow, and giving me the leading role in the business.'

How does Andrew reflect on the changes of the past few years? 'I enjoy work, but I was not a company man. Going abroad, chairing conferences and preparing strategies I found enjoyable, but I could not abide drawing up endless budgets. I also found that while I was great at having ideas, I was not so good at implementing them. What makes this business work is that Sophie is a doer, whereas I am a waffler. I much prefer to hide away in an ivory tower and plot. If left to my own devices, I would spend most of my time working out some new program on the computer instead of doing the business.'

It's a common problem, becoming so transfixed on the tools you use to do business that you overlook the winning of the new customers. This is one of the single most important causes of failure: lack of new business. 'Once people have a computer at home they ring us up and say: "Right, what do I do now?" It's like a commuter saying: "Well, I have my car for commuting. Give me a list of jobs that commuters do." There is a notion that somehow other people will be thrilled to give them work.

'What I do not miss about my former life is office politics, commuting, inflexibility of working times, compulsory drinks in the pub, especially when someone is leaving, being asked at two hours' notice to make an impromptu speech at the company Christmas party, and the company Christmas party.' The couple now have a 30-yard commute from the house to the old mill, which they've recently converted into offices so they can separate living and working arrangements more clearly.

'Our clients often like to come here rather than us to visit them in their glass towers in Bristol or wherever,' Andrew adds. Each stresses the need to get out, network and meet people as much as possible to avoid 'ending up like a pot-bound plant, devoid of nutrients', as Andrew puts it.

Ask Sophie what she misses and she replies: 'Friends.' For Andrew, the list is rather longer: 'I miss the feeling that I can go away on holiday and not have to worry about anything. I miss the feeling of security that I can do a sickie. I miss international travel, going off meeting my peers in The Hague.'

They are not keen on the word 'downshifting.' 'It sounds so negative – as though you are taking a cut in income without gaining anything,' says Sophie. 'We look at it as swopping salary for sanity. If you look at it that way, you are *upshifting*. You are taking a deliberate decision to switch off, and get a life.'

Sophie's downshifting tip

'If you have a dream, make it happen. Work out what it takes, step by step, to make it work, then do it. The bad times come good in the end if you believe in what you're doing and you stick with it.'

Andrew's downshifting tip

'If you're a couple, you need to share the vision for changing your life. The other partner has to be supportive. It won't work if, say, the wife is still expecting a clothes allowance and resents her husband being around the house during the day, or keeps asking: 'When are you going to get a proper job?'" *Details of* Better Business *are listed in our Downshifter's Directory.*

5: California dreamers

Hollywood screenwriter and producer David Weimers and his partner, ex-hospital doctor Paul Turner, quit California to take over the ailing post office at Bourton-on-the-Water in the Cotswolds. They were both coming up to 50 and Paul felt so stressed by work he feared he would not make it to retirement if he carried on in his job. David often felt isolated working at home on a script not seeing anyone all day. They financed their £426,000 purchase of the post office, shop and attached three-bedroom house by selling their three properties in California.

On a sunny October afternoon in Bourton-on-the-Water, tourists are drifting between the tearooms and gift shops, taking photos of each other in front of the honey-coloured stone houses. Village postmaster David Weimers is amused to see that his views on Arnold Schwarzenegger's election as the new 'Governator' of California have made the front page of today's *Cotswold Journal* ('Bourton's take on Arnie win'). 'Everyone and his kid brother has been asking me what I think about Arnie,' he says with a laugh.

It's exactly a year since he and Paul Turner moved to England to try and turn around the fortunes of a run-down post office in a picture-book village. They currently employ five staff, and supervise 12 postmen. Neither had any relevant experience that would have prepared them for the events of the past year.

We're sitting in the living-room behind the shop and office, with the couple's two miniature Schnauzer dogs stretched across the carpet snoozing contentedly. Paul had intended to join us, but he'd been called away to help out at another short-staffed post office in a nearby village. 'We moved here because we love the area so much, having spent holidays touring England,' David explains. 'We both wanted a lifestyle change, and to be at the hub of a community. Paul was head of the infectious diseases department at a hospital in Los Angeles, in charge of all the HIV cases.

He was getting very tired of all the administration he had to do that was taking him away from patient care. He said to me one day last summer: "Retirement is still 15 to 16 years away. I don't think I can do this any longer."'

David too was ready for a change. Having written and produced several successful Disney films such as *Tarzan*, *Winnie the Pooh* and *Clifford the Big Red Dog*, he sometimes found it isolating working all day at home writing for film and TV. 'Although I used offices at the studios from time to time, I would frequently work from home and encounter no one all day. Often I'd go and work out at the gym, just to be amongst people.'

After much discussion, they hit on the idea of buying and running a post office – ideally in the Cotswolds, preferably Bourton-on-the-Water. In the USA post offices are all government-owned, so there was no question of pursuing the plan there. Besides, the couple were set on the idea of moving to England. 'We came across one grungy little post office for sale just outside of Bath, and after two weeks of searching we saw the one at Bourton advertised on the Internet. The owners had only been there a year, but there were a few potential buyers interested in the place, and we ended up in a bidding war for it,' David recalls. They won it after grilling the owners about how the business could be improved, and paid £1,000 above the asking price. What neither of them realised was how much work they would have to put in running the business and turning it round. 'For us it was a new mountain to climb – something different. It was like, "Yeah, let's take over the post office." We've been on a steep learning curve.'

Their biggest problem from the start was recruiting enough staff: 'We had no idea how difficult it would be to get people to work in this town, which is primarily a retirement community. It's meant we have not had a day off since we took over; we're up at 5 a.m. sorting newspapers and magazines and we're working an 80-hour week. We're constantly re-stocking the shelves and talking to reps. It was never this busy working in TV!'

Although their first year's accounts aren't yet in, the couple reckon they are significantly up already on the previous year's performance. They've introduced new computer services, designing and laminating menus for local restaurants, and even producing self-published books by local authors. In the next few months, they are planning to revamp the layout so that people needing post office services and items from the shop can just use one checkout point. They plan to do some travelling as and when they get the chance, but only once they have resolved some of their staffing issues.

Financially, David and Paul are worse off than when they lived and worked in California but at the same time there hasn't been much opportunity to go and spend their hard-earned cash – on a holiday for example. Slowly they are getting on top of the workload and beginning to feel they can ease up a little. 'Our relationship with the locals is wonderful. We've turned this into a place where people can come in every day, bump into their friends and have a chat, which is great. I'm very much a people person, and I love being at the centre of town.

'It's only in the last few weeks that I've been able to resume writing – developing ideas for a couple of series for the BBC, and an animated series.'

Unlike his partner, David does have some regrets about how things have turned out. He had no idea that running the post office, and dealing with staff issues, would take up so much of his time and energy. Equally, though, he sees the benefits of changing direction in mid-career while they still have the energy and good health to make a success of a new venture. 'In the TV business, there is such age discrimination – I could definitely see it coming. The only reason why Arnie Schwarzenegger ran for governor of California is that he was over 50, and he knew the public was not going to go on buying him as an all-action movie star.

'But I think that we all have to look at ourselves in the mirror and the day comes when you ask: "Isn't it time to reinvent myself?"'

David's downshifting tip

'Remember that life is ultimately about making choices, managing your time well so that you can pursue the things you want to do, in the way you want to do them.'

6: The corporate convert

Paul Bellack, 48, gave up a high-powered, high-earning corporate job nine years ago. He lives off an investment income, is raising a young family and donates much of his time to an ethical property company of which he is a director.

When Paul Bellack, a high-flying property dealer and archetypal yuppie, walked into his boss's office at Sun Life of Canada in December 1994 and said he wanted to quit, the reaction was predictable. 'He flipped,' he recalls with a boyish grin. 'He sent me straight off to see the head of personnel and told him to persuade me to stay. They even offered me a four-month sabbatical. But they could have waved half a million pounds at me and I wouldn't have budged. I wanted a new life – outside the rat race.'

When Paul left Sun Life's London office, the insurance company had just taken over a major rival, Confederation Life, and he had been asked to run the combined property portfolios, worth £800 million. After 19 years working his way up the organisation through loyalty and hard work, he was being offered a major promotion at a time when many of his colleagues were losing their jobs. Had he stayed, his staff would have doubled in size and his salary risen from £65,000 to £95,000. Instead, he chose to walk out without a penny. 'A lot of colleagues thought I was going through a hippy phase and would snap out of it and come back after a few months,' he recalls, nine years on, from his home office in Lewes, Sussex.

After a few months spent celebrating his freedom by backpacking around India and New Zealand, Paul spent his first three years as a downshifter on self-development courses, voluntary work and the occasional property consultancy. While at Sun Life, he and a friend had bought several properties to rent out and this business provided him with a comfortable investment income to live off while deciding what career to pursue next. 'I trained as a counsellor and did yoga and meditation courses and pursued my hobbies,' he says. 'It was part of the process of leaving the corporate world behind and finding my feet and I was lucky to have the luxury of being able to take that time to work out what I wanted to do next.'

Paul's former high-maintenance lifestyle vanished with his job. He sold his car and began cycling everywhere. After years of dining in expensive, fashionable restaurants, he discovered the joys of cooking, gave away many of his expensive clothes and took up recycling 'with a passion'.

By the late 1990s Paul decided that he did not want a completely new career. 'I came to realise that I had really enjoyed my job in the corporate world, but what I wanted to do differently was firstly to be my own boss and secondly to use my skills in a more socially useful way.' The answer was the Ethical Property Company, an organisation which buys properties and then rents them at subsidised rates to charities and community enterprises around the country. As a director, Paul spends several days a week working for the publicly funded company for free. He also donates expert advice to charities from around the country which contact the EPC for help.

The rest of his time is taken up by his personal property investment business and by his family – wife Louise and daughters

Freya, three, and six-month-old Holly. In 2002 the family moved from London to Lewes, selling his fashionable west London bachelor pad and renting a house by the sea. They continue to live off the income from his rental business, enabling Paul to be a hands-on father and to donate his skills rather than charge for them. 'It was without doubt one of the best decisions I have ever made, leaving Sun Life of Canada,' he says emphatically. 'Working from home, I can get Freya dressed and take her to school. I enjoy cooking and shopping for good local food. I wouldn't have had time for these things if I was still in the corporate world.'

Paul quit the rat race several years before he was married or had children, while living an archetypal yuppie lifestyle. So what prompted such a dramatic change of course?

'I spent 19 years with Sun Life, working my way up from a 20-year-old general dogsbody to commercial and property investments fund manager. I would buy and sell properties worth £20–30 million a year. I was never stressed by the work, I loved it. But I always felt there was a gap in my life – a spiritual or life growth gap – that for years I pushed to one side.'

Two events finally brought this dissatisfaction to the fore. First, in May 1994, Sun Life sent him on a week-long leadership course in Niagara Falls where he listed his top personal goal as 'make up my mind, once and for all, about my future with Sun Life'. Then, a few months later, he enrolled on yoga, dance and writing courses on the Greek island of Skyros. 'I loved it. It was a real spiritual awakening and it made me realise there was a lot more to life than the company.'

Paul returned to work deeply unsettled and a few months later received the list of priorities he had written for himself in Canada. It provided the final spur and he decided that morning to leave the company. 'It really gave me a feeling of empowerment, to make such a major decision about my life and show that I was in charge of my own destiny.'

The reaction from friends and colleagues was mixed. His

former partner at Sun Life was deeply shocked when Paul chose to leave the company, but has come to terms with his decision over time and they remain friends. Paul's Austrian-born father and British mother, to his surprise and delight, were very supportive. So was his future wife Louise, a New Zealander whom he had met during his last few months at Sun Life.

Today, however, Paul sees more and more people jumping ship to join him. 'It's becoming an acceptable career move now, downshifting,' he muses. 'It's certainly happening more among people I know.'

Although Paul's current annual income remains significantly higher than the national average he does not believe this contradicts his downshifted lifestyle. 'I do definitely count myself as a downshifter – although I still don't like the word, it's too negative – because my energies are going in different directions than before,' he says. 'I could go out and earn a lot of money, maybe half a million pounds for a year's work, but I'm not interested.' Still a keen cyclist, he was disappointed, he says, when after six happy years without a car he finally bought one as a concession to family life.

Are there any downsides to his new life? 'Well, there are times, when the children are screaming, that I wish I had an office outside the home,' he concedes, 'but otherwise everything's great.' And what of the future? 'The greatest benefits of downshifting are a proper family life and the flexibility and control that come with owning my own business and setting my own work hours. I can't imagine ever giving all that up and going back to the corporate world.'

Paul's downshifting tip

'If your intuition is telling you "enough is enough, I need a change", then listen to it. Have the courage to start a new journey even if you're not sure what your final destination will be.'

7: Downshifting abroad

Julie Weston and Iain Simpson left good jobs and their London home in their late thirties to start over in an idyllic French village. They have three children, Ella, seven, and four-year-old twins Sam and Jonny.

Five years ago Julie Weston and Iain Simpson had a settled and happy life: a two-year-old daughter, Ella, whom they adored; good, fulfilling jobs, he as a BBC radio reporter, she as a part-time fundraising consultant to charities; and a four-bedroom home in London's fashionable Highbury neighbourhood. Then in 1999 their twin sons Sam and Jonny were born and within months their lifestyle changed dramatically.

The average cost of childcare for just one toddler in London, let alone three, is now £6,000 a year – more than the average family spends on mortgages or food. Within a year, Julie and Iain were having trouble making ends meet. 'After the boys reached 12 months I went back to work three days a week,' says Julie. 'I wasn't prepared to work full-time because I wanted to be with the children. Childcare for the three of them was enormously expensive. Even though Iain and I both had good jobs we found we could hardly keep up with the bills and couldn't afford to go on holiday any more.'

The couple were also increasingly fed up with the noise, pollution and lack of outdoor life in a big city. Finally, after months of debate, they decided they had to leave London to improve their quality of life. Some of their friends had moved to suburbs or villages outside the city where both property and childcare were cheaper, but this didn't appeal to them. 'We didn't want to commute into London. It would have been tiring and costly,' says Julie. 'The only other option was to move abroad.'

As Iain and Julie had lived together abroad while working in Asia and Hong Kong, moving to Europe did not seem like a huge leap. A visit to an ex-colleague in France left them wondering how they could follow suit. They both had contacts in international organisations, discussion with one of whom eventually led to a job for Iain in communications at the Geneva-based World Health Organisation. Several hectic months of planning and packing followed, including a long weekend house-hunting along the French-Swiss border.

Once the decision was made they acted swiftly, renting out their London home and becoming tenants themselves in a small village called Grilly, just across the French border from Geneva. Ella, then five, began attending the local state school and was soon speaking French in the classroom. Iain cycled to work in Geneva, 30 minutes away, and was home with the family by 6.30 p.m. Julie gave up work for the first few months while they all settled in and spent time getting to know their community and how things worked. Both she and Iain spoke passable French before they arrived.

Life immediately improved. There were woods and a stream just outside the house for the children to play in, as well as mountains and an enormous lake to explore at weekends. Food, utilities, insurance and petrol bills all cost much less once they were out of the city. 'We really were immediately a lot better off, financially and in every other way,' says Julie.

Less than a year after moving, the couple found their 'dream home', a five-bedroom old French house with a large child-friendly garden. As their London house had soared in value, they were able to remortgage and own both properties. But the financial strain of two monthly mortgage payments, coupled with the pressure of finding and keeping tenants, became too much and after about a year they decided to sell up in London.

'It was a huge decision for us losing our base in Britain but in the end it was a lifestyle choice,' explains Julie. 'With two houses we were basically asset rich but cash poor, just like we had been before we left London. We sat down and did our sums and thought, OK, we can both kill ourselves working very hard for ten years and keep our house in London as a nest egg. Or we can sell up and have the choice to live life the way we want: in the present, enjoying the children while they are young.'

Although Julie now works two and a half days a week as a fundraising consultant for the UN High Commissioner for Refugees she sets her own terms: working from home and not answering the phone during the children's two-hour lunch breaks when they come home from school. She could afford to give up if she needed to. 'Selling our house in London freed us from the money-making treadmill,' she says. 'I thought it would be quite a wrench to do it, but in the end it wasn't because life is so much better here. When I'm working I look out of my window and I see Mont Blanc. Instead of wanting to watch TV, the children often just gaze at the mountains. How can you beat that?'

After two and a half years in France the children, now seven and four, are becoming bilingual and Julie and Iain both speak French well. The family travels back to England quite often for short breaks, staying with relatives and using cut-price airlines in off-peak season. And, not surprisingly, they are never short of visitors. There are small downsides. They have struggled to find good after-school care on the days Julie works and drive a lot more than they would prefer.

Iain's workload has also increased recently after he was promoted. He is now rarely home before 7.30 p.m. and his cell phone often rings at weekends. But he has negotiated to start work after taking the children to school twice a week. If the strain becomes too much, he says, he could afford to walk away or try to negotiate a less hectic, more family-friendly schedule. 'I think we have our lives much better balanced now. Although I work long hours, I am flexible enough to take an afternoon off to be with the children or whatever's needed. It's a great situation to be in and we all really appreciate our new life.'

Julie's downshifting tip

'If you make your decision based on achieving a better quality of life, you can't go far wrong.'

8: Freedom in freelancing

Denise Moll, 65, set up a secretarial business from home in her mid-fifties when she was made redundant after spending most of her adult life in conventional employment.

Denise Moll lives alone, has no TV, eats out only as a treat and buys most clothes from charity shops. She survives on around £6,000 a year. Yet this isn't a hard luck story: her life, she says, has opened up in ways she never imagined possible when she was made redundant in 1993, aged 55.

'All my life I worked for other people,' she says, explaining her decision to buy a computer and fax with her redundancy cheque and set up a home-based, freelance secretarial business. 'Yes, in the beginning I had anxious moments wondering how ends were going to meet, but they always have, and I am so much happier and fulfilled and have much more time for myself and others.'

After graduating from secretarial college in the 1950s, Denise worked in London for an advertising agency, a firm of architects and a PR company before moving to the United States in 1961. There she worked as an administrator for an Episcopal church, developing a strong interest in charitable work. Back in England, she again moved from job to job, until in 1981 she settled at the Ockenden Venture, a refugee charity.

Working as personal assistant to Joyce Pearce, the charity's founder and driving force, Denise's life began to change. After years of conventional secretarial work, she became so immersed in her job – working and living with refugees and staff – that, as she puts it, 'work and play became fused instead of separate compartments'. At this time too, she says, 'my conventional Christian upbringing broadened out into a wider multi-faith, spiritual understanding' which included the embrace of simple living ideals.

This experience laid the foundation for Denise's transition to a self-sufficient, simple living freelancer. When she was offered redundancy after 12 years at the Ockenden Venture, she set up a secretarial business from her one-bedroom flat in West Byfleet, Surrey, and took on work that suited her interests and beliefs. She became general secretary of the Life Style Movement, which promotes simple, ecological lifestyles, and has since had a variety of other jobs including typing books, designing leaflets and acting as secretary for the Association of Wise Women, the Wrekin Trust and the Gandhi Foundation, among others. The work, she says, all came via word of mouth.

'Of course,' she adds, 'the kind of jobs I do pay little. But I discovered, after the age of about 55, that doing what you really want to do is more important than earning huge sums.' Her flat is owned by a housing association and she is head of her residents association. 'All these jobs, big and small, have contributed to my spiritual growth and understanding and thus provided nourishment and joy – making up, if you like, for a small income!'

Denise's flexible work schedule allows her often to use the daytime to do things she couldn't before in her conventional full-time job. She goes to mid-week matinee theatre performances, has the time to queue for standby tickets and takes leisurely country walks with friends. She has more time, too, for hobbies including reading and writing, yoga and cooking for friends. 'My whole approach to life has changed. I actually work hard, but in my own time.'

Denise had much less money to begin with than many downshifters, after working for churches or charities offering small or no pensions. Although she lives frugally, she includes organic food in her shopping, and recycles wherever she can. She has also acquired a half share in a local allotment for the princely sum of £17 a year and maintains an inexpensive second-hand car, while cutting back in other areas such as clothes-buying without any hardship. 'I thought at first that living in this poorer way would be restricting, but I find it actually liberating!' she says with enthusiasm. 'I can manage on less, don't want more, and am constantly looking for ways to reduce my possessions still further.'

Denise, who has never married, admits to being 'an inveterate shopper' when she was younger, but says such habits are not suited to her life now. 'Now and then I'm impatient when I have to count the pennies, and cast a longing eye at the Lottery. But I really don't believe it is money that brings happiness. It is how you use the resources you have – small or large – that determines how happy or unhappy you are.'

Being self-employed and flexible has also enabled Denise to broaden her horizons. She has visited Northern Ireland many times for the National Peace Council and went with UK women's groups to visit women in Bosnia. Through the International Society of Ecology and Culture she also spent a month living with a family in Ladakh, India, on their Himalayan farm. She helped with cooking, cleaning, weeding, cattle grazing and apricot picking. 'It was an experience of a lifetime,' she recalls. 'Everyone knew and helped each other in the village. I came to understand "living simply" all over again.'

Denise describes herself as a non-political downshifter and as spiritual rather than religious. She believes the steps she has taken to work part-time and simplify her life will eventually become commonplace. 'I think people will come to it in their own way. There will be a lot more leisure time and part-time working and people will be thrown more on their own resources.'

When Denise first took the momentous step of setting up on her own with so little behind her, friends were nearly all encouraging, but her sister feared that she would not be able to cope with such a huge change, or with less money. A year later she admitted she had been wrong and had never seen Denise so happy or relaxed. 'When I was working for other people I would rate my happiness at five out of ten, now it's nine or even ten,' says Denise with a smile. 'My personality has changed. I'm much more outgoing and less prone to anxiety and depression. My whole quality of life has been transformed.'

Denise's downshifting tip

'Follow your inner impulses and don't be afraid to live off less. It can be very liberating.'

9: Simple living pioneers

Euan McPhee, Nona Wright and their daughter Catriona swapped a house in Guildford for an organic smallholding in Cornwall after Euan took voluntary redundancy from his academic post.

Until they reached their late forties, Euan McPhee and Nona Wright were the embodiment of British suburban living. Like millions of other families, they lived in a semi-detached house with a small garden in a quiet suburb of a middle-sized English town. Canadian-born Nona was a librarian and Euan a further education lecturer – one of the first in Britain to teach ecology.

But the couple had always shared a strong streak of self-sufficiency and an environmental awareness that marked them out. They did not own a car, grew their own vegetables and only bought a TV set when five-year-old Catriona began to feel left out at school without one.

So when, like thousands of other families, they were confronted first with mounting job insecurity, then with the spectre of mid-life redundancy, their response was not the typical one. Euan chose to take voluntary redundancy from his job at the local further education college 'before I was pushed'. He and Nona decided to sell their house, cash in their endowment policies and buy a smallholding in Cornwall where they could create a millennial version of The Good Life.

'We didn't want to be like Tom and Barbara,' says Euan, 56, 'trying to live outside society. I still feel I have a lot to contribute, but my ambition moved away from the traditional career ladder towards wanting to see what kind of simpler, greener life we could achieve.'

Seven years after leaving Guildford, the family have fulfilled most, if not quite all, of their dreams. They have turned their nine acres of land in the hamlet of Penhalurick near Redruth into an organic smallholding, owning 30 free-range hens, 16 ducks, nine sheep and a cow. They are self-sufficient in meat and eggs and sell some surplus produce through the local economy. Euan has also planted an orchard of traditional West Country apple varieties.

Under a ten-year management plan agreed with the Rural Development Agency the family are paid to manage their orchid-filled wet meadow and heathland and to allow visitor access. Euan also teaches applied biology three days a week at Truro College, while Nona works one day a week at a theological library.

'It has been a wonderful experience,' says Euan. 'We live in a 35-year-old bungalow rather than our dream country cottage and we had to give in and buy a car to haul all the farm stuff around, but other than that we have achieved pretty much what we set out to do. Our quality of life is greatly improved.'

The couple's annual income has fallen from £28,000 to around £15,000, leaving little over for anything but essentials. But luckily Euan and Nona were well acquainted with the concept of downshifting even before they left Guildford. Together they edit *Living Green*, the newsletter of the Life Style Movement. The latter's motto 'Live Simply, That All May Simply Live' reflects its world view that rampant Western consumerism is threatening the planet's future. It is a view with which Euan and Nona whole-heartedly concur.

Their efforts to live out their beliefs in Cornwall, however, have not been all plain sailing. They bought their bungalow and small-holding with the proceeds from their Guildford home and Euan's £20,000 redundancy payment and for the first year lived on what money was left over while they applied for their countryside stewardship grant and for jobs locally. 'We had just survived the first year without starting to panic when Truro College called me up needing a replacement lecturer in a hurry,' says Euan. 'I've been working part-time ever since but money is still part of the challenge – working out how little we can survive on.'

He says they miss the London theatres and their previous two-yearly trips to visit Nona's family in Canada: 'Now there always has to be one of us home looking after the animals.' Yet the couple's greatest concern about embarking on a new life – the effect it might have on Catriona – has proved groundless. Now 16, she catches the bus to Redruth School, loves the farm animals and is considering becoming a vet. 'At first she was upset at leaving her friends in Guildford,' says Euan, 'but she handled the transition very well and has made good new friends in the farming community.'

Both Euan and Nona firmly believe that the forces shaping Britain's economy will work increasingly in favour of people opting, like them, for part-time, short-term and community-based work. Both strongly believe they are in the vanguard towards a less work-obsessed, less consumerist society. 'I think we are actually more secure now in generating income because we have diversified,' reflects Euan. 'I do not feel at all threatened or insecure about what the future holds.'

Nona agrees, pointing out that they did not have down-shifting thrust upon them. 'We are better prepared psychologic-ally than most people because we chose to do this. Many of the professional people we knew in Guildford reached 50 and were told by their companies they were no longer wanted. They had no choice about living more simply.'

> **Euan's downshifting tip**
> 'Take it slowly when you make such a big decision about your future and don't overstretch your resources, by trying to live in a house that's too big for your income, for example. Trying part-time work is always a good halfway house. Also invest in a good computer and use the Internet to keep in touch with the wider world.'

PART THREE

Preparing for Change

I ought, therefore I can.

IMMANUEL KANT (1724–1804), GERMAN PHILOSOPHER

9

Could It Be You?

It is very tempting for people exhausted by long working hours and stress to seize on the idea of downshifting, as if it were *the* key to happiness for the rest of their lives. Rebalancing your life and changing down a gear can indeed prove to be a life-transforming experience. But it is important not to romanticise the concept unduly, nor to rush into a new and simpler life too hastily. You may love it for a few weeks, treat it like an extended holiday, and then suddenly find yourself getting rat race withdrawal symptoms. That could land you in an altogether new quagmire, since it takes much longer to accelerate to cruising or sprinting speed if you've just pulled up to look at the view, or because you are suddenly bored by running.

It is crucial to talk through and plan for the financial, practical and emotional realities before you make any decision. After that, it is a good idea to sit on it for several weeks, even months if you can, until you are 100 per cent ready and eager to take a sideways leap on to a different track altogether.

The first five steps

Step 1: *Look before leaping*
If one day it hits you like a revelation that you need a change, the first thing to do is to discuss it with those closest to you. If you're single, you don't have to convince anyone else to go along with you, but for couples and families it is obviously essential that the whole household is involved in any decision. The subject should be broached diplomatically, and well ahead of any irrevocably dramatic gesture at the workplace. It is no good coming home one day and announcing: 'Guess what? I've packed it all in, and I feel *wonderful*,' because you may not get the sympathetic hearing you might expect. Many downshifters, for example, while preferring their new lives, do miss their lost income, so be aware that money could become a source of friction.

If one partner is keen to downshift, and the other not, then the sooner you know the better, so you can get on and thrash out the issue openly. Now is the time to resolve such conflicts – not after you have sold the house, uprooted the children from their schools, and bought that job lot of 25 goats and a barn conversion in west Wales. Talk about it now. A constructive way to start the conversation might be to think about the sort of life you want to be living in 10 to 15 years time. You must both be persuaded that it is likely to work, or can be made to work, before making any irrevocable moves. And don't be impatient. Getting used to the idea and talking it over from all the angles may take months rather than weeks.

Step 2: *Find out what you really want from life*
If you think you want to explore the idea further, start listing your dissatisfactions with your present life. If it is hard to put into words, try answering the following eleven questions as a starting point. If you answer yes to all or most of the questions, then a simpler, more sustainable and rational life may well be what you

are yearning for. Finally ask yourself the larger question: How would you spend your time if you knew that you only had a year to live? It may seem like a rather melodramatic question, but it is a wonderful way of concentrating the mind on what you really want from life.

Are You A Closet Downshifter?

1 Do you constantly wish you could spend more
   time with your partner/family/friends?   YES ❑ NO ❑

2 Do you feel you never have any/enough
   time for yourself, to spend on hobbies,
   gardening and leisure
   or just to relax?   YES ❑ NO ❑

3 Do you feel that your work is taking so much
   out of you that you don't have time to
   enjoy the money you earn, spend it
   or invest it prudently?   YES ❑ NO ❑

4 Do you believe your pattern of work is
   giving you health or stress problems?   YES ❑ NO ❑

5 Are you chronically or permanently
   tired?   YES ❑ NO ❑

6 Do you dread going into work in the
   mornings?   YES ❑ NO ❑

7 Do you feel your work doesn't truly
   reflect your values?   YES ❑ NO ❑

8 Are you unhappy with the contribution
   you're making to society? YES ❏ NO ❏

9 Do you think you would be happier if
   your career changed direction completely? YES ❏ NO ❏

10 Do you have so many commitments that other
   people – cleaner, nanny, babysitter,
   gardener – are impinging too much into
   your personal life? YES ❏ NO ❏

11 Do you spend much of your time fantasising
   about your next holiday and then collapse
   when you get there? YES ❏ NO ❏

Your answers may well be ambivalent. It may be, for example, that you believe your job is indeed leaving you exhausted and stressed-out with too little time for your family, but that nevertheless the work you do reflects your personal values and is helping you contribute to society. This is the kind of dilemma which currently faces millions of busy working people, particularly parents of young children. Take David Bartlett and Trisha Stead, for example. Both do jobs they love, he as a charity services manager, she as a social worker. But they also wanted more time with their young children, Ilona and Reuben. The answer for them was to move from London to Yorkshire and both work part-time so that they only needed childcare one day a week and could both have lots of quality time with the children. 'I can't imagine now doing it any other way,' says David. If this sounds like you, the next step is another paper exercise.

Work out all the possible ways of making your present life easier and more enjoyable, such as:

- asking your boss if you can sometimes work from home

- getting more help around the house

- taking more frequent breaks

If you think these changes could improve the quality of your life then take them up with your partner or manager, or both, and try and make them happen. You can always come back to the idea of more radical change later if those steps don't achieve what you had hoped.

Perhaps you should start talking about sabbaticals in your place of work, or flexi-time, or different ways of getting the job done and see how many other people are interested. Nothing will change unless people talk about change.

On the other hand, if you are convinced you cannot juggle your present life to make it more bearable, think hard about what other employment options you would rather pursue. Then ask yourself the following questions:

- Which matters most to you, job satisfaction or income?

- Would the new job option you favour give you as much fulfil-ment and income as the present one?

- Would the preferred alternative *really* give you more free time and reduce your stress levels, or might you end up still working long hours and having new anxieties to cope with? Would you really end up with the kind of balanced life you are aiming for?

This kind of exercise may make you appreciate your job more fully, whatever the day-to-day irritations and pressures. Your dream of setting up your own business might look less attractive, for example, once you've worked out the set-up costs and the long hours you would have to put in to make it work. You may realise that the advantages of sticking with it outweigh the disadvantages, especially if you have a sympathetic boss and senior colleagues who agree to take you seriously.

Step 3: *Weigh up the pros and cons*
If you decide as an individual, couple or family, that change is the only way to achieve a more balanced lifestyle, then test your gut feelings against a practical list of pros and cons. This will mark the first step from fantasising about downshifting into making it a realisable proposition. Your list should cover job satisfaction, home and personal life, earning power, emotional stresses and reactions from the outside world.

Take one of the authors of this book as an example. Early in 1996, Polly decided to consider applying for voluntary redundancy from the *Observer*, where she was Whitehall correspondent. She and her husband talked about whether she should leave her job to go freelance and work from home. Here is the list of pros and cons she drew up:

Pros
✓ A better home life with proper weekends together. At present I work every Friday evening and Saturday while Allan works Monday to Friday.
✓ Reduced stress levels and better health. As a freelance, I can better control my work levels.
✓ More time and energy to enjoy seeing my family and friends.
✓ More time to get fit through exercise.
✓ New work opportunities. The chance to diversify after seven years on one national newspaper, into working for other newspapers and magazines, researching new projects and writing books.
✓ Big redundancy cheque in the bank to help ease the transition to freelancing and provide a safety net for the future.

✓ More flexibility for the future. If we start a family or decide to work abroad it will be much easier because I will no longer be tied to a single employer.

Cons

✗ Loss of status and a guaranteed writing platform.

✗ Sharp drop in regular income. Annual salary likely to drop by £20,000 a year.

✗ Loss of job security and benefits such as paid holidays, sickness and maternity leave.

✗ Loss of camaraderie in the workplace, and the daily opportunity to spark ideas off other people.

✗ Coping with negative reactions from colleagues and others that I have somehow 'copped out' because I'm not immediately joining another media organisation full-time.

✗ Having to cut back on luxuries and expensive holidays because of a drop in income.

When Polly and Allan looked at the list it was immediately apparent that the pros were all about life-enhancement and an exciting, if slightly scary new future, while the cons were all about coping with the loss of long-held status and job security. Although the latter were by no means irrelevant, they were far outweighed by the lure of a much better quality of life.

Step 4: *Think positively*

So you have decided that the pros outweigh the cons and you want to change the direction of your life. But is it practical for you to do so, as an individual, a couple or family? Before you start thinking about what form this change is going to take, it is essential to evaluate all the risks and to make sure that the odds are on your side. You need to think about how much money you can afford to live on; what kind of essentials and luxuries you cannot do without and how much they cost; whether you are prepared to move homes to save money, and so on. All these practical aspects of your new life must be worked out in detail before you act. In the next chapter we discuss how to work out your personal finance, employment and housing needs for a downshifter's lifestyle. But for now, let's assume you have sorted out all the practicalities to your satisfaction, and concentrate on the big picture.

The psychology of downshifting is enormously important. Switching to a less hectic, more balanced lifestyle brings great rewards, and many more people are now doing it; but there are still risks. Ask yourself the following questions:

- Will this affect my close relationships for better or worse?

- Are those closest to me supportive or hostile?

- Will I be able to curtail my spending habits and live off less money?

- Will my colleagues make snide remarks to my face or behind my back if I leave for a way of life that may have less status or security?

- Do I care if they do?

- How will this new lifestyle develop?

- Where might I/we be in three or five years time?

Change is rarely easy for anyone. Many people go to great lengths to avoid it, but it has a habit of lurking in your subconscious until you decide to confront it. Prepare yourself for mental swings ranging from euphoria through doubt to possible depression if you decide to make a big change. Such mood changes are especially likely in the first few weeks or months as you adjust to a new life.

If you adjust your lifestyle a step at a time you will probably find the transition much more smooth and sustained than going all out from day one. It may take time to discover where you want to concentrate your energy and creativity, so don't rush it. Above all, remember that this is not about opting out of society, in fact you may end up contributing more to the general good than you did before – even if your consumer spending power goes down. Remember, you are far from alone – there are millions of other potential downshifters like you out there thinking much the same thoughts.

Step 5: *Test the waters*
Once you have thought through the pros and cons and worked out a rough idea of how much money you think you need to live on, and how you might earn it, spend some time in transition. This gives you a chance to see how you like living on less without committing yourself to it. So carry on with your present job (or jobs) but spend a few months living and spending in a much more conscious way. Write down your daily expenditure so you can see just where the money's going. Then try and cut back spending in the areas you have already identified for making savings. Many of the half a million Americans who have bought a copy of *Your Money or Your Life* found they could slash their expenditure by 15–20 per cent within a year just by keeping a closer eye on their everyday spending. See how much, or how little, you miss the little luxuries.

Meanwhile, think consciously about the amount of time you spend at work and getting to and from work compared with hours spent at home or on hobbies, exercise or community activities. How much do you resent not having enough time for the latter? How would you adjust your time every day to get a better balance? After six months or so, you should have a good idea whether your budget plans will work and how strongly you really want a different lifestyle. Working out how you would best like to divide up your time will also help you to decide on future employment. Compare how much time each month you would ideally spend on a paid job with the monthly income you think you could get by on. Then calculate whether the working life you had in mind would provide enough income to make your new lifestyle work. You may be planning to go part-time, or spend a period of time retraining, and you need to make sure that you can finance the change without difficulty. Remember, many people who decide to downshift are cushioned by a few thousand pounds in savings or a redundancy cheque. This is not essential. But it is certainly prudent, if possible, to build up a safety net to help carry you through the first six months or so.

The men and women we interviewed in Chapter 8 of this book seemed pretty well equally content with their downshifted lifestyle, and genuinely appeared to have few significant regrets. Yet men and women can experience quite different pressures, and ask themselves different questions when pondering whether to forsake a traditional career path in favour of a simpler, more flexible lifestyle. Let us now examine some of these issues and see what practical advice we can offer.

The Gender Agenda

You always wanted a lover,
I always wanted a job . . .
PET SHOP BOYS WITH DUSTY SPRINGFIELD, WHAT HAVE I DONE TO DESERVE THIS? 1987

What men need to consider

Even in these enlightened times of sexual equality, house-husbands and hands-on celebrity fathers led by David Beckham, most people would agree that men experience life differently from women. They worry and take pleasure and work differently to women. Their sense of identity is more likely to be derived from their work. That means their attitudes to downshifting might be completely different as well.

This competitive male world, however, has been with us for a great deal longer than the long hours culture and the 24/7 workplace.

Back in the 1960s, sociologists Ray and Jan Pahl explored why many company managers were working extremely hard. Their conclusions sound all too familiar today:

For them life is a hierarchy and success means moving up in it . . . very often it is the fear of falling rather than positive aspiration to climb which pushes these men on. Those who had an experience of downward social mobility in their family history were the most determined to have a successful career. They work, then, because they are trapped in a competitive society; above all they don't want to fall. The men were not, however, usually prepared to admit that they were driven on for selfish, materialist reasons. They would talk of 'challenge', responsibility, as well as family commitments.

Source: *Managers and their Wives*, Penguin 1971.

Yet many of the wives felt the sacrifices their husbands were making, allegedly for the family, were not worth making. What *they* wanted was to see more of their husbands.

Today, many men feel more beleaguered than ever. Work pressures have been exacerbated by the ubiquitous presence of mobile phones and e-mail, enabling us to work anytime, anywhere. Managers still toil harder than anyone else and they are feeling the strain. When 6,000 of them were polled by the WfD consultancy, a heart-breaking 84 per cent confessed they had 'sacrificed something important in their home lives' for their career.

Conflict between jobs and family is especially acute for fathers of young children. The concept of the 'have it all' Superwoman may be discredited. But many men today feel pressure to be 'Superdad', laptop under one arm, toddler under the other. James Levine, director of the Fatherhood Project at the Work and Families Institute in New York, has coined the apt phrase 'Daddy Stress' to describe this identity struggle. 'Although work is an unquestionably powerful source of male identity and satisfaction, family is equally strong,' he contends. 'What fathers increasingly want is both to provide for *and* spend time with their children.'

For those who can afford it, working fewer hours is the obvious answer. When the government polled 7,500 employees across 2,500 workplaces for its Work-Life Balance 2000 survey it found men almost as eager as women to downshift or work more flexibly. Almost half the men taking part said they'd like to work flexitime, while a quarter wanted to work from home and a fifth part-time.

Nonetheless, many men are *still* brought up to be bread-winners, protectors, go-getters, active more than passive. In a typical family, they still earn two-thirds of the income and work 20 hours a week more than their partners. During the 1990s, men's average working hours fell across the European Union – except in Britain where one in six men now put in a mind-numbing 60 hours or more. Presenteeism, where people make sure they stay at their desks or workplaces until after the boss has gone, has become a prevailing feature of today's workplace. Add commuting into the equation and it's not surprising that many men feel they are living to work, not working to live.

New men on the march

But there are signs that men are rebelling in order to re-balance their lives. Throughout the 1980s, and beyond, the expansion of part-time working was associated almost exclusively with women returning to the labour market after having children. Now more men seem to be opting for it, as more employers appreciate that switching to more family-friendly practices can increase productivity. One in 12 men now work part-time while 15 per cent work flexible shifts. Some part-timers work shorter hours because of ill-health or age, but many more do so to spend more time with family, studying or on other pursuits. The educa-tional charity New Ways to Work campaigns for a change in culture so that people with domestic commitments are treated no differently from those in full-time employment. It carried out some illuminating research on men who work part-time (or flexibly) for more than 100 public, private and voluntary-sector organisations. Practices such as redundancy, once stigmatised, were now being actively sought by many men to help build more stable and fulfilling relationships with their families and the outside world. The study *Balanced Lives: Changing Work Patterns for Men* found such men not only involved in child-care and the care of older relatives, but also contributing to the life of their communities.

Most men who downshift in this way do so quietly and anonymously. But a growing trend in male high-fliers cutting back their hours or forsaking six-figure salaries has hit the headlines. In January 2002 Suma Chakrabarti negotiated the position of permanent secretary at the Department for International Development on the basis that he would work strictly nine to five and from home in Oxford every other Friday so he could spend time with his young daughter. The same month Danny O'Neil, head of Britannic Insurance, swapped his £300,000 salary for a home-based consultancy business so he could see more of his triplets. In government, however, the options appear more limited, judging by Alan's Milburn's recent resignation from the Cabinet. The former Secretary of State for Health found that reconciling a London-based 24/7 job with a young family in the north-east had become an 'increasingly difficult' balancing act.

Charles Monkcom, former co-ordinator of New Ways to Work, feels this shift will accelerate. 'Downshifting has been going on for years, but it is now affecting a new group, male executives in large organisations, who in the past have tended to put work before home life. I think there was a fundamental deal between organisations and men, one that was implied rather than spoken, a psychological contract, where the employers said: 'You give us your time, your energy and your effort, and we will reward you with money and status.' The idea that. people stayed in their jobs for perhaps twenty years was considered OK. 'Now people starting off in work know that it is most unlikely that they will still be in those jobs for that long.' Highly skilled and well-paid men like those above obviously have a strong bargaining hand when it comes to negotiating a more flexible work deal with employers.

Yet increasingly, far-sighted employers are supporting such aspirations for the average earner. At Lloyds TSB, which offers all 77,000 staff the chance to apply for flexible or shorter hours, one in five applicants are men. The Civil Service and local councils also encourage both sexes to flexi-work. Hammersmith Council in London even went so far as to split maternity leave between a married couple it employed, so both husband and wife could enjoy quality time with their newborn baby.

Of course many employers – and many male employees – are not so enlightened. Tom Beardshaw of the charity Fathers Direct concedes that 'a significant minority of men do prefer office to home and work to family'. But dyed-in-the-wool bosses, he says, are bigger culprits. 'In male-dominated industries such as manu-facturing the assumption still is that as a man you don't have family responsibilities, simple as that.'

New rights for new dads

In April 2003 the government moved to ease the pressure on fathers and their families. Every new dad now has a legal right to two weeks' paid paternity leave and parents of children under six are legally entitled to request flexible or shorter hours from their employer. Crucially, by applying equally to mothers and fathers, the new 'duty to consider' imposed on employers removes the automatic assumption that women, rather than men, should fit work around family. Altogether 2.1 million men are eligible. Will they flock to apply for job shares and term time contracts? Will employers give them what they want if they do? It's too early to say.

The gains made by feminism in the 1970s and '80s in the workplace, the home, in politics and in popular ideology and culture were long overdue. No one can argue with any credibility that women should not have the same opportunities as men, the same access to education, to career advancement, to personal development. Women have achieved much in those directions, although they still have a great fight on their hands to translate theoretical victories into practice. But where has this left men? Arguably, even more confused than women about their role, their legitimate concerns, their responsibilities and ambitions.

Possible pitfalls

- **Coping with loss or diminution of status.** As the traditional breadwinners (particularly those over 40) men may be more resistant than women to the idea of giving up the kudos and security, of a high-status or mainstream job.

- **Adjusting to a different working environment, possibly self-employed working part-time or just working a 35-hour week rather than a 50-hour week.** The idea of spending more time working from home or outside a traditional office may not seem like an attractive option. The colleagues that you have become accustomed to having around you all the time may no longer be there when you want to talk to someone about a problem or chat about the football on TV the previous night.

- **Concern about providing for children on a smaller income.** Society still regards men as the traditional family bread-winners. Men will tend to worry about earning enough for family holidays, evenings out and so on, more than their partners. However, with the job for life now a thing of the past, it can often be a safer bet to switch to something different that you know you will enjoy and will be good at. Even if the income is likely to be lower, you will be positively transformed into a more relaxed and productive individual if you believe there is more of a long-term future in your chosen alternative.

- **Change is risky, but nothing that is worth having is without risk.** The point is that if you believe that the steps you are considering are broadly going to take you in the right direction and that the alternative employment option is exerting a strong pull over you, heart and soul, then does status really matter that much? Or does independence of mind and spirit matter more than any negative feedback you might get from your peers? Anyone who leaves a place of work is unsettling the unique equilibrium of that particular group. Subtle, and not so subtle pressure may be placed upon those who might be seen to be threatening the cohesiveness of the group, by looking beyond it.

The question for you is whether to *yield* to that pressure or *resist* it. Only you can decide.

What women need to consider

Don't you know that it's different for girls?
Joe Jackson, singer and song-writer, 1979

Many women now in their thirties, forties and fifties grew up believing that 'having it all' was a legitimate, indeed entirely rational, aspiration. They were inspired by practical life management manuals such as *Superwoman* by Shirley Conran, and their dreams were nourished by magazines such as *Cosmopolitan*. Many came to believe that it was quite feasible, desirable even, to combine parenthood with a demanding career, and still have the energy to be a passionate lover too. Some exceptional women manage to combine these roles, or at least persuade the rest of us that they do. But many more have tried and failed to live up to this ideal of modern womanhood. So relentless is our long hours culture and the competitiveness it breeds that, for many women, being a good parent, a good employee and a sane human being is virtually impossible. So badly has the Superwoman myth been tarnished that polls suggest a fifth of women under 30 will forego children rather than attempt to balance career and family. *Superwoman* author Shirley Conran herself, now chair of the Work-Life Balance Trust, has publicly exhorted career-minded women to put off motherhood until more employers become family-friendly. Although females are working in record numbers the dilemmas presented to women by their multiple roles are probably as agonising now as they ever have been.

The depth of female disillusion with rat race lifestyles was dramatically illustrated when *Top Sante* magazine polled 1,000 working women. No less than 97 per cent said they were 'frequently stressed' trying to juggle work and home life, while half were too busy to fit in exercise or an active sex life. Almost nine in ten working mothers said work-induced stress caused them to shout at their children. Amazingly, only one in ten of all the career women polled said they would choose to work full-time, conventional hours if they had the option not to.

Women are not work-shy – far from it. It is combining paid work with the 'second shift' of childcare and housework that is tipping us over the edge, says *Top Sante* editor Juliette Kellow. 'The fact is, not many women are lucky enough to have an exhilarating well-paid job, a full-time nanny and a new man. The government wants to encourage as many women as possible into full-time work but this is blatantly not what most women want – especially those with families.'

Beyond Superwoman

Clearly the stereotypical 'high-powered career woman and mother' is not quite the role model it once was.

According to the Equal Opportunities Commission, women managers still earn 24 per cent less an hour than male colleagues and only one in ten company directors are women. Although male managers are twice as likely to be made redundant as their female counterparts, women managers are three times more likely to resign of their own volition, according to the Institute of Management. Maybe women see the writing on the wall earlier than men do and they are engineering their way out of stressful, demanding work in male-dominated environments, or reducing their dependence on them before they burn out. But that could be because women are more flexible than men in balancing work and home life, and less addicted to status and the power of the peer group.

Certainly, women have always been more nomadic in terms of their employment patterns, moving in and out of jobs and self-employment, according to their circumstances. They tend to be more accustomed than men to flexibility in employment, mainly because of the breaks they take for having and raising children. In turn, they are more likely to accept insecurity in employment as a fact of life. We are not arguing that women should give up interesting well-paid jobs that they enjoy any more than we are urging women with young children to seek jobs that they neither want nor need. The only people who should make those decisions are the women themselves.

The point is that the old feminist battles have become largely obsolete. The argument now is no longer about *whether* women should pursue career or motherhood or both. It is about *how* they can best combine whichever roles suit them. Economic trends are now calling the tune and it is one women should listen to. Eight in ten new jobs created between 2000 and 2010 will go to women.

Many will be part-time. That suits most women who currently work part-time – the majority of them do not want full-time jobs. It could also favour those men and women, whether singly or in couples, who are thinking of slowing the pace of their lives and downshifting.

Our own instincts and experience of talking to the down-shifters in Chapter 8 suggested to us that women may well find that they can make a smoother transition between the one-dimensional world of fast-track career and the multi-dimensional, downshifted world, than their male friends and partners.

Possible pitfalls

- **Awareness of hostility and resentment.** Women may encounter hostility or concerns from colleagues that they are letting the side down in one way or another. 'So you couldn't stand the heat,' others might say in a superior fashion. Of course, this may be partly true, but it is still hurtful. You may also be accused of putting home life before your career and thus, by implication, putting back the cause of independent womanhood. This is a very outdated view. Flexible working patterns, home computers and so on are making the modern workplace far less essential to a fulfilling work life than it once was. And the government is encouraging employers to offer flexible and reduced hours to all employees, especially working parents.

- **Uncertainty – am I ready for this yet?** You will almost certainly have some doubts about whether you are doing the right thing in switching careers and lifestyle. This is likely to be especially true of women with young children who intend to stop working or to work instead from home and are worried, maybe even resentful, about reducing the pace of their careers. If the pressure for change is coming from your partner, you must work out whether you really want to leave your job or are being pushed. You should not go any further unless that question has been resolved.

- **Concern about losing workplace contact.** Fear of loneliness and isolation is another potential turn-off for women considering more independent employment options. Women choosing to work part-time or from home may feel cut off from the workplace camaraderie. This is often offset, however, by having more quality time with partner, friends and family. Shifting from full-time to part-time or self-employment can bring new friends and networks. Just being aware of the potential danger of isolation will encourage you to foster those new connections.

- **Loss of financial security.** If you are a single woman contemplating downshifting then you only have your own circumstances, obligations and desires to consider. If you have children, then naturally they will be major factors in the equations you have to calculate, if not *the* major factor, as will any elderly dependents you may have. If this is broadly your situation, then clearly your finances and your financial security will be uppermost in your mind. But your own personality and adaptability, in particular your willingness to take risks, will also play a crucial part in your decisions. If you are still equivocating, then there are only two pieces of advice we can offer, at this stage:

1 Bear in mind that if you are happy, the people around you are more likely to be happy too. Children take their cue from their parents in all sorts of ways, and your own parents or elderly dependents are likely to have peace of mind if you have too. It stands to reason.

2 Read the rest of this book! We are going to attempt to show you how we turn the theory into practice, how to turn mere survival back into living.

Persuade your partner – or salvage your sanity!

If you have a partner who does not share your interest in downshifting, don't despair, for there are several options open to you. Maybe the biggest obstacle is one of communication and perception. Maybe they simply don't know that there are alternatives to the status quo. Perhaps they are too busy to concern themselves with anything other than the work they currently have in hand. The first step is to start talking to your partner about alternatives. Realise that if there is any downshifting to be done, you will be the one who has to engineer the changes that lead to it.

You could reach a compromise – the variations on the downshifting theme are almost limitless as we have tried to demonstrate. You could downshift, and your partner could carry on regardless. You could both downshift, and renegotiate your personal and working relationships along lines that you both find more attractive and sustainable. This too is not an altogether fail-safe strategy. In the end, an unavoidable truth may stare you both in the face. You may have to make a rather fundamental, life-changing choice. You may have to decide what or who is more important to you – your spouse or your sanity?

PART FOUR

From Here to Simplicity: Putting Ideas into Practice

11

You and Your Money

I find all this money a considerable burden.
JOHN PAUL GETTY JNR

Whether we keep our money in a teapot or a bank vault, the way
we spend it reveals as much about ourselves to the outside world
as the way we earn it. Our cheque book stubs, credit card statements and welfare payment books can tell the story of our lives
far more succinctly and accurately than the edited highlights we
choose to record in our diaries. Inevitably, the more money you
have, the easier it should be to decide that you can get by on less
or strike out in a new direction that makes a lower income more
likely. Downshifting is not impossible without a few thousand
pounds stashed away, but it is certainly more difficult and will
probably take longer. We are acutely aware that a positive decision to simplify life, and accept the principle of living on less
money, can never be a general prescription, while there are so
many millions in Britain and the world living in poverty, or on
the brink of it. We do not underestimate the genuine difficulties
many people have in making ends meet. But at the same time, it
is worth pointing out that some of the downshifters we

137

interviewed for this book had modest incomes before they decided to change gear. Most people can incorporate some down-shifting philosophy into their lives, if they wish to do so, without having to embrace the whole package.

Make good your bad habits

When you make the decision to downshift, whether now or in the future, partly or wholly, your attitude towards the way money is earned and spent is likely to undergo a transformation. If you have fallen into bad financial habits, and your use of money is more like sado-masochistic abuse, the first point to understand is that you can change if you want to. The key question is one of motivation. If you seriously want more time to enjoy life, to study, to spend more quality time with friends and family, to learn new skills then you will probably find a way to make it happen. Having committed yourself to this goal, you now need a plan for achieving it. This plan should increase your financial independence, liberate you from bulimic 'earn it and spend it' binge living and make you feel altogether happier and more in control.

Cheques and balances: how much are you worth?

Here we show you how to give yourself and your family, if you have one, a financial health check. Whatever ails you, there is no cure or prognosis without a diagnosis. It will not require you to make wall-charts that you have to fill in every day, not will it involve a great deal of paperwork. Much of what we are recommending is simple common sense. Our main purpose is to inspire and provoke new ways of thinking about money, not to start a cult that has its own jargon, slogans and mantras. What we are recommending is not self-denial and hair shirts, but self-discovery and silk shirts (if you conclude your life would not be complete without silk shirts). Remember, over a lifetime, a great deal of money is likely to pass through your hands. Someone starting out in an average job now, earning £17,000 a year for 40 years, will earn nearly £700,000 by the time he or she retires. 'Where does it all go?' we ask ourselves. Now is the time to translate that rhetorical question into one that you can answer.

The 5-step financial health check

Step 1

Make a list of your assets. Record the main items, such as house, car and furniture, household appliances, computer equipment, jewellery, wardrobe contents, etc. Next to each heading write down your estimate of what they would be worth gross if you tried to sell them. Then do the same for any savings and investments that you have, including pensions. Do not build into any equation an expected legacy or windfall. For the moment, we are interested only in your present financial circumstances, and so should you be. Record the current value if you were to 'cash in' these investments now.

Step 2

On a new sheet of paper make a list of your liabilities, all your debts from your outstanding mortgage to the money you owe, including interest, on loans from credit card companies, bank overdraft, the £100 you borrowed from your friend last month to stop your bank balance going into the red again, and so on.

Step 3

Add up your assets and your liabilities. Subtract your liabilities from your assets. The end figure is your net worth. If you have more than you owe, the figure will be positive. If you owe more than you have, yours will be a negative net worth; this is not the most auspicious start to a newly downshifted life, but don't panic.

Step 4
Now you need to compare your income with your outgoings. Make a note of your income for the past year from earnings (your wages or salary) and from 'unearned' sources such as interest on savings, and dividends from shares, etc. Use the net figure after tax and other deductions at source have been taken away. Write down this net income total.

Step 5
Now list and cost your outgoings. These are your spending over the same period, under the relevant headings: mortgage payments, rent, food, eating out, transport, telephone, clothes, fuel, car, holidays, and so on. Try to separate out which outgoings are work-related, so that you have headings that are wholly or mainly connected with your employment for items such as lunches, travel and clothes. Write down the total.

This health check will help you to decide whether you can afford to earn less. If you cannot work out the figures because you don't keep bills and receipts, then make estimates. Thereafter, start keeping those important pieces of paper so that you can make a more accurate assessment next time. If this exercise seems too tedious a chore to contemplate, then spread it over a few days. Don't feel you can get away with not doing it. If you conclude, after taking stock of your life, that it needs a change of pace and direction, you will find it hard to make progress unless you carry out a regular personal financial audit.

A matter of life or debt

Now you know where your finances stand, and exactly how good or hopeless you are at dealing with money. Leaving aside your mortgage for a moment, let us pause to consider the question of debt, but don't put the paper and pens away just yet. Some people are almost professional debtors, spending much of their lives avoiding their creditors or getting themselves into even worse trouble trying to pay off the money they already owe. If you have significant debts, several hundreds or thousands of pounds, and you don't already have a proper strategy for eliminating them, then get one. The longer you are saddled with these obligations, the longer it will take you to downshift – you cannot proceed while weighed down by these burdens. To lighten your load you have four options: cut your spending; increase your income; realise an asset; or raid your savings or investments. Combining several of these choices rather than just selecting one, will enable you to banish the debt much more quickly. Most people in employment are able to put some money into savings or investments on a regular basis. If you have both savings *and* non-mortgage debts, then consider why you have not used the former to pay off the latter. But just remember that the interest yielded by your savings is likely to be eaten up several times over by the interest you are paying on your debt. The best course for anyone in serious financial trouble is to get some debt counselling. Your nearest Citizen's Advice Bureau should be able to point you in the right direction.

What should be far easier than getting out of debt is making sure you don't get into debt in the first place. Simplifying your life means simplifying your finances. Credit cards are an invitation to debt, so cut up all those you can live without. Try to see whether you can get by with just one. Several credit card companies no longer charge an annual fee. Once you have cleared your credit card debts, then make sure you *always* pay off the outstanding amount before each monthly deadline. Then and only then will your credit card become a convenience instead of a burden.

How we use money to keep our treadmill turning

You can now pinpoint your exact position on the two financial axes of Assets and Liabilities, and Income and Spending. You have also written down what you actually do with your money, once you have earned it. Do not throw your notes away because what you have written down may be used in evidence against you; but only if you *choose* to interrogate yourself along the lines we are about to suggest. You are about to find out whether your spending is rational or whether perhaps it is simply propping up a lifestyle that is making you weary, depressed, empty and disillusioned. You are about to discover the difference between what you *actually* spend and what you *need* to spend if you decide that your priorities in life are changing. When we pursue conventional career paths we tend to spend our money so as to *comfort*, *compensate*, *conform* and *compete*. At the epicentre of all our spending urges lie these four 'Cs'. We often use money to prop up burdensome lifestyles that we strongly suspect are completely unsustainable, rather than to help to create new sustainable, liberating ones. It's easily done. We did it. Let's look at some examples of this spending behaviour that spans all these four 'Cs', and some which fit into just one category or another. Holidays and travel are a good example of a type of spending that gives you comfort, and compensation, and enables you to compete and conform to the rat race.

'I want a week in paradise and I want it now'

Holiday destinations, what you do when you get there, and the sort of accommodation you stay in reveal a great deal about you to the people you leave toiling away in the office, the factory or the shop. Like clothes, they are subject to fads and fashions. When you work very hard and very long hours, then you feel stressed. People and their demands crowd in on you, and eventually you want to escape. A few days in paradise are what's needed, well away from all the people you have to please day in and day out. Take one of us, Judy, as an example. In 1995, when she was working as a staff journalist on the *Observer* newspaper, she took three expensive holidays and enjoyed each enormously. She went to a health farm for a week to bliss out, de-stress and have her body pampered and pummelled; to the remote west coast of Scotland and the islands of Rhum and Eigg, to enjoy beautiful landscapes, walk, explore and just 'be'; and to a quiet corner of Majorca with her then partner to do much the same thing, and to eat some good food that someone else had cooked. All perfect holidays. Cost? Getting on for £3,000 or about 10 per cent of her post-tax annual income. Judy likes to think that she went to these places simply because she really wanted the experiences; she suspects she went for comfort and compensation for the hard edges and disappointments she experienced all the rest of the year; and also because she, and her equally busy companion, left it all to the last minute, as usual, and couldn't think of anywhere else to go.

When the going gets tough, the tough go shopping

We need money and spend money in order to meet our basic physical, or subsistence needs: for food, light, warmth, hygiene and shelter. We spend money to conform to the expectations of our peers and to mark ourselves out from them, to define ourselves as members of a tribe, but also as individuals within that tribe. We also spend money to meet our own and others' emotional needs; to have fun and make up for the times when we have had too much fun working or playing.

We might as well stay with Judy, since she is in soul-baring mode. When she was in full-time employment, she reckons she spent about £100 a month, often more, let us say £1,500 a year on clothes, both to cheer herself up and to conform to the general expectation, especially applied to women, that one must look smart for the office and not wear the same clothes too often. (Within four months of taking redundancy she had spent only £35 in total on clothes.)

Judy's supermarket bills were inflated by the 'comfort and compensate' factor. There was a high proportion of readymade meals, bought to save time on cooking and by the need to get round the store so quickly that she never looked at the prices. Food, general household spending, dry cleaning, and luxuries such as cut flowers (the cheer factor again) came to about £100 a week for herself and her companion, or about £5,200 a year of which her share was £2,600 a year. It has since fallen by half. We could assume that £1,000 of that was job-related comfort and compensation spending. Despite having copious quantities of convenience foods at home, the idea of actually heating them up was often just too exhausting to contemplate, so takeaways would sometimes be sent for, or impromptu restaurant jaunts made during weekday evenings. Annual cost? Probably about £750. Popping out for lunch with colleagues, say three times a week, and the occasional round of drinks on a Saturday night after the paper had gone to press would set her back about £30 a week, or over a 46-week working year about £1,380. Then there were tube fares for getting to and from the office Tuesday to Friday, and petrol and car parking money on Saturday. About £800 a year. She also used to have a cleaner coming once a week, because there never seemed to be any time to keep the house straight herself. The cost of that was £1,300. Judy now does her own cleaning. Maybe we should at this point add up all these figures to find out how much Judy was spending simply to comfort, compensate, compete and conform in relation to her job. She makes it a grand total of £9,730. In other words, nearly one-third of her disposable income, just over 30 per cent, was spent on propping herself up at her work, just maintaining her position in the rat race – not improving it, not moving ahead, just surviving. Now pick up the pen and paper again, and work out what proportion of your spending is devoted to propping yourself up in your job, just keeping the treadmill turning. You may be every bit as aghast as Judy was, and as some of the downshifters we interviewed were after they carried out similar calculations.

Getting more from less: the four new 'Cs'

You've now worked out your annual rat race membership fee – the amount you spend just to perpetuate this one-dimensional, career-oriented, anxiety-inducing lifestyle. Naturally, the figure is likely to be a great deal higher if you take into account the type of house you live in and the kind of car you have, and all sorts of other expenditure that is peculiar to you and your life. We have not gone into all conceivable variations on the expenditure theme – only you can judge whether your house, your car, your hang-gliding lessons, and your top-of-the-range camcorder give satisfaction and good value.

However, you may well have concluded by now that too many of your spending habits reflect the needs that we have already ascribed to Comfort, Compensate, Conform and Compete. If so, what do you do? How can you develop a more rational, healthy and effective way of managing and spending money? Here's a suggestion: think about whether your spending patterns might change if you placed four new 'Cs' at the top of your list of priorities. What would they be? We suggest you try out Control, Challenge, Compatibility and Creativity.

Turning Excess Into Success: Reviewing Spending Habits

Rat Racer	Downshifter
Comfort	Control
Compensation	Challenge
Conformity	Compatibility
Competition	Creativity

Give yourself a break – take control

Let us explain what we mean. The people who feel fulfilled and generally content are often the ones who have a strong sense of having influence and *control* over their lives. They believe that they, not fate, shape their destiny and they consciously take responsibility for doing so. The way that they spend money expresses that feeling of control. These people usually have a good idea what they want from life. They have goals and plans for achieving those goals. Their spending is tailored to these and money is a means to these ends not an end in itself. Money, for this type of person, is a tool rather than a comforter. If this person sounds like you and you discover you are motivated to do so, then you are likely to make a highly successful and enthusiastic downshifter! If you decide that your *goals* in life are changing, then your *behaviour* will change accordingly. So too will the way you think about money and the way you spend it. What's more you may decide that the way you earn your money needs a thorough re-think. If you are unhappy in your current job, try to pinpoint the source of that unhappiness. It's quite possible that the key problem is one of control, or the lack of it. If you are frustrated at not being able to do your job your way and that you are wasting your talents on an organisation that does not deserve you, self-employment could suit you perfectly. It is by no means a soft option. There is no one else to blame when it goes wrong, but win or lose it is all down to you.

The power of the consumer

We can also use money to *challenge* what we don't like about our lives and the world around us. As we have described earlier, the consumer is sovereign in Western cultures and that supremacy has brought about an excessive plundering of finite natural resources. But the flip side of the 'sovereign shopper' idea is that people can use their money to challenge business and commerce to clean up their act. You don't need to be a member of Friends of the Earth or Greenpeace to be a useful and active environmentalist, just someone who shops and spends money sensibly and sustainably. If you don't like the way battery hens are kept, don't buy their eggs; if you disapprove of exploitation of certain developing countries by oil companies, don't buy their products. If you make a connection between commercial cause and environmental effect, follow that connection through when you select the goods and services you are buying. Nothing concentrates a business executive's mind more effectively than an emerging or threatened consumer boycott, as Shell's U-turn over the deep sea disposal of the Brent Spar oil rig demonstrated. He or she has no option but to listen and do something to placate the angry consumer. The political power of the sovereign consumer is huge and usually underestimated, if contemplated at all. Use it!

Spending + believing: do they add up?

When you spend money to challenge the status quo it can make you feel influential, and rightly so. In turn, this helps you to feel more in control of life. Now let us examine the third 'C', to find

147

out how much *compatibility* there is between your spending habits and your personal philosophy. Unless you are a monk, a saint or a hermit, there is likely to be some degree of mismatch between your use of money and your general outlook on life. Let us take the motor car to show you what we mean, because it is a classic example of our schizophrenic attitudes as citizens and consumers. People love their cars, find them indispensable, lavish money on their upkeep, and even – heaven help us – give them names. Often these are the same people who are careful to recycle all their bottles, jars and newspapers, seek out organic food, and in most other respects shun environmentally damaging behaviour. Of course very few people will be able to eliminate incompatible spending and consumption patterns for all sorts of good reasons. Realistically, the best you can aspire to achieve in dealing with this kind of inconsistency and mismatch is reduce it. Maybe, for example, we should aim to use the car only when there are no other viable alternatives. The more we use public transport, and walk or cycle to places, the easier it will become to do so because the pressure to improve provision and facilities will increase through simple people power.

Give your right brain a free rein

Finally, in order to feel that we can reduce our dependence on money to comfort and compensate, to conform and compete, we need to build more *creativity* into the way that we spend, save and invest it. We rely too much on advice from bank managers and other financial advisers when managing our money. Many of us are too busy earning to think enough about making our money work for us, through savings, investments, and pensions. Financial planning should never be an optional extra in anyone's life. Remember it's your money, and your future we're talking about. It is never too early to make plans for a comfortable, and enjoyable old age free from money worries. Thinking creatively about our finances means breaking out of our short-term 'here and now' mindsets, the unthinking rituals of earning and spending. Creative money management involves planning, foresight, intuition, checking out hunches, keeping in touch with new services and offers. It means trying to get some pleasure and satisfaction from our investments as well as maximising returns. Here are some tips for injecting some creative and lateral thinking into your money management:

• Too much money sits in bank or building society accounts earning paltry amounts of interest. That money could be earning its keep better elsewhere. Check in the weekend broadsheet personal finance sections each week to make sure you are getting the best rate of interest available. You may have more in your instant access accounts than you really need for emergencies. If so, consider putting part of that sum into a higher-earning account for three months, a year or five years.

• Try not to delegate too much financial management and planning to others. Your money can be badly invested, when you are too busy to keep track. Moreover, unless you are careful to avoid it, the money that you put into your savings, investments and pension funds may go into all sorts of undesirable trades such as tobacco manufacturing, arms trading or despoliation of rain forests.

• The whole business of investing money wisely so that we do not gain from others' misery and loss, now or in the future, is so vast that it properly belongs in another book. There is a huge and growing literature on corporate and social responsibility (CSR) tracking the shift from the way the private and public sectors have traditionally operated (for decades) towards more openly accountable systems for shareholders, and ultimately the general public. Legislation and market trends are slowly reflecting this in terms of the fast-changing world of pensions and investments. There is now a plethora of ethical investments that invite you to hand over your spare cash so that you can save for your retirement, and build up nest eggs for other purposes with your conscience intact.

- As everyone who has followed the Equitable Life and Robert Maxwell pensions scandals will know, saving for your old age can be a can of worms. At the time of writing, the government's pensions policies and strategies are under review. How best can society support an ageing population that may not have saved enough to secure a decent quality of life in retirement? The jury is still out. All we can do is to reiterate the advice of financial advisers in recent years. Don't put all your eggs in one basket – take reliable advice from people you trust. Property, pensions, savings and investment plans: a good spread of these, wisely distributed, is most likely to be your best bet. This reduces your risk of calamity if and when one or another goes pear-shaped.

- A recent survey from the Bristol Business School warned against 'over-reliance' on property to provide people with an income in retirement. The research found that 40 per cent of people questioned were either using, or considering using property to help pay their way in old age. Among younger people (aged 25–34), this figure was 55 per cent. Professor Merlin Stone said that too many people appeared to be banking on a continued rise in house prices: 'There is no guarantee to this, and some market commentators predict that over the next few years UK property prices could fall by around 20 per cent, with the south-east being the hardest hit.'

- Make a will. Everyone over the age of 18 should make a will, downshifters included. If you die intestate (you did not make a will), you are simply adding to the distress of loved ones that you leave behind. Not only will they have to sort out your affairs, they may also be denied part of your estate that you would have wanted them to receive. Instead, it might go to the tax man. Making a will eliminates the extra hassle relatives would otherwise experience, and ensures that they get what you would wish them to inherit.

12

New Ways
To Work

Next week there can't be any crisis. My schedule is already full.
HENRY KISSINGER, FORMER US DIPLOMAT

With our jobs no longer supplying guaranteed security and identity, Britain is ripe for a revolution in 'flexibilisation' of work. The
aim? To help us as individuals to find a better balance between
family, job and all our other commitments and activities.

In this chapter we help you to turn daydreaming about finding
this nirvana of a balanced life into reality. We suggest ways of
figuring out what kind of work would suit you best and lay out
the alternatives open to full-time conventional employment. We
hope you will be pleasantly surprised at the number of options
which beckon from the world beyond the rat race treadmill.

A Changing Workplace . . .

When we authors left our newspaper jobs seven years ago the
only real option was to go freelance. Polly thought about staying
on for a four-day week but was warned she would have to forfeit
her staff job and pension and go on a much less secure rolling

contract. She might have stayed if she could have negotiated a job share on staff or a short-term three-day week or career break to rejuvenate. But at the time few employers in any industry would have made such an offer.

Today the outlook for would-be downshifters is much brighter. A quarter of all employees work part-time (44 per cent of women and 8 per cent of men), while 24 per cent work flexitime, 21 per cent work shifts and 12 per cent work during term times only. The government is pumping millions of pounds into helping employers from bus depots to coal mine operators to introduce work-life balance programmes. And all employers now have a legal duty to consider seriously all flexible working requests from parents with a child under six or disabled child under 18.

Of course the country is still full of dinosaur employers who would as soon fire you as let you work through lunch and leave an hour early to catch an exercise class. It is also true that some organisations embrace flexible working and family-friendly hours in principle while encouraging staff to work late and at weekends in practice. Nevertheless, a growing posse of employers, led by banks, supermarkets, the health service and local councils are seriously trying to help their staff achieve less stressful, better balanced lives. Why? Because they have discovered that it pays to do so. Research has shown that productivity gains and reduced absenteeism and staff turnover far outweigh the costs of introducing generous flexible working and leave schemes. Lloyds TSB is saving £2 million a year, while the AA has discovered that its home-based workers are 30 per cent more productive than those in the office.

Ten steps to a new life

Many people don't get past the stage of bellyaching about their employer, sitting at their desks daydreaming of escape. If, on the other hand, you are unhappy enough to seriously consider leaving your present job you will now be faced with a be-wildering, but exciting choice of alternatives.

You will need to ask yourself whether you want to switch to another permanent, full-time job in the same field or a full-time job in another. Alternatively, you may prefer to try working part-time, re-training or working for yourself from home. Maybe you want to juggle some kind of career with being a mother or house-husband. Whichever course you think you might like to follow, it is essential that you think it through and plan ahead in great detail before making any moves. You may be surprised to find that the course of action you thought was the most attractive, wouldn't work at all well for you in reality.

The first step to take is to carry out a paper exercise to help you work out what you really want to do and – just as impor-tant! – whether your particular skills are suited to fulfilling your goal. If not, you may need either to re-train or to modify your plans. The following simple ten-step exercise is designed to help you on your way.

Step 1: *goals*
Try and work out what you really want to do. Start by listing and ranking the things you dislike about your present job or employ-ment. Then ask yourself honestly how far short your job falls from meeting your aspirations. You may come to the conclusion that changing your employer but staying in the same field would solve most of your problems. If so, then that is probably the best course of action – at least in the short term. If not, then more drastic action is called for.

Step 2: *identify your strong points*
Ask yourself what kind of work you would shine at. List all your achievements since starting school, not just academic, but hobbies, sports and community activities too. Look at the list and pick out the six achievements you felt best about. What was it in

each activity that gave you a buzz? It could have been, for example, acting as part of a closely knit group, or alternatively making a success of going it alone. It could have been working outdoors; a sense of danger or security; the adrenalin of physical activity; or the excitement of solving a problem or conducting some penetrating piece of analysis.

Step 3: *highlight key skills*
Go back over each of these episodes and highlight the key skills you used to achieve the result. Then do an audit of your current skills and specialist knowledge. How many marry up with your list of rewarding activities? Are there any gaps that a bit of training, on or off your job, could fill if necessary?

Step 4: *mix and match*
Review your two lists and see what themes keep recurring. Did the skills you used to apply, and which made you feel good, involve mainly data, ideas, people or things? Were the activities carefully planned and structured or did they evolve as you went along? What kind of working pace did you feel most comfortable at and to what level of pressure do you best respond?

Tease out which skills from past and present give you most satisfaction of all to point you in the right direction for the kind of jobs which would be most suitable.

Step 5: *highlight dislikes*
Do the same exercise as above for the six activities in your life which you have least enjoyed, isolating what it was about each which turned you off. Was it boredom, no time to think, dealing with people, working on your own, too much pressure or travel, or not using your hands or your brain? This will help you identify what not to do in the future so that you don't jump from the frying-pan into the fire.

Step 6: *get feedback*
We can all be self-deceiving. Ask two friends who have known you a long time what they think are your greatest strengths and weaknesses. Check this against your own list.

Step 7: *count up opportunities and pitfalls*
Note any opportunities in the offing which may help to smooth the way for you to change your working life. These could include a redundancy cheque, the fact that your children will soon be leaving home, or the possibility of linking up with friends who have similar goals, dreams and ideas. Then write down everything which might constrain your options and choices for the future. Do you have expensive school fees to pay or elderly relatives you may soon be caring for, and so on? But don't be too intimidated. Treat this as a list of hurdles to be crossed and accommodated, not a catalogue of excuses to do nothing.

Step 8: *budget ahead*
Take a good hard look at your cash flow. Whatever your next career, it is likely that you will take a cut in income, at least initially. So look back at the calculations you made after reading the last section on finance and work out what you need to survive, as opposed to how much it takes to maintain your current living standards. Then compare this figure with the kind of salary you will expect to earn by following the new career path of your choice. You will quickly see whether it is financially viable in the immediate future or not.

When doing this, remember to calculate whether your new working life means that you will be saving on things such as commuting, business clothes and working lunches. What's more, if the aim is to switch to a less stressful way of working, you are also much less likely to need the expensive retail therapy such as frequent restaurant meals or weekends away to keep you going. But don't overdo the slash and burn. It is important to be able to enjoy simple pleasures and treats in life and if you end up permanently worried about making ends meet you will be just as stressed as you were in your high-pay high-anxiety job.

Step 9: *dream your impossible dreams*
Let go and write down everything you dream of doing – however way out or ambitious it may seem. See how many fit in at all with the lists you've prepared. Then eliminate the dreams to which your talents and likely earning power (barring that lottery win!) are clearly unsuited and aim for those which are realistically achievable.

It may be, for example, that you've always wanted to try living abroad for a few years, but that is just not compatible with your family commitments and your employment options. On the other hand, you may also have always wanted to live in the country and if your skills are suited to working from home either through self-employment or telecommuting, then this dream may be realisable sooner than you had dreamed possible. A good idea at this point is to imagine your ideal life in five years time – the work you're doing, where you're living, your family set-up, how you spend most of your time. This will help you with Step 10.

Step 10: *set aims and objectives*
Sort out your aims and objectives before you begin to actively explore new ways of working or prepare to hand in your notice. Your aims are the grand strategic visions for fulfilling your realistic dreams five years ahead and beyond. Your objectives are the stepping stones to get you there. They are tactical, measurable and you can set deadlines for them.
Your aims may be:

• gain control of my life

• work fewer hours

- spend more time with my family

- move to the country

And your objectives may be:

- within a fortnight to draw up a *curriculum vitae* and send it to potential employers in the new field I'm interested in

- within three months prepare a detailed plan for my own home-based business

- within one month put the house on the market

What will work for me?

The guide above will help you identify what work you are likely to be good at. Many of you reading this and looking to downshift will already have a very clear idea of what it is you want to do. Others may be planning to carry on as normal while their partner downshifts. But what about those of you who don't have a clear vision? Well, as we said earlier, there are a whole range of options available, and a growing number of specialist handbooks on offer to help guide you. Below we take you through the new ways to work which are likely to become the mainstream employment patterns of the future. Remember, you are not alone! At a glance, the main options open to you are as follows:

Flexible working

1 full-time hours

2 part-time hours

3 job share

4 term time working

5 teleworking

Self-employment

1 from home

2 in an office

Unpaid work

1 volunteering and community activity

2 homemaking

Flexible working 1: full-time hours

If what you are looking for is more control over when and how you work, but you don't fancy going it alone, then flexible working is probably the right path to follow. A quarter of people in full-time jobs now work flexitime. Many jobs are now advertised in newspapers or on recruitment websites with flexible hours of work which mean employees can negotiate to work during the day outside the standard hours of nine to five, or work evenings and/or weekends if it fits in better with their outside commitments.

Beware however any attempt by a present or future employer to make employing you on flexitime an excuse to reduce your job security and employee rights. It may be, for example, that a potential employer might offer you full-time flexible working to suit your need to work evenings rather than full days, but may try to deny you pension rights or full sickness cover. It is essential to check the fine print before signing any flexitime contract.

A more recent trend, particularly among professionals, is to work full-time hours in a 'compressed' working week. Usually this means a four-day week or a nine-day fortnight. About 6 per cent of employees work this way.

Pros: Flexitime can be a godsend to people with commitments such as school runs or sports teams. Compressed working hours allow you to have a long, three-day weekend without losing pay.

Cons: Flexitime can result in loss of overtime payments if you are working outside nine to five by choice. Ten-hour days are tiring, especially if combined with other work such as looking after children or elderly relatives.

Flexible working 2: part-time hours

If you are looking to work less hard and can afford a reasonable cut in salary then part-time working could well be the answer. Traditionally, part-time employment usually meant a low-skill, low-paid job such as cleaning or piecework. But increasingly, part-timers are becoming accepted in office jobs and in the professions.

Job shares are proving especially popular among high-fliers in the Civil Service, NHS, banking and local government. Part-time workers also now have the same legal rights as full-timers to holidays, pensions, sick leave and other benefits – on a pro rata basis.

If you opted for part-time work you would be very far from alone. Almost 6 million women now work part-time including two in three working mothers with children under five. One in ten men, too, work reduced hours, double the number in 1984.

The most popular method is simply a shorter weeking week, usually two, three or four days. Others include job shares or term time working (see following pages) or 'voluntary reduced work hours' (V-time for short) which enable employees to cut their working hours and salary for a limited period – usually six months – before returning to full-time hours and pay.

Of course, many of these people will have been forced to take part-time work after losing full-time jobs. Nevertheless, switching to working maybe 20 hours or even 30 hours a week after the endless drudgery of a full-time 48-weeks-a-year job is liberating and rewarding if done by choice. It can allow you to fit work around everything else in your life – family, friends, hobbies – instead of your job always coming first. With this better balance is likely to come greater peace of mind and a healthier, if more frugal, lifestyle. For all these reasons, part-time workers are often better workers.

If you're planning to take the plunge, however, do think through future expenses. If you were thinking of moving to a bigger home, for example, you may have to shelve your plans. And if you are likely to start a family in the near future, or to be caring for an elderly relative, you need to make sure your new income (perhaps plus savings) will cover the extra expenditure.

Pros: A simple solution allowing many to stay in their same job. It can help parents cut costly childcare bills.

Cons: Lost income. It can result in over-work if you are not careful to stick to the hours you're paid for. In old-fashioned organisations it can affect promotion prospects.

Flexible working 3: job share

Job sharing is another flexible friend which is finding favour with both employees and employers. It involves two people sharing one full-time job between them. They usually divide the working hours, pay, benefits and holiday entitlement down the middle. So, if you job-shared a solicitor's post, for example, you might end up working 20 hours a week on around £15,000 a year and be entitled to two weeks annual holiday and half a full-time employee's pension entitlement.

Job sharing is now an accepted way of easily introducing part-time working into traditional full-time occupations. High-profile examples include a joint chief executive of an NHS trust and senior Whitehall officials Maggy Piggott and Judith Killick who have split jobs for 14 years. Their latest post is as joint head of judicial appointments policy in the Lord Chancellor's Department.

If you enjoy your present job but find the long hours or the pressure of work exhausting, why not suggest a job share to your boss? You might be surprised at how positive a reaction you get. Employers who don't want to lose talented staff are growing more amenable to being propositioned like this from below – and they may well prefer to offer you a job share than see you walk out.

If you are offered a job share with your present employer or elsewhere, however, do beware that you are not being asked to do more than half a job. Otherwise, you'll be heading straight back towards square one.

Pros: Offers your boss a way to help you work part-time in a job that requires full-time hours. With two people sharing a role holiday and sickness absence causes less of a problem.

Cons: Problems can arise if job sharers do not communicate clearly and hand over work smoothly halfway through the week.

Flexible working 4: term time working

Term time working is an ingenious way of giving parents who would otherwise not be able to hold down a paid job the chance to do so. Initiated by enlightened employers, it gives workers with children the same conditions of service as full-time or part-time employees but allows them to take unpaid leave during school holidays. This is obviously an ideal arrangement if you are a single mother or father. Often single parents are put off getting a job by the cost of childcare which can often be so high that the family is better off on welfare benefits. Under a term time working arrangement, a parent can both earn a living and be the prime carer of his or her children.

About 8 per cent of employers now offer term time working, otherwise known as holiday leave contracts. The drop in pay is often spread across the school year. Pioneers include schools, local councils, the Civil Service, banks and building societies and many leading retailers including Boots, B&Q, Asda, Marks & Spencer, J. Sainsbury and Littlewoods.

Pros: Helps parents avoid the nightmare of trying to find suitable and affordable holiday childcare and spend more quality time with their kids.

Cons: Your drop in pay could be as much as 15 per cent and should be calculated against childcare savings. Colleagues may be resentful if summer annual leave is all booked up by parents on term time contracts.

Flexible working 5: teleworking

Teleworking is perhaps the best publicised of the new ways of working. Made possible by the huge advances in information technology and the explosion in home-owned computers, it allows people to work at home some, or occasionally all, of the time. Teleworkers keep in touch with their managers and outside clients by telephone, fax, e-mail, text message and the Internet.

At present 1.5 million people in Britain telework at home for a single employer, all or part of the week. Teleworking is popular among managers and professionals working in central and local government, voluntary organisations, banks, building societies and other customer-based companies such as BT and the AA. The swelling ranks of the self-employed also include hundreds of thousands of teleworkers, working via computer from home for several employers. Not only does teleworking make sense for employees with expensive commuter journeys, but it makes sense for employers too. People often work more efficiently from home, especially in short bursts, than in the office where there are constant interruptions. And employees who are allowed the flexibility of working from home some of the time are likely to be happier and therefore more productive. It is important, however, to establish ground rules from the start. You may want the flexibility of working from home, but you must make sure that your employer is not going to baulk at paying for your phone and fax bills.

If you think teleworking would suit you, why not raise it with your employer? For all you know, there may already be other people in the building who have negotiated just such an arrangement. Similarly, when applying for new jobs, sound out prospective employers. It may well be easier to establish such a working arrangement from day one rather than persuading your boss a few months down the line that you should spend part of your week working from home.

Pros: You will save time and energy spent on commuting. Unless working hours are set in stone you can work around family needs or other commitments.

Cons: Working from home can be lonely and isolating. Domestic issues may intrude, making it hard for you to concentrate. It may be awkward to get technical support if your equipment breaks down.

Doing the Deal – Five Golden Rules

If you decide to try out a new deal with your current employer, we suggest these negotiating tips:

1 Accentuate the positive

Emphasise how changing your hours will be a win-win scenario. Allowing you flexibility will enable you to stay with the firm and be more motivated and productive.

2 Don't lay down the law

Be flexible and open-minded. Start by talking about 'what ifs' rather than making demands. Consider more than one option if you can.

3 Be sympathetic not confrontational

If discussions go badly or slowly avoid making it a personal issue. Focus on your job rather than your feelings. Give your manager time to talk and think through your proposal and he or she may well come round.

4 Keep a written record of your negotiations

If the worst comes to the worst and you end up in an internal dispute or at an employment tribunal, your records of who said what and when will stand you in good stead.

5 Get an agreement in writing and read the small print

When you reach a deal, ask immediately for a written contract. Make sure any reduced pay is pro rata and your holiday, sickness and pension entitlements all continue on a proportionate basis.

Self-employment – is it right for me?

All the above are, of course, variations on the theme of the traditional permanent post with one employer. But it may be that you are ready for something more radical. Perhaps it is not so much the long hours, the commuting or the stress that have got to you, but the fact that you are working for someone else. Maybe you would prefer to set your own agenda, be in control of your own working life, even, dare we say it, make your own mistakes. If so, then switching to self-employment may well be your best course of action.

In the past, small-scale self-employment was mainly limited to a fairly limited range of jobs, such as running small shops or pubs, cleaning people's homes, plumbing and decorating, or free-lancing as a typist. Until the last decade or so, most of us worked in traditional full-time jobs. But in recent years there has been an explosion of freelancing in many areas of employment. One is our own field, journalism; others are legal work, computer programming, IT and website design, PR, marketing and secretarial work, graphic and interior design, book-keeping and accountancy.

Charles Handy, in his best-selling book *The Age of Unreason*, points to the need to re-invent work through what he terms a 'portfolio' approach. A portfolio lifestyle, as defined by Handy, involves five kinds of work: (1) waged, with money paid for hours worked; (2) fee work, for results delivered; (3) homework, from looking after children to shopping, cleaning and washing the car; (4) gift work, done for free outside the home, for friends, charities and so on; and (5) study work such as learning a new language or training for a sport.

This kind of lifestyle, which aims for a balance between traditional work, i.e. a job, and the demands of home, community and study is easiest to assume if you are self-employed. People in one job can still aspire to a portfolio lifestyle, but all too often, the job eats up so much time that there is little left for anything else.

The joy of self-employment is that, so long as enough money is coming in, you can balance your life to suit your own needs, not the company's.

Have I got what it takes? Asking this question is vital, as it is no good embarking on a life of self-employment in a fit of enthusiasm if going it alone doesn't suit your personality or skills. Most practical books on self-employment, otherwise known as starting a micro-business, agree on the necessary qualities you need to possess to be a successful entrepreneur. They include:

- a high degree of motivation and self-belief

- drive and determination

- a willingness to listen – and learn

- a very clear focus on what your goals are

- resilience, self-discipline and self-reliance

- effective time management

- good communication skills

If you've got all these in abundance, you've got the makings of a successful self-employed person. But it is as well, also, to consider the potential pitfalls of being your own boss. In *Go It Alone*, a book on self-employment by Richard Greensted, ten interviewees who went solo talk frankly about the pitfalls they encountered.

Their jobs were diverse (they included a literary agent, a marketing adviser, an interior designer and a surveyor) but they encountered many common problems. These included loneliness, a feeling of isolation from the outside world, frequent ups and downs as work poured in and then dried up, and sometimes serious problems with cash flow when clients paid up late.

Before you embark on self-employment it is vital that you think through how all these pitfalls, and any others you can think of, would affect you. Would you take it all in your stride? Or are you a real worrier who would find it impossible to switch off if you were going through a thin patch?

Remember also to take into account the concrete benefits you will lose when you are no longer employed by someone else. These include paid annual and public holidays, sickness pay, paid maternity leave, and employers' contributions to pensions. Added together these can be worth a lot to you as an employee – and should not be discarded lightly.

Self-employment 1: from home

Where do I work from? Once you have decided that being your own boss would indeed work for you, the next question is where to make your base. For many people the answer is blindingly obvious: home.

Working from home may sound to you like a backward step, inextricably linked in your mind with housework. Yet in fact home-working is likely to provide the biggest revolution in modern working lifestyles of them all. The Henley Centre for Forecasting estimates that 7 million full-time employees, 1.6 million part-timers and 1.3 million of the self-employed (based in offices and other workplaces) could all successfully work from home right now. While the overall numbers of self-employed have remained constant for a decade at 6.8 per cent of employees (with construction workers and estate agents the most numerous occupations) those working from home are rising steadily, especially among the over-35s. No longer a cottage industry, the availability of relatively cheap fax machines and personal computers have allowed a huge range of professional, creative and business people to work from home.

For those seeking an independent approach to work and

living, being based at home has many advantages. One of course is that it saves the costs of commuting which are often considerable. Another is that you can write off many work expenses, such as the use of one or more rooms as workplaces, or a percentage of your phone bill, against tax. Similarly if, as a self-employed person, you become VAT-registered, then you can also claim back 17.5 per cent VAT on desks, shelves, the cost of installing a business telephone line and many other expenses.

Once you have seriously decided to try home-working, it is sensible to appoint an accountant, if you don't already have one, to help you run through all the costs and rebates which may not have occurred to you. Alternatively, you could buy one of the many how-to-do-it books on setting up a business at home, or find a course on home-working – many local authorities run them for free. It is essential that you work out in great detail how much money you will need to cover your costs for the first 12 months, including overheads and living costs. Then work out how much money you have to make a day, a week or a month to break even. Is this realistic? If not, you may have to rely on savings or modify or delay your plans.

Before handing in your notice and telling your employer you are going it alone, it is also important that you think through the loss of all the crucial support systems which you take for granted as someone else's employee.

Your company or employer pays your telephone and fax bill, supplies your stationery and posts your letters. They also market and advertise the company's products or services. If you go it alone you will no longer only have to use your well-honed and proven skills as, say, a researcher, a computer programmer or a plumber. You will also have to wear several other professional hats. You will need to be able to sell your business to potential clients with confidence, to run your own book-keeping and accounts (unless you pay someone to do it), to organise your own office equipment and to do your own budgeting. If any or all of these are things which you hate doing or think you would be no good at, you must think carefully before going ahead.

The other crucial element to home-working is making sure that your work and family lives won't conflict. Many people believe working from home will give them much more time with their partners and family, only to find themselves locking the study door to get away from the children who are constantly interrupting their work.

To work successfully from home, you must draw clear boundaries between your work time and your home time. Statistics show that homeworkers are a startling 30–100 per cent more productive than their office counterparts, so working from home should indeed allow you to spend more time with the family. It's just a matter of shutting off from family life during those hours when you are working. One obvious way is to set yourself fairly rigid daily or weekly hours of work and stick to them. Also, keep a room or part of a room for work only and make sure that family life (in the form of children's toys, for example) doesn't intrude into your workspace.

Finally, it is obviously vital to get the support of all those you live with before embarking on a home-based career. If your partner is based at home and is worried you will be under his or her feet, you've got a problem. Suddenly spending a lot more time at home can alter relationships and create unexpected tensions. Women, in particular, often find that when they take up home-based working their partner also expects them to run the household more or less single-handed on top. If these kind of problems emerge, it is crucial to sort them out early on. Even better to think and talk them through before you make the final decision to set up at home.

Having said all this, if it suits your personality and circumstances then working from home can be the ideal way of having all worlds. Both of us, as freelance journalists, are enthusiastic converts. We find that not only do we work faster and more efficiently, but we have saved considerably on commuting costs and the trappings of high-powered and high-salaried jobs. Most importantly we have greater control over our lives.

Self-employment 2: in an office

Those who find it impossible to work at home, surrounded by distractions such as children, or a sinkful of dirty dishes, may prefer to rent an office space to help them re-create the discipline of a nine-to-five working environment. The only major drawback to this solution, of course, is that it costs more money than working from home. But that is a calculation which you will make when working out your finances for your new working life.

Unpaid work 1: volunteering and community

Many of our interviewees in Chapter 8 had found new rewards and fulfilment in voluntary work for community or environmental groups after leaving full-time employment. All, without exception, preferred their new lives to their old. But it is important to plan for such major life changes, and to make sure you are suited to them and that you can afford them.

A 'portfolio' lifestyle, where you consciously include time for unpaid work, is probably the most rewarding you can achieve in modern society. Working for a voluntary group, for example, may solve a long-held need to contribute in a certain area, such as animal welfare, or may open up entirely new horizons for you.

Many charities pay volunteers' travelling costs and lunches. And they often provide a whole new world of contacts and friendships.

Unpaid work 2: homemaking

Similarly, switching to a job with fewer hours or less stress to allow you more time and energy for home life and children brings obvious rewards. Apart from the emotional benefits, it can allow you to spend less money on expensive childcare. But, again, it is essential both to think through such a move and to work out in advance whether you can afford it. It is no good swapping the stress of long hours and no time with the children for the stress of not having enough money to pay the bills. Neither is it any good choosing to spend more time at home out of a sense of duty when really you want to be in the office going flat out for your next promotion. Don't be pushed into making the wrong decision. As with all the employment options we have run through, the crucial point every time is to choose a new direction which will suit you and your family and bring you all a happier, more balanced life.

13

Home Front

Houses are built to live in and not to look on . . .
FRANCIS BACON (1561–1626), ENGLISH POLITICIAN, PHILOSOPHER AND ESSAYIST

Just as we use money and our jobs to comfort and compensate us, so we use our homes in much the same way. Who hasn't left the office dog-tired and depressed only to revive when we reach the safety and comfort of our own surroundings? As the outside world becomes more unfriendly, so more and more of us are retreating into our personal worlds based around home, family and friends. We may feel insecure and undermined at work, but at home we are in control. This shift in attitude is reflected in many areas – our growing enthusiasm for DIY home improvements, gardening, takeaways and home video viewing, to name but a few.

To feel completely autonomous in our own homes, most of us want to own them. Owning an attractive, comfortable home makes a huge difference to our morale and well-being. Yet it can also bring stress and hardship to those who over-stretch themselves.

In order to own the homes we want many of us still take on

mortgages which stretch our resources to the limit, despite the tough lessons of the late 1980s. This often means having to scrimp and save in other areas. The unnecessary financial stress can even end up straining personal relationships. Moving up the property ladder usually also goes hand in hand with spending more on furnishing and decorating. All too often, we end up using credit or loans to buy that gorgeous new sofa or wardrobe – and end up paying well over the odds in interest charges.

If you are looking to simplify your life, it is worth thinking hard about where you really want to live and what, to you, are the essential elements for an ideal home. Many of us would undoubtedly be able to lead freer, more spontaneous lives if our housing costs ate up a smaller slice of our salaries.

Wanted: the downshifter's dream home

If you have decided to downshift, or are considering doing so, then where you live is a vital part of the equation together with the employment you choose and the income you expect to earn.

When you first sit down to decide your future life, try and be open-minded about where you live, both in terms of location and size of property. Being flexible about your home may make a big difference to whether or not your plans to downshift will be viable. Of course, your decision will be governed by many considerations including the size of your family, where you plan to work from, and whether or not your dreams include moving from city to town or country. Bearing this in mind, we list below the most obvious options open to you:

1 stay where you are

2 stay in the same area but opt for a lower mortgage or rent

3 move to a smaller property or to a street in the same area where properties are cheaper

4 sell up and move to a new area

5 work from home

6 move into shared or communal accommodation

1: Staying put

If you, your partner or family are wedded to your present home then it doesn't make sense to leave when your aim is to achieve a happier, more balanced life. Instead, you will need to build all your plans around staying where you are. It is quite possible to downshift without moving, but you will have to make careful calculations about what you can afford.

If your rent or mortgage is high, and your family income is going to drop then you will obviously have to cut back in other areas. But don't despair! We have already pointed out how cutting out commuting costs and other work-related expenses can save people thousands of pounds a year.

Try and calculate all the money you have spent annually on your home and garden over the past two or three years. Then see how much of the expenditure covered jobs which you yourself could do in future. For example, you may have paid a gardener to cut the lawn or a plumber to do a simple job like replace a tap washer. You may have employed a weekly cleaner and you may have paid a decorator several hundred pounds to re-paint your living-room. All these are activities which any able-bodied home-owner could do given the time, the equipment and the patience. If you are prepared to take such jobs on in the future, you could reduce your annual housing costs substantially.

2: Re-mortgaging or renting

Of course, the biggest holes in your housing costs are made by your monthly mortgage, council tax and rent payments. But here, too, you'll be pleased to hear, there are ways of cutting your bills significantly.

Most building societies offer deals to tempt people to switch mortgages. In the 1990s, and early 'noughties', re-mortgaging became big business with tens of thousands of families profiting by negotiating a lower monthly payment with a new lender. Most of these deals tie you in with a lender for at least five years. In return, householders receive a reduction of anything up to a third on their monthly repayments for the first few years of their new mortgage agreement. Although it is a hassle switching your mortgage, and you will be charged a couple of hundred pounds in administrative costs, the potential gains are substantial. If you are paying back, say, a £75,000 mortgage at £550 a month, you should be able to find a deal which cuts your repayments by up to £100 a month.

Scan the money and business pages of the broadsheet newspapers for easy-to-read and up-to-date information about re-mortgaging.

Another course of action would be to switch from owning your own home to renting. The monthly rent might be a similar amount to your monthly mortgage repayment and, of course, you still have to pay the bills. But all those expensive overheads – repairs, re-decoration and unexpected disasters such as a flooded bathroom – will be dealt with and paid for by the landlord. Renting is probably a good option to consider if you are flexible in your lifestyle and are looking to save as much money and reduce your responsibilities as much as possible.

3: Trading places

If you want to stay in the same area, but are happy to move home to suit your new needs, this is obviously an ideal opportunity to save money. Whether you live alone, in a couple, or as part of a family, sit down and work out systematically, room by room, how much space you really want or need.

It may be, for example, that you now have a guest bedroom which is almost never used. You may also have a junk room which you wouldn't need if you gave or threw away all that junk, which you never use anyway. You may have a garage, but do you really need it?

Once you have decided how much space you need, think about locality. If you are living in an expensive but small inner-city flat, you may be able to save substantially by moving to a less fashionable area a little further out of the centre. On the other hand, you could get somewhere bigger, if that's what you need, for the same price. In the same way, if you are living in a three-bedroomed house in an affluent suburb, you could save a lot of money by selling up and moving to somewhere smaller, or the same size in a less up-market neighbouring suburb.

Take some time visiting neighbourhoods in your area to see how you like them. Check with friends who live in cheaper localities what the advantages and disadvantages are. And make sure the new locality you have in mind has good local transport and shopping facilities which don't involve much more travel than at present, and preferably less. There's no point saving on the mortgage if you have to start using your car for work or driving five miles to get to a decent supermarket.

4: Pastures new

For many people, moving out of the city into the suburbs or, better still, the real countryside is a cherished dream. As we mentioned earlier, hundreds of thousands of us have been pursuing this dream since the early 1980s. But, if you are planning to join this exodus, stop and think first. Remember that a downshifted lifestyle – perhaps growing some of your own food,

and getting more involved in your community – can be successfully pursued in town or city as well as in the countryside. And
be aware that starting again in an idyllic rural setting carries
disadvantages as well as advantages. Below, we offer a short list
of pros and cons to living in both town and country.

Living in the country: pros

✓ Fresh air and natural surroundings.

✓ Life is usually quieter and slower-paced.

✓ Accommodation is often cheaper than the more affluent city
suburbs and there is often more land or garden with the house.

✓ Children will probably have more and safer playing space;
neighbours are likely to be friendlier and local activities may
be easier to become involved in.

✓ Parking problems are rare and housing and car insurance rates
are lower.

✓ Easier to obtain locally grown food.

✓ Easier to find a plumber, electrician or builder, and overall
cost of living may be lower, depending on area.

Living in the country: cons

✗ Choice of housing is much narrower than in cities and planning permission for home extensions and improvements may
be restricted.

✗ Weather may be inhospitable in winter – cold, foggy, windy
or snowbound; farm smells can be off-putting; tourist areas
can be over-run by summer visitors.

✗ Isolated houses in exposed positions can be costly to heat and
there may be no mains gas or sewage drainage.

✗ Street lighting may be poor and local transport sparse, while
the GP's surgery, local hospital and schools, chemists and
supermarket may be some distance away.

✗ Social life is likely to be much more restricted and, with local
transport limited, it may be harder for guests to visit you.

✗ Longer, and maybe more expensive, commute to work.

✗ Employment options may be narrower.

Living in a town or city: pros

✓ More choice of neighbourhoods and houses; flats, limited in rural areas, are plentiful.

✓ More public transport, schools and health care are available.

✓ Shopping is much more diverse and convenient.

✓ More entertainment, leisure and sports facilities; children may benefit from having more youngsters nearby to play with.

Living in a town or city: cons

✗ House prices are higher; you may have to accept a smaller house and/or garden than in the country and children's play space may be restricted.

✗ Closeness to neighbours may mean a lack of privacy, especially in terraced housing.

✗ Faster pace of living and higher noise levels from traffic, people, shops and factories.

✗ Health and welfare services are more likely to be over-stretched and large inner-city schools may have more discipline problems.

✗ Neighbours may be unfriendly and you may feel isolated in the midst of so many strangers. Friends may have to be made through your job or children's schools.

✗ Parking may be difficult and more expensive.

If you do decide to go ahead and move to a new part of the country, think through the lifestyle changes this will involve and how they will affect your budget. For example, it's not only your mortgage and council tax payments which may be much higher or lower. What about fuel bills if you are moving to a colder climate? And telephone bills? If you are moving away from your friends and work colleagues, you are therefore likely to be making many more long distance phone calls in future. Also, think through your new travel needs and the amount of routine upkeep your new home is likely to need. Again these items may substantially affect your budget either way. You may be saving even more than you thought by moving. Or you may find unexpected expenses to offset against the savings you have estimated that your new home will bring.

But, if you have decided to head for pastures new, how do you find your new home? House hunting in a new part of the country is not an easy business. Spending weekends or even holidays touring around looking out for 'For Sale' signs may be fun once or twice, but it soon becomes tiring, time-consuming and expensive.

There are several ways for you to get round this problem. Find out the names of the weekly or evening papers in the areas you are interested in and then order copies by post for the days that their property advertising comes out. If you are wired to the Internet, it is also worth a quick trawl. Limited accommodation listings are now provided for most of the country.

This initial research will give you a good idea of the range of accommodation available and how much it costs. Armed with this knowledge, you could then link up with an estate agent in the area, specifying what you are looking for. Members of the National Association of Estate Agents will provide a referral service for people moving from one area to another. Just walk into an agent's in your home town and tell them you want to take advantage of the National Homelink Service.

5: Mixing business with pleasure

Like many downshifters, you may be tempted by the idea of working from home. If so, you must think through the implications not just for your career, but also for your housing arrangements. Working from home, as we said in Chapter 12, can be a wonderful experience, allowing you more time with family and friends while saving you money on commuting and other work-related expenses. But it can also bring unexpected savings in accommodation costs.

If you work from home, you can set some of the costs of the room/s you use as a study or workshop against tax. Likewise a proportion of your telephone bill. And when you want to buy a new piece of furniture, such as a desk or shelving, you can again claim back tax so long as the items are used, at least in part, for business purposes. If, as a self-employed person, you become VAT-registered, then you can also claim back VAT on office equipment, the cost of a business telephone line and other items you may tot up in the initial outlay of setting up a business from home. The financial bonuses can be substantial.

If you want to move, then work out how much more space you would need to work from home and then look for properties of that size in the area you're interested in. It may be that you will have to look in a slightly cheaper area than you'd originally planned in order to find a house with adequate work space which is within you budget. On the other hand, remember to calculate how much money you will be saving on commuting and other work-related costs, giving you a bigger monthly budget to cover your mortgage.

If you want to work from home but would prefer to stay where you are, be inventive about the space you have. Moving is a costly business, however efficiently you do it, and it may be that your home has unfulfilled possibilities. You may have a well-kept loft or cellar which could be converted into a study without too much expense. Or, if you need a large workshop, how about converting your garage or a garden shed? You may need to park your car on the street in future but that should be a small price to pay compared with the benefits.

If you are stuck in negative equity then a home conversion is a particularly good idea. Not only will it create the space for you to work at home, but it will raise the value of your property and make it easier for you to sell in the long run.

6: Sharing a roof

If you need to save money to create a new lifestyle then how about sharing accommodation? This could mean either opening your own doors to a lodger; moving into someone else's flat or house; or sharing a rented house with several other lodgers.

If you own your own home, but want to dramatically reduce your outgoings, one option would be to sell your flat or house, pocket the profits and move to rented accommodation in a cheaper part of the country. Your rent may not be a huge amount less than your mortgage but all those overheads will disappear and with luck you'll now have decent savings in the bank to fall back on. Of course, such a change of direction would need to fit in with your employment and living plans. It is a course of action probably best suited to the young and single, or to couples without children. But there is no compelling reason why any of us should feel we have to keep our feet on the housing ladder if we have other, more pressing priorities for our money.

If, on the other hand, you are a home-owner who wants to live off less but would prefer to keep your property, how about renting out a room? Everybody has horror stories about the lodger from hell, but if you think carefully about the advertisements you place, making clear your likes and dislikes, and take your time vetting would-be housemates, you should be able to avoid making a bad choice. If you are very nervous about it, stipulate a three-month trial period and make them sign up to it on the dotted line. Then if things go quickly wrong, they'll be out before you know it. There is a big market for rented rooms and you should be spoiled for choice. But remember, to do it legally you will need to declare your earnings from rent to the tax man who will deduct tax at the same rate you pay on your salary. Up to a certain threshold (currently £4,250 per year) income from letting part of your home to a lodger is tax-free.

For the bolder downshifter, another option may beckon: communal living. In the individualistic 1980s buying your own home became a national craze and communal living a national joke. Remember the cult TV comedy *The Young Ones*?

Although not particularly widespread now, there are opportunities for those attracted to communal or community living. One high-profile example is the Findhorn community in Scotland which draws thousands of visitors every year. Another is the award-winning BEDzed development at Beddington, Sutton, an environment-friendly, energy-efficient mix of housing and work-space on the site of an old sewage works.

PART FIVE

Living Better on Less

Civilisation, in the real sense of the term, consists not in the multiplication, but in the deliberate and voluntary reduction of wants. This alone promotes real happiness and contentment.

MAHATMA GANDHI (1869–1948), INDIAN NATIONALIST LEADER

How to use this section

In this section, we build on the 'strategic lifestyle planning' advice given in the previous section on finance, work, and housing. Now we are going to show you how day-to-day living can become happier and healthier with less money, but more time to enjoy what really matters to you. Some of the suggestions and ideas we offer are, individually, fairly modest steps, while others are more radical.

Nowhere in this book is it our intention to lay down the law, for downshifting is not a cult. It's simply a way of living, with a strong philosophical basis. All we want to do is set out the best information that we can find to help would-be downshifters or those already embarked on downshifting, and to give some suggestions and markers that simplify the process and make your goals easier to achieve. Only you can decide what steps amount to impossible sacrifices and which burdens you can happily shed. Only you know what is negotiable, and what provokes the response: 'That's ridiculous,' or 'Hmmm, well, maybe it's worth thinking about.' The radical downshifter, of course, will harbour no such doubts and will go the whole hog at every opportunity!

In each of the forthcoming seven chapters, we will show you examples of free or cheaper alternatives to the way you may currently eat, travel, run your households, and so on. But cost is not the only guiding principle underpinning our advice – better health, environmental sustainability, and ethics are equally important.

14

Food and Drink

By forcing the damn fool public to pay twice over – once to have its food emasculated and once to have the vitality put back again, we keep the wheels of commerce turning.
DOROTHY L. SAYERS, MURDER MUST ADVERTISE, 1933

Never underestimate the importance of good food – making enough time to shop for it, prepare it well, and, above all, to enjoy eating it. Your health and sense of well-being is critically dependent upon it, so if you cut the wrong corners you are simply cheating yourself and the people whose diets depend on you.

The whole business of eating and drinking should never be an afterthought. We are what we eat. With every mouthful, with every supermarket expedition, with every visit to your allotment, if you have one, it is your chance to get healthier and happier, but not only that. The way you spend your money on food and drink also shapes the livelihoods of other people, and so their health and well-being too.

Shopping is far from a trivial business. Like any other activity, it is a set of skills that can be learned, honed and improved. It is also about making political choices. We have a responsibility to get it broadly right. It's your opportunity to help to change the world and yourself. Your stomach, your brain and your wallet are inextricably linked, and it is for you to decide whether all three should benefit from this inter-dependence, or not. Here we suggest ways of reviewing your shopping, eating and drinking habits, changing some of them, and getting more from less money.

Before we outline our alternative plans, we offer some general thoughts on the art of shopping.

Where should you buy your food and drink?

Ask yourself whether the shops and other outlets you use deserve your custom, and whether their activities are consistent with your beliefs. You may worry, for example, about the quality of produce available in supermarkets and modern mass production practices. The ingredients of processed foods are often mystifying. The fruit and vegetables on offer often look better than they taste and their nutritional content may have diminished in transit. Do you have a decent market locally where you could save pounds on fruit and vegetables?

The Women's Institute runs superb little fresh produce markets around the country. See if there's one in your area, or a similar enterprise run by another voluntary organisation. If not, and you grow some food yourself, think about getting together with other like-minded souls and starting your own market.

Many people believe that eating well costs a lot of money. In fact, the key barrier to healthy eating is not simply the *price* of the food itself, but whether people have *affordable* access to it. An out-of-town supermarket may make all kinds of impressive claims about the quality, freshness and price of its food, but none of it is the slightest use to the person who is unable to get to it. The answer is not to encourage more car use, but to increase the incentives to shop locally. That sets off a positive chain reaction.

If more people shop locally, the choice and quality of goods available will rise, and prices will fall. So community and neighbourhood life benefits, the environment wins because car dependence declines, and you save time and travelling costs because you can get good food round the corner.

Take the inspiring example of what's been achieved in the Worcestershire town of Droitwich Spa. Many superstore chains run loyalty card schemes which entitle customers to various discounts and money-saving vouchers, once you clock up enough points. In Droitwich, the local *Advertiser* newspaper and Wychavon District Council have got together to provide a card that fosters loyalty between the town's residents and traders. More than 50 local retailers and other traders offer discounts and other benefits to cardholders.

When is the best time to shop?

Avoid going shopping when you are hungry or thirsty or very tired. Your defences against subtle advertising, and the seductive atmosphere of a well-stocked supermarket, will be down. You will emerge with a trolley heaving with ready-meals, processed foods and other 'comfort and compensation' items that can waste your money. Meanwhile you may forget to get things that you *do* need. If you use a supermarket, try to go when it is likely to be quiet, and you are in a reasonably positive frame of mind. For many people, impulse-buying increases with stress levels. The quicker and more easily you can get around, the more rationally and cost-effectively you are likely to shop. One exception to this rule that could save you even more money is to shop when prices are cut on goods that are nearing or have reached their 'sell-by' dates. Saturday afternoons, and the hours before a shop closes for a public holiday, could be prime shopping times for downshifters with their new flexibility.

How can I best resist temptation?

With the benefit of a succinct shopping list. It helps you to cut down on impulse buying, and forces you to think about the next few days' meals in the relative calm of your home rather than in those temples to temptation where we tend to buy our food. If you need more reinforcements against temptation, then leave all plastic cards at home. Only take with you the cash you intend to spend at the shop. And a calculator to keep a running total as you cruise the aisles: it works every time.

Who to shop for food and drink with?

Ideally, no one. Shopping with small demanding children, who have yet to absorb the liberating philosophy of downshifting, is likely to present practical problems to anyone trying to save money and to buy healthy food. Some of the more enlightened supermarkets have supervised play-areas, where you can drop off the children, and some offer confectionery-free checkouts.

Why shop for all your food and drink?

Think laterally. You could grow some of it yourself, barter with friends and neighbours, organise the delivery of locally produced organic or conservation grade food to your door, and finally toast your success with some home-made wine, beer or lemonade. Food and drink is fundamental to our enjoyment of life. Why delegate so many decisions and so much of your spending power to unseen, anonymous, profit-driven supermarket chains and multi-national food producers? Might not eating and drinking become more pleasurable and meaningful when you know more about its origin, how the food was produced?

What sort of food and drink should we consume?

Most people need to eat more fresh fruit and vegetables to get the vitamins, minerals and fibre they need to stay healthy – five portions a day is the amount recommended by the World Health Organisation. Many should boost their consumption of starchy, fibrous foods: this means eating more bread, pasta, potatoes, pulses and cereals and building at least some main meals around these foods. These should make up about half your daily diet. Luckily for the downshifter, a healthy diet need be no more expensive than an unhealthy one, and may cost less although as we pointed out earlier you may have to travel further to get hold of the freshest ingredients.

Buy foods that give good nutritional value and are versatile – dried pulses are a great standby for making soups, casseroles and savoury bakes, they are cheap and they keep for months if stored in an airtight tin or jar. When you shop for groceries, try to cut down on the tinned and pre-packaged food. Supermarket 'own brands' are usually cheaper than other varieties and often just as good as their better-known counterparts. Processed food, such as cakes, biscuits, crisps, pre-packed pies, sweets, chocolates and tinned meats, can never match fresh, whole food for providing what your body needs to function well. These items also tend to be packed with saturated fats. Most people would benefit from eating less fatty foods. And don't forget, the longer food is kept, and the more it is cooked, the less nutritional value we get from it.

Now we accept that one person's meat is another's poison and that you will take much advice about your diet with a pinch of salt (no more than a few grains ideally). So we will focus on giving you a few facts so that you may draw your own conclusions.

Living off the fat of the land

As a nation we consume more fat than is good for our health. Most of this excess comes from meat and dairy products such as cheese, milk and butter, and the heart disease created by this excess kills thousands of people every year. Moreover, we are profligate in the way we use precious land to produce food. Most animals reared for meat are fed on crops that could be eaten by people, yet livestock only convert a fraction of the crop's energy into food.

To yield one kilo of beef, you may need as much as ten kilos of grain. If a one-hectare field used for beef production was given over to bean and vegetable growing, it would produce ten times as much protein. So it makes sense for those concerned about the planet, their health, and their pocket to reduce their consumption of meat and dairy foods, and increase consumption of vegetables and pulses. Try substituting some of your meat-based meals with vegetarian ones. If you are already a vegetarian, and veganism holds no appeal, then you can concentrate on other ways of saving money. There are plenty to pick from; for most people.

From plot to plate

Britain has some of the finest and most fertile arable land in the world. Yet rather than grow most of it here, we prefer to fly in exotic fresh food, often produced by cheap labour in countries thousands of miles away. The pollution caused by transporting all this food on roads and by air is huge, and the produce loses a fair proportion of its goodness *en route*. Processed food is often well-travelled too by the time we eat it. The ingredients are sent to processing plants, perhaps in other countries, then on to warehouses, and then supermarkets, before finally being loaded into our cars. So food production cycles can measure several thousands of miles. Alternatively they can be a couple of miles, or even just a few feet. The aim of the downshifter, we suggest, should be *to shorten these distances between plot and plate*. Obviously, it is for you to decide how modest or radical this shortening should be. But remember, the fresher the food you eat, the healthier your diet.

Some like it hot

As a general rule, fruit and vegetables are best consumed either raw or lightly cooked. *Do* wash your fruit and veg, or scrub it very gently if it is dirty, but try to resist the temptation to peel the skin off everything, because the most nutritious elements are often in the skin or just beneath it. *Don't* boil away all the goodness. Try steaming vegetables or briskly stir frying. Instead of dribbling oil into your pan, you can now spray it in so that the oil goes further and you stay trim and gorgeous. There are now oil sprays on the market, which cost next to nothing, but will save you pounds in the long run. That way you can afford the tastiest and healthiest oil – extra virgin olive oil – *most* of the time, not just as a special treat.

It's the real thing: H_2O

There is only one liquid that our bodies really need in order to function well, and we do not drink nearly enough of it. Sales of bottled water have rocketed since the 1970s in the UK market. We spend a total of £1 billion a year on the stuff, partly because so many dislike the taste of tap water, but also because we tend to think of the bottled variety as healthier. This is not necessarily true. Many people worry about the nitrates content of their tap water, but it is quite possible that the level is even higher in some types of bottled water. Provided that your drinking water supply lies within legal safety limits, there is no real reason for buying bottled water other than on grounds of taste or fashion. A slice of lemon or lime in a glass of tap water can improve the taste enormously, so think seriously about whether it's really necessary to pay twice for your supply. Alternatively, consider investing in a water filter jug.

Tea, coffee and soft drinks

Tea and coffee contain caffeine, a chemical that stimulates the metabolism. These drinks may be habit-forming, but there is no credible evidence that they are addictive. The question for down-shifters is whether they might wish to substitute at least some of the cups of tea and coffee they drink for something rather less stimulating, such as fruit or herb teas or cereal-based drinks. If you want to take steps to slow the pace of your life, you will probably want to cut down on stimulants like caffeine that would otherwise charge you up again. What might help you do this is to buy real coffee, not instant, and loose tea instead of teabags. It will take longer to make so you will probably drink less of it! As for soft drinks, fruit juices, with no added sugar or sweetener, are healthier than canned fizzy drinks such as colas.

Alcohol

Scientific studies have shown that moderate drinkers sustain less heart disease and have lower levels of cholesterol than those who drink to a greater extent. Most independent health experts regard drinking up to two units a day for women and three for men as moderate. A unit is the equivalent of a glass of wine, a half pint of beer, or a single measure of spirits. Beer and wine contain certain vitamins and minerals. The down-shifter has three main options on the question of alcohol: to become teetotal (perhaps you are already); to save money by drinking less; or to save money by making their own beer or wine.

If you want to go the whole hog

Here are five more tips for people who wish to downshift more radically:

1 **Only buy organic food, as far as possible, and support local producers who work to nationally recognised certification standards.** Most shop-bought vegetables and fruit are sprayed with pesticides which can cause environmental damage. Organic boxed vegetable schemes are now widely available, delivering direct to your home or from a nearby pick-up point.

2 **Giving your custom to shops and markets that you can walk or cycle to may mean you can gradually cut down supermarket chore visits.** Find your nearest wholefood shop and start stocking up on dry foods that store well. Pulses such as chick-peas and lentils are among the cheapest and best sources of protein available. With pulses, vegetables and herbs you have the core ingredients for the most delicious soups, casseroles and bakes that cost little and are packed with goodness.

3 **Look out for Fairtrade labelled products such as tea, coffee and chocolate.** Available from Oxfam and many supermarkets, these products are ethically sourced, ensuring that producers in developing countries get a fair price for their goods.

4 **Form a money-saving co-operative with like-minded friends and neighbours to buy wholefoods direct from wholesalers.** Minimum orders can range from around £100 to £350 and delivery is usually free. Wholefood wholesalers include Lembas based in Sheffield (www.lembas.co.uk, Tel: 0845 458 1585), Green City in Glasgow (www.greencity.co.uk, Tel: 0141 554 7633) and Infinity Foods in Brighton (www.infinityfoods.co.uk, Tel: 01273 424060).

5 **Save restaurant visits for really special occasions.** Make sure your family and friends take their turn at cooking so you get a break from it. Get into the habit of taking picnics and packed lunches when you go out for the day.

Further reading and contacts

Find out where you can obtain organic food from the Soil Association (details in the Downshifter's Directory). Recommended reading: *Food for Free* by Richard Mabey (Cygnus, 2001); *The River Cottage Year* by Hugh Fearnley-Whittingstall (Hodder & Stoughton, 2003).

15

Transport

The train company Connex South Central has announced that it is cutting 40 services a day across Kent and the south-east of England. The company said the move was designed to improve punctuality.

BBC RADIO 4 NEWS, 2 SEPTEMBER 2003

Travelling has never been easier – or more complex. We get around on foot, by car, bicycle, bus, tram, train, ship, ferry, hover-craft and aeroplane. The choice is liberating and phenomenal. So much so that we have become lazy and unthinking in our habits. We take the car for the shortest of journeys when we could just as easily walk. Instead of jumping at the opportunity of getting fit by cycling, we prefer to drive everywhere. Then we go to the gym – and work out on bike and running machines! And when we take a foreign holiday we criss-cross the globe in jets without a second thought for the huge amounts of energy consumed and the pollution created.

Those of us not scraping by on low incomes and benefits also tend to forget or ignore the costs of transport, just as we ignore the cost to our time of sitting in rush hour traffic jams. We reason that we deserve the luxury of our personal space and would rather be stuck in a queue than on public transport.

The average British family spends 14 per cent of its weekly budget on transport, compared with 12.6 per cent on eating at home. Yet we think much less about cutting back on travelling costs than we do about saving on other essentials such as food and housing. Transport is therefore a living expense ripe for reform by budget-slashing downshifters. And the good news is that finding cheaper ways to get around can be fun, healthy and nothing like as inconvenient as you might imagine. Below we suggest seven ways forward, ranging from the easy and obvious to the much more radical.

Step 1: *cheaper driving*

Two-thirds of British households own cars, so let's assume you own one or maybe even two. You may be one of the millions who commute to work every day or you may just use it for leisure, shopping and school trips. Either way, you probably believe that your car is indispensable or that you can't bear to part with it. If this is the case, the priority is to cut down your car maintenance costs. There are many ways of doing this:

Ditch the second car

If you are a two-car family, then seriously consider selling one. Even if one partner had to switch to a long commuter train journey, the expense would be highly unlikely to outweigh the annual cost of a second vehicle.

The Environmental Transport Association estimates that for people who travel less than 2,000 miles a year, the fixed and running costs of motoring work out at £1 a mile, making it cheaper to travel the full 2,000 miles by taxi! For those covering 5,000 miles a year by car, ETA estimates the total cost per mile at 59p. If their owners sold their cars and travelled a third of the mileage by taxi, a third by train and a third by bus, they would each save £600 a year. So, if you're trying to save money, running two cars doesn't make sense unless you are both working in places so inaccessible that they are impossible to reach by any other means.

Buy the car you need, not the one you fantasise about

The next step is to consider changing down a gear in your choice of car. If you've bought your latest model for speed or fashion status, regardless of your actual needs then trade it in. Cars with rapid acceleration and top speeds up to 120mph drink up petrol and you can hardly ever make use of what you've paid for unless you break the speed limit. Instead, buy a car whose hallmarks are safety and reliability, and which has cheap spare parts. Safe, reliable cars are generally considered a low risk by insurers, and this will help keep your annual premium low.

Also, however tempting the TV ads, be careful to buy a car no bigger than you need; one that matches rather than exceeds your day-to-day requirements.

Another must is to shop around for the best deals. If you live in London or the south-east, it might be worth a trip to the north of the country where saleroom prices can be considerably cheaper. You will almost certainly get a better deal if you sell your current car privately rather than trading it in. Finally, try and choose a fuel-efficient model which doesn't burn up the petrol. Depending on their engine size, BMWs drink up between 9 and 19 litres to travel 100km in urban areas, while a bottom-of-the-range Ford Escort uses up 8 litres and a Fiat Uno only 4.6 litres. Over a year it will make a sizeable difference to your pocket.

Buy green and save money

If you want to limit your car's environmental impact as well as saving money, you have plenty of choice. The market in energy- and fuel-efficient cars is booming, helped by the government's graded vehicle excise licence system which rewards smaller-engined and fuel-efficient cars with cheaper licences. As a basic rule of thumb, ecofriendly cars have low engine capacity, economic fuel consumption and a low top speed.

For the more adventurous, cars and vans with dual fuel engines powered jointly by petrol and LPG (liquefied petroleum gas) are now sold by several UK-based manufacturers, led by Vauxhall. As well as being kind to the environment by greatly reducing pollution emissions, they squeeze 180 miles from every £10 spent on fuel compared with 100 miles for petrol-only cars. Across Europe there are 5.5 million dual fuel cars in use. So far around 50,000 UK motorists drive them and several hundred garage forecourts nationwide now offer LPG facilities. As an added incentive, LPG vehicles receive a discount on the central London congestion charge.

Keep it running

Now you've got a car which is reliable and cheap to run. The next priority is to keep it on the road for as long as possible. The longer you own a car, the slower the depreciation rate. To help keep your car healthy:

- find a garage mechanic you like and trust, and stick with him – you're more likely to get a good cheap service that way

- repair little ailments such as fan belts and worn tyres as they come along, to avoid bigger bills later

- check your oil level frequently and make sure you change it when the owner's manual suggests

- get your car tuned regularly. Badly tuned vehicles drink up petrol as well as being highly polluting

Drive cheaply and safely

Set a personal speed limit, preferably below 60mph. Driving at 50mph (80kph) on motorways rather than 70mph (112kph) burns up far less petrol and cuts emissions substantially.

Don't leave an idle engine running. A stationary engine uses up fuel and pumps out unnecessary pollutants. Never leave your engine running for more than 60 seconds and switch it off when stuck in a traffic jam.

Step 2: *consider car pooling*
Car pooling or sharing – for commuter journeys, school, shopping and leisure trips – is an excellent way to save money while helping to reduce the number of cars on the road. By sharing trips you will help both to reduce pollution and congestion and to speed up your own journeys. Car sharing is still limited in Britain but has taken off in Germany and Holland where extensive networks help people find suitable partners to commute or travel over distances of hundreds of miles. The average commuter car in Britain carries just 1.2 occupants, or six people for every five cars. Not surprisingly, the roads into every major city in the country are jammed with monotonous regularity every rush hour. The introduction of the congestion charge in London has shown what a difference it can make when people use shared transport (in that case buses and tubes) to enter a city centre.

To make car pooling work successfully, you need to find one or more colleagues who live nearby, work in the same building or close by, and who have inflexible, identical working hours to your own. Mutual goodwill is obviously crucial to making the arrangement succeed. For example, if one of you wants to stay behind in town one evening, the other either has to make similar social arrangements or one of you will have to get home by another means. It may take a little effort to get started, but the benefits – halving your commuter costs and the time you spend behind the wheel in stressful rush hour traffic – are substantial.

Car sharing between neighbours and friends for domestic journeys, school runs, shopping trips and so on is more widespread than commuter pooling. Suggest to your neighbours that you might like to co-ordinate your weekly shopping trip, taking it in turns to drive. Do the same with the parents of your children's classmates. It's an easy and sociable way to cut down your driving costs. Car pooling is especially useful in rural areas where bus services can be very limited.

Company programmes encouraging commuter ride-sharing are also increasingly popular around the country with employers helping staff to identify colleagues taking similar routes to work via written databases or Intranet systems. Sometimes several small employers in a business park or town centre create a joint ride-sharing pool. At Derriford Hospital in Plymouth, 7 per cent of the 4,500 staff are ride-sharers. Why not suggest to your employer that they set up a car pool database and promote it to staff? Or enlist the support of one of several on-line ride-share matching services such as www.Liftshare.com, www.Shareajourney.com or www.villagecarshare.com.

Step 3: *get into cost-free travel – rediscover walking and cycling*
Most of us get into our cars for the shortest of journeys without thinking. Three-quarters of journeys in Britain are under five miles long, half are less than two miles. Yet a staggering 69 per cent of these journeys are made by car. Short journeys at low speeds are costly in petrol use and add unnecessarily to traffic pollution and congestion. If your journey is only half a mile away, it's a fine day and you have plenty of time, then walk or cycle. Gradually build up the distance and the number of trips you make without driving. You may even end up walking or cycling to work. If you do, don't worry that you will have to set aside more time to get there. Government statistics show that a 7 kilometre (4.4 mile) rush hour journey takes 41 minutes by car, 51

minutes by bus, 45 minutes by train or tube, 51 minutes on foot
– and only 22 minutes on a bicycle. We use our cars even more
for shopping trips than for commuting but here, too, bicycles are
a good substitute. Major bicycle outlets now sell attachable bike
trailers made of a light alloy metal frame lined with a tough
plastic which can easily carry a week's shopping for a family of
four. Enlightened employers, such as the Environment Agency,
Pfizer and Orange, are also helping health-minded staff to
purchase bikes by offering interest-free loans and/or encourage
cycling to work by providing mileage allowances, racks and
showers.

Not only will walking and cycling save you money, it will make
you fitter. The Sports Council and Health Education Authority
recommend regular aerobic exercise as essential for healthy living.
Walking and cycling both fit the bill perfectly, improving strength
and stamina, lowering the risk of heart disease and helping you
to stay a trim, healthy weight.

Step 4: *rediscover public transport*
If your job or children's school is too far away for you to walk or
cycle, try rediscovering buses and trains. Many local authorities
are now actively trying to revitalise public transport networks,
after years of neglect, to reduce the number of cars on the road.
Despite all the bad publicity about major south-east commuter
routes, you may be pleasantly surprised by the standard and
frequency of your local service. To save money, always find out
about cheap weekly, monthly or annual tickets and about non-
premium times to travel – usually after 10 a.m. – when prices are
much cheaper. In London, Ken Livingstone's transport revolution
includes cheap family tickets for those travelling with children
after 10 a.m. Why not check out some of the lower priced, advance
booking rail tickets deals and let the train take the strain for your
next business trip or weekend away? For those living in rural areas
where public transport is scarce, seek advice on organising

alternatives from the Community Transport Association on 0845 130 6195 or at www.communitytransport.com.

Step 5: *give up your car*
It may seem difficult, especially if you live in remote countryside, to get around any other way, but if you re-think the way you live, it is possible to greatly reduce your car dependence and get around instead by foot, bicycle, public transport and the occasional taxi.

First investigate public transport alternatives for getting to work and for other essential trips like shopping and school runs. Then decide which journeys you can feasibly make by public transport, walking or cycling and which, if any, are out of the question. You could then try not driving for a month or two and see how practical and enjoyable – or not – such a lifestyle would be.

This sounds dramatic and time-consuming, but may well fit in with the changes you are already contemplating. For example, if you are deciding to work from home in your new downshifter's lifestyle, then one knock-on effect would be that you would no longer need a car to commute.

Similarly, if you were prepared to switch your shopping habits from a superstore to local shops, a car would again seem much less indispensable. Home shopping, which is beginning to take off in Britain, is an even better option. No transport is needed because your order is delivered to your door (see also Chapter 14, Food and Drink). Likewise, if you are planning to move to a new area, make the choice partly on whether essential facilities such as schools and a hospital are in easy cycling, walking or taxi distance. If you are planning to stay where you are, then investigate the public transport. On the surface, it may seem cheaper to run your car than use a bus or local train service, but don't forget to factor in the big annual lump sum costs of tax, MOT, annual service, depreciation, and so on. The

Environmental Transport Association calculates that, for those travelling 5,000 miles a year by car, the running costs total £692 and the fixed costs a whopping £2,291. If the distances involved are not too great, then invest in a bicycle which will cost only a tiny fraction of your annual driving budget. Major bicycle outlets these days boast a wide range of choice, including folding bicycles which can be easily stored in trains, buses or the back of cars. And don't overlook tandems for couples. If you have young children, family bicycles, which can carry up to four people, are now on the market.

For those living in areas with poor public transport, another route is to join or start up community initiatives. These could include lobbying the Post Office and local councils for Postbus services to take on passengers as they now do in many rural areas. Another option is to get a group of residents together who agree to share local taxis for weekly trips into the nearest town, and so on. It is already quite common for taxis to offer cheap daily school pick-up services between rural villages.

Club together

Of course there are times when car travel is simply the easiest and most convenient way to get from A to B, particularly if you have several destinations en route. The good news here is that car share companies, otherwise known as car clubs, are flourishing in major cities. These allow you to book a car by the day or hour when you need one – without any of the costs of owning a vehicle yourself. Around 30 car club companies operate in cities including Bristol, Bath, Swansea, Leicester and Edinburgh and the Countryside Agency is funding 13 pilot schemes in rural areas. Car club members pay a joining fee and annual membership which typically costs £125, less than the standard tax disc. Each time they use a car they pay an hourly hire rate of £2–3 plus 15–20p for every mile driven. Most clubs guarantee to have a car parked within ten minutes' walking distance of your home or office. Many local authorities work with car clubs, marking designated parking bays in congested city centres for users. To find out more call Carplus, the car clubs' association, on 0113 234 9299 or visit www.carclubs.org.uk.

Further reading and contacts

Available from most newsagents, *Which Car?* is a reliable guide to value-for-money vehicles.

Cutting Your Car Use, a short, pocket-friendly book by Anna Semlyn, offers readers a 'personal traffic reduction guide' full of useful tips. Available from Green Books on 01803 863260 or via www.greenbooks@gn.apc.org.

The Environmental Transport Association can be reached at 68 High Street, Weybridge, Surrey KT13 8RS. Call 01932 828882 to order a copy of its green car buyers' guide. To review its services, which include emergency recovery for both cars and bicycles, see www.eta.co.uk.

The Cycling Touring Club (CTC) provides information on the full range of bicycles and accessories on the market. Alternatively call 0870 873 0060 or visit www.ctc.org.uk.

16

Household Management

Have nothing in your houses that you do not know to be useful, or believe to be beautiful.

WILLIAM MORRIS (1834–96), ENGLISH DESIGNER, SOCIALIST AND POET

Clutter is the enemy of efficient household management. In this chapter we are going to help you get rid of what you don't want or need, by recycling or selling it. We will also give you some tips on cutting your heating, water and lighting bills, to save you money and help the environment.

Clutter spreads like a virus, and you are unlikely to summon all your powers of decisive action to dispose of it unless you establish exactly what it is, and why you allow it to accumulate. Try this practical exercise. Inspect the contents of each room, drawers, cupboards. Just look at everything you have and list every item that fails to pass the 'William Morris Test'. Don't forget any sheds or attics, well-known breeding grounds for this insidious species that colonises our domestic worlds.

We will recognise most things as either useful or not, but a significant minority will fall into a grey area that we could sum up as: 'Well, You Never Know, It Might Come In Handy.' This grey area is actually stuffed full of clutter. Steel yourself for some pretty challenging questions. Does that hairless, one-eyed teddy bear under the stairs still justify your lifelong hospitality, not to mention your house space? If it has been several years since you played your old records, could it be time to give away or sell the record player – and, yes, even the records?

If in doubt, throw it out

Once you have your own clutter report, think about how you came to have all these items still lying about the place. That should help you stop it all building up again after the clear-out we suggest you now undertake. When you are busy, it is all too easy to ignore clutter and find a drawer that you can still open to store your most recently acquired knick-knacks. Then there are all the broken items that you always meant to repair, but never did. In addition, there will probably be items that you strongly suspect you will never use again, but you simply cannot face making a decision about their future.

Here is a five-point plan to help you transform your clutter list into a satisfying achievement, and an act of altruism to your fellow man and woman. Do not despair, panic or prevaricate. The chances are that you will suffer absolutely no withdrawal symptoms, but will feel liberated by creating a new, more spacious habitat in which to enjoy the delights of simple domesticity. Remember, it means less to keep clean and to insure, less to lug around the country when you next move home, and less to worry about!

1 **Get** some cardboard boxes. Place in them all the items on your list that you know are incapable of being recycled – tins of congealed paint for instance, and long dead paintbrushes. Take them to your local council tip, or arrange for someone from the council to collect them. On the same trip take all the re-

cyclable bottles, cans and newspapers that are lying about to put in the 'eco-banks' that you generally find at these official tips.

2 **Gather** together all the things that you simply hate, or no longer need but which others may be able to use, or even find aesthetically pleasing. It might be worth offering first refusal to relatives and friends before making any irrevocable disposals!

3 **Generate** some income! Car boot sales thrive on gatherings of people who are undertaking clear-outs. You can make some money by taking your unwanted paraphernalia to one. If there is room in your car, take your neighbour's unwanted items too. Alternatively, you can contact a dealer in secondhand furniture and knick-knacks, who will come round and offer you a deal.

4 **Give** it away! Take it to charity shops, and such virtuous behaviour will be its own reward. Make sure it really is in good condition, otherwise you are simply passing on your responsibility to junk your junk to someone else. If you don't want the hassle of travelling to such shops or the logistics are too difficult, then it is worth phoning them, telling them what you have got and ask whether they will collect. Some areas have charity or volunteer-run recycling centres. Check if there is one near you, and again they may collect if you can persuade them that it would be worth their petrol money.

5 **Go On** recycling, every day week and month, not simply as part of the annual domestic clutter audit that we urge you to undertake. Make it part of your life, enjoy being part of an endlessly replenishing loop of renewal and regeneration.

What happens to your rubbish?

By now we hope you are convinced of the need to recycle and cut down on the volume of rubbish you put out each week for the binmen. In case you still harbour doubts, let us give you some facts about what is in the rubbish we create and what happens to it.

What a Waste!

• The UK produces enough waste every hour to fill the Albert Hall. The amount we produce rises by 3 per cent a year.

• Nearly 80 per cent of our domestic waste goes into land-fill sites.

• Nearly one-quarter of all UK production of the green-house gas methane arises from landfill sites.

• England recycles a lamentable 12 per cent of its waste, compared with Germany (52 per cent) and the Netherlands (47 per cent).

Source: Cabinet Office Strategy Unit 2002

As if the release of methane was not bad enough, there is also a liquid called leachate that can seep into underground streams and rivers, and finally into surface water that causes pollution. Then consider the pollution caused by lorries taking the waste from your front gate to the landfill sites. You can see the environmental damage piling up.

If you recycle or compost more of your waste, you're helping to reduce pollution. What your household produces may seem

212

negligible in the grand scheme of things but if everyone made an effort, it would make a serious difference.

How you can help cut waste

Reduce what comes into your home. Ensure what you buy is durable and useful. Cut back on short-life items such as ordinary batteries, disposable razors. Use cloths rather than kitchen roll. Take your own carrier bags when you shop.

Re-use products and containers. Buy washing-up liquid, laundry and cleaning fluids in refillable containers. Use yoghurt pots to grow seedlings for a kitchen garden, or indeed to make your own yoghurt.

Recycle kitchen and garden waste to make compost to top your flowerbeds.

Replace worn-out or broken items with second-hand, recycled or energy-efficient alternatives e.g. lightbulbs, glassware.

Bargain hunting

Only a generation or two ago, buying and selling second-hand or barely used goods was commonly regarded as rather Bohemian, if not completely naff. Now, it seems, almost everyone is at it. The world's largest car boot sale – eBay – operates round the clock, most high streets now have at least one if not several charity shops, and business at architectural salvage yards is booming. There's rarely been a better time to kit out almost your entire house and garden with other people's cast-offs, if you know where to look.

New careers in general trading have been launched on the back of eBay and other auction websites. If you've never tried this way of buying and selling just go to some real auctions and see how they work before going on-line. If you are interested in finding out more, visit www.government-auctions.co.uk. This website has a huge database of auctioneers and other specialist companies that organise sales for disposal of bankrupt stock, liquidations, government property and so on.

Keeping warm at home

Investing in energy efficiency in your home means you pay lower fuel bills in the longer term and you are doing your bit to tackle global warming. Here are some tips for keeping the heat inside your home, instead of disappearing through doors, windows and chimneys:

- **Draught-proof your windows, outside doors and letterboxes.**
  Use easy-to-fix brush or PVC seals. Thick, lined curtains will help keep the heat in at night.

- **Fill gaps in floorboards or skirting boards.**
  Newspaper can sometimes do the job, or beading/sealant. Stripped floorboards can look fantastic, but putting down carpet or some other floor covering will help keep your home warmer.

- **Ensure your hot water tank is properly lagged and, if you have one, the attic is fully insulated.**
  Grants may be available.

- **If you have an open fire, consider the alternatives.**
  Multi-fuel burning stoves, though costly, are much more energy efficient than a traditional fire.

Once you have done at least some of the above, try turning the central heating thermostat down. Some of the more go-ahead local councils now have energy efficiency units, which may be good sources of local information. Grants may be available for low-income households living in a draughty home. Information and guidance on energy efficiency is available from the Energy Saving Trust (www.est.org.uk).

If you want to be really green, then you might consider switching to an electricity supplier that reinvests its profits in non-polluting renewable sources such as wind. Until fairly recently, these renewable energy suppliers have tended to charge more than conventional ones. Ecotricity (www.ecotricity.co.uk) is one exception.

Greening your cleaning and maintenance

The marketing of many conventional household cleaning and laundry products is fairly shameful. We are led to believe that our homes are dirty, dangerous places, where every lurking germ has to be rooted out and urgently exterminated. What the adverts don't tell you of course is that the cleaning products in question may be potentially far more damaging to health and the environment than the grime they are intended to tackle.

Ordinary cleaning products and detergents often contain various petrochemicals and phosphates, which may not be biodegradable. If and when they get into watercourses, via drains and sewers, they can harm aquatic life, plants, fish and invertebrates. On the whole they are best avoided. Much cleanliness can be achieved (notably in fridges and on work surfaces) by soaking a cloth in warm water containing a spoonful or two of bicarbonate of soda, wringing it out and applying with elbow grease. It's that simple. Here are some more tips that can save time, money and effort without adding to pollution:

SUBSTITUTE chemically based household cleaners and laundry products for gentler alternatives. Ecover (www.ecover.com) produces a good range of environmentally friendly substitutes. These are widely available from health/wholefood shops, which may provide refills if you wash and take back the containers.

WINDOWS AND MIRRORS can be adequately cleaned with pieces of scrunched-up newspaper dipped into a bucket of water. Add a splash of white vinegar if you can be bothered.

TEA TREE OIL makes a good disinfectant, but go easy on it. Remember that many, if not most, bacteria are either harmless or positively beneficial. Our immune systems thrive on dealing with them. As long as you observe basic rules of hygiene, particularly handwashing after going to the loo, handling animals and before preparing food, calamity is unlikely to strike if your work surfaces are less than sparkling and sterile. Remember it's your home not an operating theatre.

DECORATE your home with traditional, non-toxic water-based paint. You may find that it is more expensive than the solvent-based paints that most of us use, but think of all the money you are going to save by following our other tips! Water-based paint comes in a range of gorgeous colours, and leaves no nasty smells while it is drying out. If you find it hard to obtain locally, a number of firms provide a mail order service. These include Fired Earth (www.firedearth. co.uk), Tel: 01295 814399 and Farrow and Ball (www.farrow-ball.com) mail order, Tel: 01202 876141.

17

Growing Your Own

Many gardens and allotments of the villagers had already received their spring tillage, but the garden and the allotments of the Durbeyfields were behindhand. She found, to her dismay, that this was owing to their having eaten all the seed potatoes . . .

THOMAS HARDY, TESS OF THE D'URBERVILLES, 1891

Growing at least some of your own food is one of the greatest delights of downshifting. Whether your home is in a tower block, a bedsit, a suburban semi or a rural smallholding, gardening will enhance your life. It's healthy, sociable and it will save you money. Not only that but if you garden organically, as we suggest you do, you will be helping to create a healthier planet too. This is because you will be creating a balanced eco-system to match your newly balanced lifestyle.

Newcomers to gardening first need to size up the opportunities for growing. You may want to start in a small way first, with a few seedlings or young herb plants in pots on a window sill, just to see how it goes. Those who fancy growing out in the fresh air can exploit patios, backyards and window ledges if there is not much space elsewhere. Maybe the idea of an allotment appeals, in which case register your interest with the council quickly. In some parts of the country, available allotments are rare, so get your name on the waiting list while you are still thinking about it. You can always drop out later if you change your mind – there will be plenty of others after your plot!

Having room to grow flowers, shrubs and produce is frequently a major reason why people want to move house, sometimes out from an urban area to a rural one. However, it must be emphasised that if and when you catch the gardening bug you will find happiness and satisfaction in your gardening wherever you are. We aim here to give some advice to beginners and more advanced gardeners, who may be interested in switching to organic methods. More importantly we want to inspire and galvanise those of you who tend to think that gardening is what retired people do. Think again, you are never too young or too old to enjoy it. Gardening is for life.

It's cool to compost

Composting creates an excellent natural fertiliser for all your gardening and growing. You can recycle in this way at least 20 per cent of your household waste that would otherwise end up being driven by a gas-guzzling lorry to a distant landfill site. Once you get in the habit, you will find composting is fun, and your garden produce will be all the better because of it. It takes a while for your kitchen and garden waste to decompose to the point where you can spread it on your flowers and vegetables, so there's no time like the present to start a compost heap or bin. Some councils can offer discount deals or money-off vouchers for buying composting bins and water butts. Check out your local authority to see if these are available. Don't forget, you don't need a garden to make compost.

Warm to a worm: your best flexible friend!

If you are pressed for space, a wormery might be the answer as they are smaller than many traditional composters. There are various types on the market but one of the most widely recommended is the Can O Worms, available through Herefordshire-based Wiggly Wigglers (www.wigglywigglers.co.uk). Prices start from around £80 for a starter pack including the housing – a series of circular trays on top of one another – coir bedding, instructions and 500g of worms.

The company also produces compact and attractive 'baby beehive' wooden composters (painted or unpainted) of different sizes. Give them your kitchen vegetable waste and they will repay you with beautiful rich compost for your plants. Contact details: Wiggly Wigglers, Lower Blakemore, Herefordshire HR2 9PX. Tel: 01981 500391.

Composting in the great outdoors

People with gardens need no paraphernalia to compost, except for a piece of old carpet or thickish polythene to keep the rain from washing it away. Those who like paraphernalia can buy or make a container for it from wood or recycled plastic. An old dustbin is perfect, provided you punch some holes in the sides and stand it on bricks so that air may circulate. The more varied the composting input, the richer and more nutritious the output. So start with some stemmy material, such as prunings, to help the air circulate at the bottom, then alternate layers of soft and tougher material. Most organic waste can be usefully composted, but here's a rough and ready guide. These items are ideal:

• vegetable and fruit peelings, or raw whole pieces if they are beginning to decompose in your rack or larder

- tea leaves or bags

- eggshells

- undiseased plant remains

- grass clippings

- small amounts of wood shavings

- waste from rabbit and guinea-pig hutches or hamster cages

- shredded newspaper

Avoid the following:

- cooked kitchen scraps, even cooked vegetables

- raw meat or fish – they can attract vermin or make nasty smells

- any non-plant based artificially made material, such as plastic, metal or glass

- cat and dog faeces

- persistent weeds such as bindweed, couch grass and ground elder

It can take several months for the first batch to compost. It depends on the ingredients, how you mix them and the temperature. The original material should be unrecognisable when it is ready to use. It should be crumbly, dark or black, sweet-smelling and earthy in texture. The longer you leave it the better it will be, and so will your home-grown produce, shrubs and flowers. Don't forget, every time you compost, you are renewing your connection with nature, and giving it a helping hand. Don't worry too much about the technicalities like layering – it is better to just have a go and get on with it than concern yourself about perfect layering. When you have got your compost going, what next?

The answer lies in the soil

Those of you with gardens need to become better acquainted with soil. Use one of the home-testing kits you can buy at garden centres to find out what will grow best in it, in short, whether it is alkaline or acidic. You should be able to tell from digging a fork into your soil and handling it whether it is mainly clay or chalky or sandy. Sow and plant accordingly. One of the best aspects of gardening is that you can do it all year round. In the case of vegetables and herbs, which we are mainly concerned with as downshifters, there should always be something delicious and nutritious to pull, wash, chop and serve at the dinner table. You don't have to buy a lot of books, although there is a huge variety to choose from if you feel so inclined. You can borrow from the library, join a local gardening club, or just ask a gardener.

Complimenting your neighbours on their impressive-looking leeks or carrots is a great way to get to know them better, and to glean some valuable information to start you off on this exciting journey. There is nothing an established gardener or grower likes more than being complimented on his or her produce, and being asked: 'Tell me, how could I grow some like that then?' Before you know it you will have a fund of knowledge which you can later pass on to some other curious gardening innocent, a bagful of free produce and some cuttings and seeds. This precious commodity of gardening knowledge and enthusiasm is passed on free, from one to another like a never-ending Mexican wave. Books can do this too, if your nearest neighbour lives a few miles down the road! So can television and radio, even the Internet.

If you don't have much space, one idea is just to grow herbs in pots on sills and ledges. Get into the habit of using them every day in cooking or salads. Perhaps you have plenty of space outside but the ground is covered by weeds. This is not a problem; it is what gardeners call a challenge. You can save the nettles for composting or for nettle water to spray on aphids. While clearing away the weeds – ask others to help you – start designing the garden you want to create in their place.

Imagine what different styles would look like, and how much work each would require of you. Think seriously about whether you want a lawn. Many people have decided that it is simply not worth the time and effort they put into creating and maintaining an immaculate lawn. The prospect of global warming and the exceptionally dry summers some parts of the UK have experienced in recent years (notably 2003) have prompted more gardeners to question the quintessentially English love of lawns. But what are the alternatives?

Design your own downshifter's garden

Simplicity, balance, eco-friendliness and a degree of edibility! These must be the essential features of a downshifter's garden. Whether you are starting from scratch or you have inherited someone else's plot, try bearing those four features in mind when designing and planting. Here are ten tips that will help you create a downshifter's garden:

1 **Trees and large shrubs**
These will give shade, shape, character and privacy to your garden, so try to include some in your designs if there are few or none at present. We should try to plant new trees where and when we can.

2 **Dig a pond**

A pond will attract wildlife, in particular frogs, which will eat some of the pests that would otherwise eat your plants.

3 **Grow less grass**

Think about what else might grow where your lawn does. You could get rid of it altogether and turn it over to wild flowers and vegetable growing. Or you could make it into a small circle at the centre of your garden, and part-pave the surrounding area leaving random or designed gaps between the stones for herb-growing.

4 **A place to sit**

Watch how the light and shade changes in your garden, and decide where would be the best place for a seat or table and chairs. Build this into your plan.

5 **The compost heap**

Decide where the compost heap will go. The closer it is to the house the more often you will use it. If the end of the garden is the only available place, keep a minibin, with cover, in the kitchen so you don't have to go out in the rain.

6 **Catch that rain**

Acquire or buy a water butt, to catch the rainwater run-off from your roof. Maybe you could convert a large plastic barrel or drum. This way you may still garden and grow while others' activities are stalled by drought-induced hosepipe bans. Rainwater is soft and may be better for your plants than tap water. Dogs and cats often prefer to drink rainwater too.

7 **Which plants to grow?**

When deciding what to plant, choose plants that require little or no watering. These include lavender, lilac, tulips, sunflowers, carnations, wall flowers, jasmine, holly, broom, buddleia and crocus. Plants that need a lot of water include willow, elder, bamboo, clematis, primula, and azalea. Incorporate plenty of organic matter, such as compost, into the soil. It will condition the soil and help keep moisture around the plants' roots.

8   **Which plants to keep?**

Remove from your garden anything that you hate, or that obscures one of your treasured plants. Remember the 'William Morris Test' that we suggested you applied to your home in Chapter 16? Well, repeat it in your garden. Bear in mind that what you may find irksome now, may look glorious in six months. So just draw up a hit-list at this stage and monitor those plants that you list. One year from now, get out your list and only then decide which plants can no longer justify their existence. Give an offender a stay of execution – ask a neighbour or a gardening contact if they would like it. If there are no takers, then dig it up. Where practicable, shred it and put it on the compost.

9   **Water with care**

Water your plants in the evening, and surround the stems with a layer of mulch to reduce evaporation. Cut the bottom out of plastic bottles and push them, top first into the ground next to those plants that need plenty of water. When watering just fill the bottle from your watering can. It will take the water directly to where it is needed, wasting virtually none.

10 **Share the work and enjoy the results**

Gardening can be solitary and some people like it that way. There are ways of making it more sociable, even if you cannot interest other family members or it is not feasible to join a club. If you have a friend who gardens, maybe you could arrange for him or her to come and help you with your gardening and for you to do the same in return. You could alternate the sessions monthly or weekly. It would give you a sounding board for your gardening plans, an extra pair of hands, and an instant cuttings and seed-swapping partner. It may be fun to dream up some joint projects – like growing some plants to give away as birthday or Christmas presents. After a couple of hours of hard labour, you can then sit down with a cup of tea, catch up with each other's news, and admire your joint handiwork.

Bring your garden into the office

Gardening can be a great adventure, so be bold in your vision and think laterally. So many millions love gardening, so bring your new-found knowledge and enthusiasms into other areas of your life. Make new connections through gardening, meet new people, get to know colleagues and acquaintances better. Who knows what new doors will open for you?

Let's imagine you are still working at your career or job and are wondering how you can downshift without leaving your employer for whom you have toiled long and hard. Here's an idea for making your working life more enjoyable and for getting your boss to allow you to go part-time or flexitime, or to do more of your job from home. Put a notice on the office noticeboard (or e-mail your colleagues if you can), inviting them to join you in a 'Gardener's Question Time' session. You could hold it in the function room at the pub round the corner, or in the company's board room, if your boss agrees.

Everyone brings along a cutting or some seeds to swap, or else a gardening problem that one of your green-fingered colleagues could probably solve. This is an excellent wheeze for bonding with colleagues and bosses alike. Office politics will be cast aside as you have a jolly good chat about Nina's sweet peas or David's problem with honey fungus, and you leave with something new and intriguing to put in your window box or garden. If you can relate to the colleagues around you at work as people, gardeners preferably, the easier it will be to negotiate that switch to part-time or home working, or win that sabbatical you have always hankered for. If your question time session goes with a bang, you then have the makings of a workers' gardening club. Remember, you don't need to be an expert to garden successfully and enjoyably. You need only genuine curiosity, a demonstrable enthusiasm for gardening, and a few social skills.

Allotment contentment

Parks are often described as the green lungs of urban areas, but so too are gardens and allotments. There is a distinctive romantic appeal about allotments, these hidden havens of DIY food production, mutual support and co-operative endeavour. Visitors accustomed to a built-up environment are also often struck by the vast expanse of sky that suddenly opens up above them, but also by the friendliness and character of allotment holders. A sensible first step is to contact your local council to get some general information and advice. They should be able to put you in touch with allotment associations in the area. Alternatively, the nearest allotments association is likely to be listed in your phone book or Yellow Pages. A plot will cost a few pounds a year to rent, and provided you put in enough effort, it will give you and your family virtually free food. Moreover, you will never be stuck for a gift!

If you hanker after something bigger than an allotment – a smallholding in the country for example – we advise you to try allotment gardening first, for this will help you decide whether you are temperamentally suited! As you will have read in our interview in Chapter 8 with downshifters Dan and Bel in remote rural Wales, smallholding has unique rewards, but it is also fraught with possible difficulties, requires tremendous energy and is potentially isolating. Do plenty of research before putting your house on the market!

Further reading

The Easy Care Gardening Expert by Dr D.G. Hessayon (Transworld, 1996); *The Complete Book of Self-Sufficiency* by John Seymour (Dorling Kindersley, 1996).

Leisure and Pleasure

For a long time, leisure was for the rich, while slaves or the working classes did the work. Now we can all have leisure and we have to decide how to spend it.
MICHAEL ARGYLE, THE SOCIAL PSYCHOLOGY OF LEISURE, 1996

'In our day, we didn't have television – we made our own entertainment,' so millions have been told by their parents or grandparents. Now that television is probably the most wide-spread leisure activity of the modern world we will use this chapter to explore some alternatives. The person who has no TV is regarded as an eccentric curiosity by almost everyone else, but he or she may be leading a fuller and happier existence.

If you have ambivalent feelings about your television, it might be worth logging how much time you spend watching it and pondering whether life might be better without it. Consider doing what your parents or grandparents did. Make your own entertainment. The enthusiastic downshifter will take this message to heart more than most!

He or she will give serious thought to the following idea: swap or sell your television set and video, or cancel your agreement with the rental company. That way you will have much more time to try any or several of the options outlined in the preceding chapters, or to pursue your own alternative leisure ideas.

Ten ideas for cheap thrills, and lasting pleasure

1 Readers and borrowers

In the 1980s and early nineties, there was occasional talk of privatising libraries. This threat appears to have since receded, but perhaps greater commercial involvement can be expected in the next few years, as use of their traditional services has waned. Since 1992, library visits in England have gone down by 17 per cent, and book loans by almost a quarter. Over the same period sales of books have risen by 25 per cent.

In 2003 the Department of Culture, Media and Sport published a blueprint to modernise libraries and increase their appeal to younger people. It stressed their valuable roles as learning and information centres helping to fulfil the government's commitment to universal Internet access (the number of 'on-line hours' available to users had grown to 52 million in the previous year) and as promoters of literacy among all age groups.

Although free book borrowing seems set to continue for the foreseeable future at least, lending charges for videos, tapes and similar items could well increase. Much will depend on library users themselves and their awareness and resourcefulness as lobbyists to uphold the ideals on which the public library system is founded.

The reference sections of libraries are nerve-centres for down-shifters. These are free information points for local, regional and national activities and organisations. They should be able to help you track down most of the addresses and phone numbers you need to find out about hang-gliding, spaniel-breeding or what-ever new leisure activity you plan to pursue. Don't forget the British Library, London, which is seeking to create a 'virtual library' for the future, not only of the written word, but of computer graphics, even architectural drawings. The idea is to make increasing amounts of information available over the Internet.

Finally, a word about library staff. They are generally extremely helpful, and often respond heroically to courteous requests for help. What's more, most of their services are free.

2 Volunteering

Whether they shake a tin in a shopping centre for charity, do committee work, visit prisoners or hospital patients or help out with their child's playgroup, volunteers are the backbone of any community. We dealt with some aspects of volunteering in Chapter 12.

Many voluntary and charitable bodies are short of willing hands. According to the 1997 National Survey of Volunteering in the UK, the proportion of adults engaging in such had fallen from 51 per cent in 1991 to 48 per cent. But those who do it are putting in more hours – about four hours a week compared with 2.7 hours in 1991. The old adage of 'If you want something done, ask a busy person' appears to be true: people in work are more likely to volunteer than the unemployed or the retired. Sports, education and social welfare are the most popular spheres for voluntary work. If you can spare some time on a monthly or weekly basis, then decide to whom you would like to offer your services. This might be a national charity that you already support financially, or a new organisation. The chances are that you have read or heard about one recently that has struck you as particularly worthwhile. Decide whether hands-on practical work suits you, indoors or out, or whether you'd be happier doing committee work and report writing.

One idea is to find out if there is a Groundwork Trust in your area. This is a voluntary body that employs volunteers, and some paid workers, to regenerate the natural and built environment in run-down or derelict urban areas. Sustainable development is the common thread running through its projects, so both the environment and the local community benefit as jobs are created.

3 Buy less, make more, do it yourself

As we have seen, rat racing leaves us with little personal time, so we end up buying clothes, food, furniture and furnishings that at one time we and our families would have made ourselves. We 'contract out' domestic and household services far more than we used to, for the same reasons. Clearly, it would be unrealistic to expect more than a very small minority of people to aspire to total self-sufficiency. However, inherent in the downshifting philosophy will be a hankering to do some of the work ourselves that we currently farm out.

The trick is not to think of it as work, but leisure with attitude, leisure with purpose. What you can do is think now of one or two jobs that need doing around the house or garden, or items that need replacing. Then pick out those that you fancy having a shot at doing yourself. It can be jam-making, particularly if your garden has a fruit tree, making a lampshade, a brick wall, or laying a patio. You have to really want to do it, otherwise you probably won't get around to it, or you won't accomplish the task as well as you might. Motivation is all-important. Maybe you could rope in some friends to help you, other downshifters perhaps, whom you could repay in kind at a later date.

Another secret of successful DIY is to set yourself generous deadlines, or not to set them at all. Many of us have had a basinful of deadlines, enough to last a lifetime. Let your leisure activities evolve at your pace, no one else's. Those jobs that need doing urgently, which you don't really have the time or inclination to do, are probably best given to someone whom you pay.

4 Learn as you earn

If you've already spent too much of your life hunched over your computer screen why not take a course in some active, practical but pleasurable pursuit where you can learn new skills at your own pace. The range and quality of adult education courses available in most areas has improved considerably in recent years under the government's 'Lifelong Learning' initiative. Colleges and universities are falling over themselves to sign up adult learners for their courses, and many of the more popular ones can now be taken either during the day or evening. As well as giving pleasure and stimulation, these courses can spark off ideas for more satisfying ways to earn money.

5 Get to know your mother's father's Uncle Horace

Researching one's family history could become a fascinating and rewarding lifetime's project. If you write it up into a narrative, complete with family tree, you and your family will have a unique record to keep and ultimately pass on to the next generation. Circulate chapters of your *magnum opus* as you complete them as Christmas or birthday presents. Don't wait until you have finished the whole work because if you do it properly, it will probably take years. Some of your relatives may not live that long! Writing up a family history will give a new focus to your relationship with your kith and kin.

Older relatives will probably be only too pleased to be asked to rummage around for letters, photographs and family documents for you to borrow and glean interesting material. Don't forget to 'interview' them too – getting your parents' or grandparents' memories recorded. You can spread this over several sessions, each one focusing on a different era or major life event. To make it easier you can use a tape-recorder, or even a video-recorder. Encourage your willing participants to make their own video diaries; you provide the technology, they will provide the memories.

Of course, the whole enterprise will have to be handled with tact and diplomacy, especially if there are a few skeletons rattling in the family cupboard. But most families are likely to be grateful that one of their number has agreed to undertake this task.

6 Set up a reading circle
Libraries are not the only sources of free or cheap reading matter. Another one is reading circles. Get together with a few friends, agree on a book that you would all like to read. Take it in turns to borrow or buy the book then pass it on to the next person, and so on until everyone has read it. Then meet up in each other's homes to discuss what you liked or disliked about it. Start all over again with a different member suggesting the book you all read. Obviously it makes sense to keep the numbers fairly small – half a dozen or fewer, and ensure you live quite close together.

7 Write a novel, short story or play
Everyone has a story to tell – their own – and it can provide the basis of any piece of fiction, or simply inspire it. Many overlook shorter forms of creative writing in pursuit of the novel, which is fine if you have the self-discipline, staying power and the talent to sustain such a long piece of work. If you want to get your work published, you are probably more likely to strike it lucky if you divide your writing ambitions into more manageable chunks. There are plenty of writers' workshops and creative writing courses to choose from. One excellent way to start is to read the guidelines published by BBC Radio for new writers of drama and short stories. For other markets, look out for the *Writers' and Artists' Yearbook* or *The Writer's Handbook*.

8 Become a dog-walker
To have all the pleasure of being a dog owner and none of the responsibility, you can offer your services as a dog escort to elderly or disabled neighbours or their carers. You will suddenly assume great popularity, especially if you live near a park!

9 Enjoy your parks

Treat your local park or open space as an extension of your garden or its substitute, if you do not have one. If there is some aspect of it that puts you off, such as vandalism or excessive litter, do something about it. Form a local Park Watch group, perhaps through an existing organisation such as a residents' group or a Neighbourhood Watch Scheme.

10 Giving to the person who has everything

Present-giving and entertaining friends, relatives or colleagues can be a delightful, life-enhancing experience, or it can be a time-consuming, duty-laden ritual for both donor and recipient. It can be extremely expensive, but the money spent does not necessarily equate with the enjoyment had.

Why don't we give each other more pleasant experiences as presents instead of buying things? Why don't we go and spend more time with the people we care about instead of compensate for our long periods of absence by handing over beautifully wrapped objects that they may neither want nor need. A walk in the country and a picnic; organising a home-made dinner, get everyone to bring a different course or dish – it will save you time and money, and possibly be more fun for everyone; or arranging a surprise visit to or from a mutual friend or relative is likely to be a far more memorable and meaningful way of marking a birthday or an anniversary. We all long for more spontaneity and serendipity in our lives, but we don't use our imaginations or make the time to make these things happen.

We prefer to spring our surprises on others in the form of purchases, which are just as likely to disappoint as to thrill unless we have asked some pertinent and searching questions in advance. If the best things in life really are free, why do we behave as though they cost a lot of money, and that the more we spend the better they are? The answer, in many cases, is that we don't stop and take time to think about it often enough, or that we do know it to be true but are too busy to act on it. So maybe the next time you want to do something nice for someone who has 'everything' give them something that they almost certainly have not had enough of recently; your time. Essentially, you don't have to be more generous with your money to make life better for you and the people you love. You simply have to be more generous with yourself.

Further reading

Public libraries generally have details of adult education courses, and any family history societies, in your area.
Writers' and Artists' Yearbook (A & C Black) and *The Writer's Handbook* (Macmillan) are each published annually and are indispensable guides to new and established writers in all market areas.

Holidays

One of the symptoms of approaching nervous breakdown is the belief that one's work is terribly important and that to take a holiday would bring all kinds of disaster.

BERTRAND RUSSELL (1872–1970), ENGLISH PHILOSOPHER AND MATHEMATICIAN

Opportunities for global travel and tourism have never been greater. And we Britons, always an adventurous race, are taking up the challenge in our millions. A third of us now take two or more holidays a year. In 2000 we spent £16.8 billion booking flights and holidays through travel agencies, while domestic tourism raked in a further £48 billion.

As a nation, the much-predicted move towards a more leisure-oriented society has yet to materialise. Instead we have an over-worked majority and an idle, jobless, impoverished minority. But if you belong to the ranks of the over-worked, switching to a downshifter's lifestyle should allow you more time for both leisure and holidays. And instead of spending your precious time off lying flat out on a beach recovering from a stressful job, you will be able to explore new, more fulfilling ways of spending your leisure time.

Of course, your new downshifter's lifestyle may also mean you have less money to spend. But having an enjoyable holiday doesn't have to mean splashing out a thousand pounds on a week-long skiing trip or a rushed visit to Florida or the Caribbean. There are many cheap, exciting alternatives which just take a little more time and energy to explore. Read on to find out what they are.

Cheap packaged paradise

Most of us take package trips for our annual holidays which we often book several months in advance. While this is a safe, hassle-free approach, especially when we only have a few precious weeks a year, it is much more expensive than waiting for last minute bargains. For those who don't mind which particular resort or even country they are visiting but just want a beach with sunny weather or a good skiing centre, then waiting for late deals is a good investment. And if you have flexible working patterns or are self-employed then taking a last minute holiday is much easier than when you have to clear dates with bosses and colleagues weeks in advance.

Most High Street travel agents advertise last minute package and flight bargains throughout the year, with prices down to as low as a third of the original price. Or you could scan the newspaper travel sections or trawl through the holiday listings on Ceefax and Teletext in the comfort of your home. Look out in particular for the growing number of travel agencies which specialise in cheap late bookings. These include on-line specialists such as Lastminute.com and expedia.co.uk. Last minute packages to the Caribbean out of the peak season can sell for as little as £450, two week trips to Kenya for as little as £400 and packages to Goa, India, can drop as low as £300. One word of warning, however. Do make sure that whoever you book with is a member of ABTA or ATOL, the two trade associations, just in case your last minute holiday goes wrong. If you are misled by your agents about your destination, you want to have a legal comeback.

Shoestring travel

If you want a more adventurous time than a fortnight's package deal will offer but have restricted funds, then take advantage of the range of very good budget guides now on offer. These are a very good investment, guiding the shoe-string traveller to the best sites and cheapest decent hotels in the farthest-flung corners of the world. Among the best and best-known are the Lonely Planet travel survival kit guide-books and the Rough Guide series, both available from major bookstores. They provide in-depth city-by-city information on budget transport, accommodation and restaurants in every country they visit as well as lots of cultural and historical background. Once you have covered the expense of your air fare, it is quite possible to live much more cheaply than at home in many foreign countries, especially those in Asia and Africa. If you're planning to travel for several months rather than weeks, another way of eking out your funds is to take temporary work abroad. English is by far the most used of the international tourist languages, so English-speakers are particularly in demand for bar, restaurant and hotel jobs in resort areas the world over.

House swaps at home and abroad

For the less adventurous who don't fancy roughing it in cheap foreign hotels, house-swapping could be the perfect answer. Since the early 1990s recession, house-swap holidays have grown in popularity as families desperate for a break, but unable to afford splurging out on two weeks in a hotel, began advertising their homes in national and overseas newspapers and magazines and websites. Most swaps take place between families living in different parts of the UK, although swaps with second homes in France, Italy and America are also growing in popularity.

Agencies have now sprung up to help the process along and to offer back-up to families nervous about opening their homes to strangers. Usually all you have to do is supply a description and photograph of your house and details of the type of area you want to holiday in, seaside, mountainous or whatever, and they will put you in touch with a suitable householder on their lists for a reasonably small fee. Homelink International, one of the biggest agencies, has 12,500 members worldwide. Its UK website, full of tempting listings, is www.homelink.org.uk. One enthusiastic British member featured in *The Sunday Times* had arranged over 100 exchange holidays in 16 countries over the past ten years! A second longstanding agency, Home Base Holidays, is based in London (see Downshifter's Directory for contact details). Members pay an annual fee of £29 to advertise their home and access other swappers.

If you would prefer not to go through an intermediary, try advertising in national newspapers or in the local papers of the area you want to visit. This should only cost you £20 or so a time. The advent of the Internet has also produced new opportunities to find house-swap partners the world over. You can scan through a comprehensive list of holiday homes across the UK at your leisure or advertise your own home to interested parties in Britain or overseas. We recently heard of someone who advertised to swap his north London home for a family house in Boston for two weeks. He received three inquiries and telephone numbers within a week!

A variation on the house-swapping theme is house-sitting. This involves looking after someone else's home for a short period in return for free accommodation in a nice location. Most house-sitters are not expected to do more than keep the house clean and tidy, water the plants and feed and walk any pets. Often people choose house-sitters they know or by word of mouth, but house-sitting agencies are now starting to spring up. These advise house-owners to draw up a written contract of duties the sitter is expected to perform. Sitters also usually agree to pay gas, electricity and phone bills during their stay. A web-based organisation, www.housecarers.org.uk, matches sitters and owners from around the world. Homelink International also offers an international house-sitting exchange service but it makes up only 2 per cent of its business.

If there is a specific UK area you are interested in visiting, you could also try placing an ad in the local paper advertising your services.

Activity holidays

Try a more active holiday than those of the beach and sightseeing variety. Your vacation should turn out to be cheaper, healthier and at least as rewarding. Activity holidays can allow you to indulge a favourite hobby or to try your hand at something new you've never previously had the time for. They include long-distance walking and cycling, hiking and bird-watching, fishing and canoeing. All of these can be pursued either within the UK or abroad, and the growth in specialist holiday companies means there is plenty of advice on hand.

Just look up advertisements in newspapers and magazines and then ring up for the brochures. You can either opt for a ready-made package, which is likely to be quite expensive, or cull the company brochures for information on good locations for your activity and then go it alone, hiring bicycles, canoes, or hiking equipment and staying in bed and breakfast accommodation or small hotels.

Other agencies also offer impartial advice on activity holidays. The Sports Council, for example, in the interests of public fitness, publish a register of firms offering guided walking holidays. The National Trust also provides a long list of nature walks around

Britain (it owns 57 nature reserves and over 400 sites of special scientific interest), while the Youth Hostels Association has compiled a comprehensive directory of walks to suit all ages and interests. The Car-Free Leisure Network, initiated by Transport 2000 (see Downshifter's Directory), co-ordinates and promotes efforts by local authorities to make popular tourist destinations more accessible by bicycle, train, bus and foot.

Camping and caravanning can also be classed as activity holidays in that they involve more physical effort – and more personal freedom and adventure – than booking into a hotel. Both are still very popular in Britain, particularly, but not exclusively, in the summer months. Both caravan and camping sites cost peanuts compared with hotel prices, especially for families. If you're looking for a site near a nice clean beach, the best bet is to invest in a copy of the annually produced *Good Beach Guide* or to look it up in your local library. The guide gives beaches star ratings depending on the cleanliness of the water and the sand and the quality of the amenities. Then check whether camping and caravanning is available on or near the beachfront.

Working holidays

Working holidays may sound like a contradiction in terms, but they are cheap and can be great fun. They also offer a good opportunity to get away from it all and contribute to a good cause at one and the same time.

Many farms around Britain offer working holidays with free food and lodging in return for a good day's work in the fields, helping to harvest crops or fruit-picking. For those who want to work in the wider countryside the British Trust for Conservation Volunteers (BTCV) – details in the Downshifter's Directory – organises a wide range of conservation holidays from dry-stone-walling to re-planting hedgerows and ponds at very reasonable rates. Accommodation is often communal but prices are cheap and holidays or weekends such as these are a great way to meet like-minded people.

The National Trust also runs hugely popular working holidays tailored to all ages from 17 to 70. It offers 470 trips throughout the year costing from £55 a week including food and hostel-style accommodation. Participants help with feelgood activities such as dry-stone-walling, wildflower surveying and restoring the grounds of national landmarks such as Fountains Abbey. For details call 0870 429 2428 or browse their on-line brochure at www.nationaltrust.org. Yet another option is the WWOOF – Willing Workers on Organic Farms – which places working holidaymakers on farms throughout Britain and Europe. You will be expected to help out on your host farm during the days but get to stay in basic accommodation for free and eat your fill of organic produce. Some WWOOF hosts welcome children. Visit www.wwoof.org or call 01273 476286. Also overseas, many US state parks have volunteer programmes allowing cost-free camping and camp facilities in return for 20–30 hours' work a week, ranging from flower-planting and mulching to clearing up trash.

Holiday at home

This may sound like another contradiction in terms, but think about it. We don't mean literally stay confined to the house, but use your time off from working or household duties to get to know your locality better. It's much less hassle and requires much less organisation than preparing for a trek abroad. Take time to sit down and enjoy simple pleasures such as listening to music and reading books. Catch up on the gardening you've been falling behind with and the exercise you haven't had time for. Discover, or revisit, local beauty spots, garden centres or wildlife havens. Most cities and large towns now have city farms or nature activity centres on their fringes. Then there are all the films or plays you've been wanting to see, the friends you haven't had time to visit and the new restaurant which you were saving for a special occasion. The week or fortnight will fly by in no time, and you'll feel relaxed and refreshed without having left the comfort of your own home!

Be a green tourist

Now we've given you lots of ideas about how to holiday more cheaply and – we hope – more enjoyably, how about taking a little time to think about the impact your wanderings make? Tourism now ranks as the world's third largest industry and its impact on the environment is enormous and growing. Planes emit far greater amounts of greenhouse gases, per passenger, than any other form of transport and coral reefs are being damaged beyond repair by tourist boats and careless divers. Many beautiful parts of the world have been ruined by overdevelopment, with little of the travel companies' huge profits being ploughed back into the local economy in compensation. But concern is growing about damage from tourism, fuelled by the growth of green consumerism. If you count yourself among the latter, here are a few guidelines on how to choose a holiday which allows you to tread lightly on the Earth.

1: Don't take a mainstream package holiday
They may be cheap, but package tour holidays operate in a cut-throat, cut-price industry where protecting landscapes and beaches from environmental degradation comes close to the bottom of the priority list.

2: Support green tour operators
As an alternative a growing number of travel companies are jumping on the green bandwagon and are offering eco-tourist holidays and/or are making contributions to conservation

efforts either in Britain or in the countries where they operate. Many of these more specialist firms are members of the Association of Independent Tour Operators, which operates a responsible tourism rating system. For the green-minded tourist, AITO's website www.aito.co.uk lists several dozen members warranting two or three stars. For the adventurous, canoeing and kayaking have little environmental impact. Canoeing holidays in two-seater canoes are common in America and Canada, and takers are usually rewarded by coming close to a rich array of wildlife.

While on your travels, watch out for the sale of products made from endangered species, such as elephant ivory trinkets and tortoiseshell jewellery. Consumer power is the quickest way to stamp out such activity and help protect the remaining animals in the wild.

3: Holiday in the UK

Travelling abroad, either by plane or boat, uses large amounts of energy and creates pollution. So the serious eco-tourist should take holidays within Britain as much as possible. And there's plenty to see. Our ten national parks, for example, offer a great variety of holiday opportunities amid spectacular natural beauty. For those wanting to spend their time off in actively green pursuits, there are now lots of opportunities including working holidays and field study tours.

Bird-watching is another activity holiday with a decidedly green tinge. Most specialist firms are conservation-minded, limiting the size of their tours so as not to over-disturb the birdlife and its habitat. They also often hire conservationists to give lectures to tourists.

Making a Better Community

No man is an Island, entire of it self . . .

JOHN DONNE (1571–1631), ENGLISH METAPHYSICAL POET

People power

Life-changing events such as bereavement, redundancy or divorce tend to affect people in one of two ways, in our experience. They can go to pieces, retreat into a shell and just try to muddle their way through the rest of life as best they can. Or they gain strength through adversity, grit their teeth and fight on. In doing so, they can inspire others to do something positive to support others either in their communities or elsewhere. The women of the Rylstone and District WI in Yorkshire posed nude for a fundraising calendar after the husband of one of them died of leukaemia. They raised more than £500,000 for research into the disease and their story was turned into a film, *Calendar Girls*, starring Helen Mirren and Julie Walters, released in 2003.

As mentioned earlier, volunteering – making time to help others – is generally on the decline in the UK. It must be one of the great challenges for politicians of all parties to persuade more people to engage actively in local community life, and help make their streets and neighbourhoods, villages, suburbs and towns better places to live.

Many people feel cynical and alienated from the political process. National policies favour devolving power to the lowest possible level, and yet there is a widespread shortage of candidates standing in local town and parish council elections. The estimated average age of these councillors is 57. How can we tackle apathy and NIMBYism (stands for Not In My Back Yard), and make politics and active citizenship more attractive and relevant to the lives of young people and disadvantaged groups? What can be done to help close the yawning gap between government and the governed? How best are we to build stronger, more cohesive communities?

Creating a favour economy

The regeneration of communities from within is the idea behind time banks, which have recently been implemented around the UK following success in the USA. Law professor Edgar Cahn developed them originally as a way of providing non-medical services for elderly people, helping them to stay living in their own homes and keep healthy. They are based around the simple notion of mutual support – a kind of economy in which favours, rather than money, are exchanged.

The way they work is like this. You 'deposit' the time you are prepared to give in the bank by giving practical help and support to others, but it's not just a one-way street. When you need help yourself – with gardening, or a lift to a hospital appointment, for example – you can make a 'withdrawal' from the bank. In other words someone comes to provide that assistance that you need. Everyone's time is worth the same and the bank is run by a broker who keeps records, links people together and makes sure the giving and receiving is kept in balance. They can help break down barriers between generations – linking schoolchildren with residents of old people's homes – and different social groups.

In September 2002 there were 36 such schemes operating around the country and a further 13 banks in development. A two-year evaluation of UK time-banking schemes was carried out by Dr Gill Seyfang, of the University of East Anglia, funded by the Economic and Social Research Council and Time Banks UK.

Juggling time and money

'Our current definitions of success load aspirations towards money and the market economy, yet having money and little time can lead to a lowered quality of life, stress, poor health and depleted, unfulfilling relationships. Time, put to good use, can refresh the parts that the market economy is not designed to reach – growing relationships, building social networks, and the core economy of friends, neighbours, family, community'.

Source: *The Time of Our Lives: Using time banking for neighbourhood renewal and community capacity building*, New Economics Foundation, October 2002

The study found that time banks were successfully attracting participants from socially excluded groups such as low-income households and those who had little or no experience of traditional volunteering. The main motives for getting involved in time-banking were primarily social (meeting people and making new friends) and altruistic (helping others). Earning time credits – getting someone else's time back in return – was the least common motive for joining.

Some time banks are based around a hospital or a health centre. The pilot bank that has grown around the Rushey Green GP practice, which operates from two sites in Catford, south London, evolved from discussions with patients and users of the practice.

By the end of April 2001 it had 60 members including five organisations, and had clocked up nearly 3,000 hours of mutual support. Among the services rendered were befriending, running errands, giving lifts, woodwork, poetry writing, teaching sewing and the piano, form-filling, fishing and lifting heavy items. The time bankers' ages ranged from 16 to 91. One of the themes is helping elderly people get out into the community and feel they are contributing something useful – not just sitting at home, feeling lonely maybe, and on the receiving end of others' help.

Among the visible successes of the Rushey Green pilot was the transformation of the garden around the main surgery building in Lewisham High Street. The time bank obtained a grant from the environmental charity Groundwork to enable them to replant the flowerbeds with mature shrubs and plants to help attract wildlife. Health visitor Lavinia Johnson described the difference it made: 'The flowerbeds at the front of the building were dismal – full of weeds and rubbish – and they had been like that for years. Then the members started taking care of it. Mothers coming to our clinics often comment on the change, especially the wonderful display of daffodils in the spring. It cheered them up and made them feel better even before they got to see a health visitor or GP!'

There are countless ways of contributing towards a richer, stronger community and many of you will already be doing so. See the Downshifter's Directory for more details about time banks, community development work and volunteering.

10 ways to build a better community

1 **Get** to know your neighbours, if you don't already. Showing a courteous, friendly interest in your neighbour's affairs is not busybodying – it's good citizenship, and the first essential step to becoming involved in your community. At best you will make a new friend by making the first move and at worst you

will get to know your enemy if he or she turns out to be the neighbour from hell.

2 **Join** your local residents or tenants association and see whether there are any skills you could offer to keep the wheels turning. It's a quick and easy way to get to know people in the area and find out what community projects are worth pursuing or setting up.

3 **Stand** for your local parish, town, district or borough council. You do not have to be a member of a political party, nor indeed harbour party-political ambitions. Some of the best councillors sail under their own 'independent' flag.

4 **Plan** a street party to help drum up ideas for making improvements to the area, and identify common interests.

5 **Become** a school governor, or volunteer for hospital or prison visiting.

6 **Buy** and read your local paper to find out what are the burning local issues. You may want to get involved. Write letters for publication in local and national papers – it's an easy way of contributing to political debates at all levels, and you don't have to leave the comfort of your home.

7 **Support** your local theatre or arts group. Even if you are not interested in performing or exhibiting work, you can be helpful behind the scenes.

8 **Become** an adult literacy tutor – help adults who left school without knowing how to read and write: most libraries will have details of local schemes.

9 **Make** better use of a spare room if it is empty for long periods – get in touch with your local college or university to see whether they could use it to accommodate students or visiting youngsters on exchange schemes. If your town, village or suburb is twinned with another overseas, your local council should be able to put you in touch with the local town-twinning organisers.

10 **Consider**, if you have young children or elderly relatives,

setting up a baby-sitting or granny-minding circle, so you can get out more and get stuck into wider community involvement.

PART SIX

Simplify and Save –
50 Life-Changing Tips

- **Give the gift of time** Instead of a costly present, donate your time as Christmas or birthday gifts to busy, stressed-out family and friends. You can be sure a promise to walk the dog or babysit once a fortnight will be gratefully received.

- **Embrace simple style** When clothes shopping, ignore stripes, polka dots and patterns and choose simple colours and classic designs which won't go out of fashion overnight. White, black, cream, grey and camel mix and match extremely well and you can also liven them up with a bright scarf or belt or dramatic piece of jewellery.

- **Indulge in DIY beauty** Instead of booking into a salon for a facial, do your own cleansing, exfoliating (rub vigorously with a warm flannel) and steaming (fill a deep bowl with steaming hot water, cover your head with a towel, lean over the bowl and enjoy). Finish off with a gentle face pack of natural yoghurt containing squeezed lemon juice and put thinly sliced cucumber on your eyelids.

- **Live in the present** Wasting time worrying about things that may or may not happen and over which we have little or no control is a disease of modern life. Try and inhabit every moment as you live it and cut off wandering or negative thoughts as soon as they enter your head (a few deep breaths will help). You'll save lots of time and mental energy if you do.

- **Have a potluck dinner** Hugely popular in the States, potluck dinners are a way of having an informal supper party or celebration without spending a fortune on food and wine. Each guest brings a dish or a share of the drink.

- **Entertain at home** Instead of the ritual Friday night pub crawl, which costs you £50 in rounds, take it in turns with your friends to host a weekly cocktail party. That way you'll only be forking out once every few weeks.

- **Take care of the pennies . . .** and the pounds will take care of themselves. It may be a cliché but no less true for that.

- **Curb your inner shopper** When you see that must-have pair of trainers or beautiful dress through the shop window try walking past and waiting a week before you go back for it. Chances are the urge will have gone.

- **Make active choices not passive ones** Simpler living is all about making choices: about where and how we live and work, how we spend our time, what we eat, where we shop, how we get around. Don't let your life passively wash over you, own it.

- **Know when to say no** Taking on too much is a recipe for stress, tense relationships and a complicated life. Be there for a friend in need; but don't sign up for community volunteering or PTA duties if you can't realistically fit them in.

- **Ignore the phone** Don't be a slave to our instant communications age. If you're too busy to talk, let the message machine do the work. If you're worried people will be offended, drop call waiting.

- **Discover free exercise** Why waste your hard-earned pennies at an expensive gym? Why run indoors when you could do it in the fresh air for free? Why cycle in a room full of sweaty bodies if you have a bike sitting in the garden shed?

- **Pay down your mortgage** If you have any monthly savings, this is a very cost-effective way to use your money. By paying down the interest ahead of time, you could save tens of thousands over the life of your mortgage.

• **Kick the lateness habit** Being constantly late for appointments is stressful, rude and can throw out your well-ordered plans for the day. If the habit of cutting it fine is deeply ingrained, try setting all your clocks five or ten minutes ahead of the real time.

• **Cut down on TV** It may be cheap entertainment but getting too involved in the dramas of made-for-TV friends can distract us from our own lives and loved ones.

• **Don't get hung up on housework** Dirt is unhygienic and has to be kept at bay, but who cares about a little dust? Remember you can reduce time spent on domestic drudgery as well as paid work.

• **Enjoy life's simple, free pleasures** Sit on a park bench, walk in a wood, study the night sky. Watch young children and learn from them.

• **Avoid the upgrading urge** Your video recorder and CD player are only two years old but already you're thinking of buying a DVD player. You are happy with the picture and sound quality you already enjoy and upgrading will cost hundreds of pounds. Why do it?

• **Learn to let go . . .** It's not easy to let go of the trappings of conventional success, especially when people around you still live that way. Try to do it with optimism and enthusiasm rather than regret. Don't think of what you've lost (the fancy car, the second foreign holiday a year): think of what you've gained (control, better health, more time with the people you love).

- **Be idle** According to psychologists, some of our best, most creative thoughts and ideas often come to us when we let our busy, over-heated brains just drift. Time to buy that hammock!

- **Make your own morning coffee** Buying one cappuccino a day on the way to work will set you back £30 a month or £360 a year. And you have to queue for the privilege.

- **Ignore junk mail** If you waste even ten minutes a day reading it, that amounts to an hour a week or 52 hours a year. Put it straight in the recycling bin.

- **Read newspapers in the library** Most libraries stock a selection of national and local papers and magazines. You could easily save yourself £5–10 a week. And avoid piling up old newsprint around the house.

- **Avoid queues** If your schedule is flexible enough, avoid queue angst and save time by shopping at quiet times of day such as mid-morning or late evening. Ordering food, clothes or gifts over the phone, by mail or via the Internet are other alternatives.

- **Start a simplicity circle** Increasingly popular in the States, simplicity circles are mutual support groups for neighbours and friends who want to de-clutter their lives. If you know people who have already downshifted or want to, why not suggest starting a circle to share tips and experiences?

- **De-clutter daily** There's no point getting organised if the mess mountain reappears a week or a month later. Losing or mislaying stuff amid clutter costs you needless time and money buying replacements.

- **Go up the wall!** When you're stuck for floor and surface space, mount shelves, brackets, hooks, rails, fridge magnets for vertical storage. When you run out of wall space, use the ceiling – lengths of plastic-coated wire and pegs – for hanging important bits of paper. Saves you bending to rummage through low-level chaos.

- **Avoid buying dry-clean-only clothes** . . . and view 'dry-clean only' labels with suspicion. Many such items can be machine washed quite adequately, without being wrecked, on low temperatures.

- **Make second-hand your first choice** You can kit out entire houses, wardrobes and garden sheds from good charity shops, car boot sales, second-hand dealers and house clearance operators. If you have a computer, scour eBay for e-bargains.

- **Use local shops and services** Dump your national or global superstore loyalty cards. Local loyalty reaps bigger dividends in the long term, as neighbourhood shops and producers get to know you personally – and the kind of stuff you like and need to buy. Saves on transport costs and traffic rage.

- **Cook in bulk and freeze** Sounds like a lot of faff, but with a well-planned cooking or baking session once a week or month you will save hours of shopping and agonising over menu-planning. Very therapeutic.

- **Get up earlier!** If you get up an hour earlier, you may find you whizz through the chores, get more satisfying things done and feel generally more in control of events.

- **Recycle stationery** Open your mail carefully and re-use as many envelopes as possible. You'll save money and, over the years, a few trees too.

- **Avoid Xmas shopping in December without being a Scrooge** Spread present buying through the year, starting with the January sales to avoid the pre-Xmas commercial madness and consequent pressures to binge-spend.

- **Hit the supermarket after 5 p.m.** Prices on fresh produce are slashed as they approach their sell-by deadline. If you have the storage space, stock up on three for the price of two deals while you're at it.

- **Give door-to-door salesmen the heave-ho** Avoid the hard sell when your defences are down by putting a sticker in the window saying you neither buy nor sell at the door.

- **Use a birthday calendar** Remember special days and anniversaries before the event and you'll be less inclined to spend more on late, guilt-induced olive branch offerings.

- **Learn to haggle** Don't assume the price on the label is sacrosanct – it can be the starting point for negotiation. Traders at car boot sales, junk shops and markets are often open to sensible offers, or a cheery 'What's your best price on this?' Just remember things are worth only what buyers are prepared to pay for them.

- **DIY wall decoration** As an alternative to mass-produced framed pictures, use your own photographs, children's paintings – anything you fancy, to brighten your walls for next to nothing. Beauty, after all, is in the eye of the beholder.

- **Be spontaneous** Your diary is there to support the smooth administration of your daily life, not to enslave you. Plenty of unfilled white space in a diary is a downshifter's badge of honour, not a mark of failure. It means you can act on the spur of the moment as inspiration strikes, and deal with the unexpected with graceful aplomb.

- **Leave your wallet or purse at home** If you don't intend to spend when you go out, just slip a fiver or some loose change into your pocket and leave your wallet, and temptation, at home.

- **Tackle pester power at source** Reduce your children's exposure to the tyranny of TV advertising. Strictly ration TV time, tell them to switch over or press the mute button when the ads come on and, most importantly, give them someone real to interact with – yourself.

- **Make your own greetings cards and stationery** If you have a computer, you can save a lot by personalising your greetings/ notepaper/ correspondence cards etc.

- **Don't be envious** If the grass looks greener on the other side of the fence, it's probably either a trick of the light or Astroturf. If you can find satisfaction in simple pleasures – a good conversation, sharing a home-cooked meal, a walk with your mates, a well-written letter – you'll be the one who is envied.

- **Make time for downtime** It's not selfish to look after yourself and take time out from domestic, family or work duties to do whatever you choose. Don't let anyone make you feel guilty for doing this on a regular basis. If you behave like a doormat, don't be surprised when people walk all over you.

- **Remember happiness is the best revenge** If you're upset or hurt by someone's actions, you'll waste time and energy plotting ways of getting back at them. Don't get mad – get a life.

- **Keep friendships under review** If some of your friends, their problems, needs and endless sagas are taking up too much of your time and energy, gently let them know. It may be hard but sometimes it's necessary. Introduce them to each other – ideally they soon won't notice your absence.

- **Start planning for the hereafter** When preparing or updating your will, write down (and circulate to your loved ones) what sort of funeral you want, the songs, hymns or poems you'd like read, and so on. It'll be a relief to have done it, if not a joy to do. Leaving it to your survivors to sort out what they think you would have wanted will only add hassle to their grief.

- **Consider a green funeral** Take your thrift and your simple living principles unto the grave. A woodland burial in a willow or cardboard coffin is a realistic alternative these days to a traditional one, and it tends to work out cheaper!

- **Be the change you want to see in the world** As Gandhi pointed out, everyone can be a role model for change in their everyday behaviour.

PART SEVEN

The Downshifter's Directory

In this section we feature details of 50 organisations that can offer further information, ideas and inspiration to help you achieve your downshifting ambitions.

Finance

The Co-operative Bank

PO Box 101
1 Balloon Street
Manchester M60 4EP
Helpline: 0870 600 0328
www.co-operativebank.co.uk

This is the banking arm of the Co-operative Movement, founded more than 100 years ago. It takes a robust ethical stand in all its operations – no investment of customers' money in oppressive regimes, the export of weapons to such regimes, in activities that needlessly or illegally damage the environment or companies involved in animal experimentation for cosmetic purposes. It does actively encourage and support organisations that monitor their impact on the environment and that help people to help themselves, such as *The Big Issue*, the magazine that is sold by homeless people, and Groundwork (see below). Above all, it regularly canvasses opinions from customers about what the bank should and should not be doing. It offers on-line banking to transfer funds, pay regular bills, request statements and standing orders. Compared with the main high street rivals, it is small but it is the best known bank that espouses 'small is beautiful' principles. The Co-op's insurance subsidiary CIS offers a range of pensions.

Ecology Building Society
18 Station Road
Cross Hills, Near Keighley
West Yorkshire BD20 7EH
Tel: 0845 674 5566
www.ecology.co.uk

The society was born in 1981 out of concern about the impact of existing lenders' preferences and practices on the environment. In cases where a lot of renovation was required, the lender tended only to release part of the funds needed or even retain the whole advance until the work was completed. This meant that borrowers were often pushed into taking on costly bridging loans and contractors to carry out the work swiftly. The net result of this, says the EBS, was a lending policy that devalued self-reliance, repair and renovation and encouraged the wasteful use of natural resources. The EBS promotes green house-building techniques, energy efficiency and low-impact lifestyles.

Ethical Investment Research Service (EIRIS)
80–84 Bondway
London SW8 1SQ
Tel: 020 7840 5700
www.eiris.org

The ultimate ethical sleuths. Established by a group of Quakers and other Churches in 1983 to help 'socially responsible' investment funds to screen potential investments, EIRIS (pronounced 'iris') provides information rather than makes moral judgements about the companies it analyses. It does the research and lets the individual investor decide whether to put in money or not. It offers services to private investors, independent financial advisers and companies, and produces a quarterly newsletter, the *Ethical Investor*.

Triodos Bank
Brunel House
11 The Promenade
Bristol BS8 3NN
Tel: 0117 973 9339
www.triodos.co.uk

A 'social' bank that only supports businesses and projects that are socially, ecologically and financially sustainable – projects that benefit the community, enhance the environment and respect human freedoms. It offers a wide range of green and ethical savings accounts for individuals, businesses and charities. Recent additions include an organics savers' account. Triodos comes from the Greek word trihodos which means a threefold path – a view of society that emphasises education and culture, human rights and economics.

Work and learning

Better Business (formerly Home Run)
Cribau Mill
Llanfair Discoed
Chepstow NP1 6LN
Wales
Tel: 0845 458 9485
www.better-business.co.uk

A magazine published ten times a year available by subscription only. It aims to bring useful and timely advice and information to the self-employed and small businesses, whether based at home or elsewhere to help them work more effectively and to provoke fresh thinking. How to recover debts, and increase your chances of swift payment, how to find new clients and keep abreast of the latest technology are typical subjects covered. There are plenty of case studies and interviews with people who work for themselves from home, giving their own secrets for success and pitfalls to avoid. Money-saving tips. Also publishes guides on different aspects of running a business.

Crafts Council
44a Pentonville Road
Islington
London N1 9BY
Tel: 020 7278 7700
Fax: 020 7837 6891
www.craftscouncil.co.uk

An independent, government-funded organisation that promotes the contemporary crafts in Britain. The council provides start-up grants for makers who are within two years of setting up a business and whose work meets the scheme's criteria. Every two years it produces a free guide, the *Crafts Map*, which lists craft shops and galleries selected for the quality of the work on display. The council's reference library contains a database of more than 4,000 UK craftspeople. It also sells *Running A Workshop*, a 250-page guidebook on how to set up and run a crafts business, including chapters on exhibiting, selling by commission, selling abroad and promotion and publicity. Order a copy from the gallery shop on 020 7806 2559.

Department for Education and Skills (DfES)
Sanctuary Buildings
Great Smith Street
London SWIP 3BT
Tel: 01345 665588
www.dfes.gov/learning&skills

The department provides factsheets on Training and Skills

Councils, local organisations which provide information and guidance on training schemes and courses such as NVQs (National Vocational Qualifications). Its website also lists NVQ courses available around the country and provides information on apprenticeships and on claiming tax relief on training. If you are not sure which new learning and career path you want to follow, the DfES also funds www.learndirect-futures.co.uk which helps you identify your strengths and match your skills and interests to opportunities in the workplace. Visit the site or call 0800 900 900.

Department for Trade and Industry Work-Life Balance Team
1 Victoria Street
London SW1H OET
Tel: 020 7215 6249
www.dti.gov.uk/work-lifebalance

To promote flexible working practices, the DTI publishes the free *Essential Guide to Work-Life Balance* which advises individuals on different types of flexi-work and negotiating with employers. It also includes many case studies. The publication can be viewed on-line. The DTI work-life balance website also gives information on parental flexible working rights, leave rights and part-time workers rights; links to employment agencies specialising in part-time and flexible jobs; and advice for businesses looking to introduce flexible working programmes.

Flexexecutive
Shropshire House
179 Tottenham Court Road
London WIT 7NZ
Tel: 020 7636 6744
Fax: 020 7636 5627
www.flexexecutive.co.uk

A flexible recruitment consultancy for employees and employers. Advertises management and professional jobs including teaching on part-time and flexible basis. Also offers factsheets on different working practices. Contact the agency by e-mail or phone if you would like to send in your CV.

New Ways to Work
1–3 Berry Street
London EC1V 0AA
Tel: 020 7253 5358
Fax: 020 7253 7263
www.new-ways.org.uk

For 20 years, New Ways to Work has been the leading UK organisation providing advice on alternatives to conventional full-time employment. It advises individuals and companies on flexible working hours, part-time work, job sharing, term time working, career breaks, voluntary reduced work time, sabbaticals and working from home. It also publishes books, leaflets and case studies for media use. Recently, New Ways to Work merged with Parents at Work which campaigns for flexible working options and rights for parents.

Telework, Telecottage and Telecentre Association (TCA)
c/o Alan Denbigh
Nailsworth
Gloucestershire
Helpline (members only): 0800 616 008
Fax: 01453 836174
E-mail: alan.denbigh@telework.org
www.tca.org.uk

Europe's largest teleworkers' organisation. Members include the self-employed, company employees working from home and companies introducing teleworking into their organisations. Membership benefits include a network of 150 telecottage resource centres, teleworker training, lobbying force to promote interests of teleworkers, group discounts on home office insurance, stationery, computer equipment and software, and an advice line. The association also publishes the bi-monthly *Teleworker* magazine and members receive a weekly e-mail bulletin of news and full-time and temporary teleworking job opportunities.

Trades Union Congress (TUC)
Congress House
Great Russell Street
London WC1B 3LS
Tel: 020 7636 4030
www.tuc.org.uk

The TUC has produced a range of publications to help people in flexible or part-time jobs understand their rights and make sure they are recognised. It campaigns against Britain's high overtime levels and produces a free, fortnightly bulletin of news and advice on work-life balance issues. Entitled *Working Times*, you can find it at www.tuc.org.uk/changingtimes. The TUC also advises employers on recruiting and assimilating part-time workers and can advise individuals planning to switch career on which union to join or contact for advice.

Workers' Educational Association
Temple House
17 Victoria Park Square
London E2 9PB
Tel: 020 8983 1515
Fax: 020 8983 4840
www.wea.org.uk

The largest voluntary provider of adult education in the UK, founded in 1903, with more than 650 branches nationwide providing 10,000 courses for adults of all ages and every walk of life. Courses are created in response to local need and often run in partnership with community-based organisations. Part-time evening and day-time classes are offered on a wide range of subjects including history, archaeology, literature, philosophy, visual arts, music, science, health and personal development and information technology. For details contact the national association or your nearest branch office.

Food and growing

Henry Doubleday Research Association (HDRA)
Ryton Organic Gardens
Coventry
Warwickshire CV8 3LG
Tel: 0247 630 3517
www.hdra.org.uk

The national centre for research and promotion of organic gardening, farming and food. A mine of information that all organic gardeners should consider joining or at least visiting at its HQ just outside Coventry. It has an inspiring demonstration organic garden on its 22 acres, an excellent shop selling books, guides and everything you will need to garden without pesticides and chemical fertilisers. It also has a café/restaurant.

Permaculture Association
BCM Permaculture Association
London WC1N 3XX
Tel: 0845 458 1805
www.permaculture.org.uk

The association promotes the spread of permaculture – self-empowerment through living in balance with nature whether in town, city or country – and provides information to raise the profile of sustainable development. The ideas that led to the formation of this educational charity were developed by two Australian ecologists, Dr Bill Mollison and David Holmgren. Groups, projects and associations practising permaculture operate in more than 100 countries.

Soil Association
Bristol House
40–56 Victoria Street
Bristol BS1 6BY
Tel: 0117 929 0661
www.soilassociation.org

Founded in 1946 by a group of farmers, nutritionists and others concerned about the way food was produced. The association campaigns for and certifies organic farming and growing in the UK. It sets standards that producers must meet to be able to label their food as 'Soil Association approved' organic. The association gives helpful advice and information to consumers, and works with government and other bodies to improve the climate for organic farming. An extensive range of books and other publications is available.

Shopping and Household

Fairtrade Foundation
Suite 204
16 Baldwin's Gardens
London EC1N 7RJ
Tel: 020 7405 5942
www.fairtrade.org.uk

The foundation works to secure a better deal for disadvantaged producers in developing countries, and improve employment practices, where necessary. More than 100 coffee, tea, juice, sugar, honey, chocolate and cocoa products carry the Fairtrade Mark, awarded by the foundation, which was set up by CAFOF, Christian Aid, Traidcraft, New Consumer, Oxfam and the World Development Movement.

Good Deal Directory
PO Box 4
Lechlade
Gloucs GL7 3YB
www.gooddealdirectory.co.uk

Updated annually, this book tells you how to find bargains at factory shops and end-of-line sales. More than 3,000 discount shopping outlets are listed on its website. Noelle Walsh, a former editor of Good Housekeeping, is the author. You can buy the book by credit card by ringing 01367 860177.

Traidcraft
Kingsway
Gateshead
Tyne and Wear NE11 ONE
Tel: 0191 491 0591
www.traidcraft.co.uk

Traidcraft is the UK's leading fair trade organisation. Traidcraft plc's sales top £12 million a year and its food products are sold in most major supermarkets. Income from sales reaches poor farmers and craftspeople in 30 developing countries. Traidcraft works with local partners in these countries to fight poverty by developing sustainable trade outlets. Ethical shoppers can also purchase clothes, gifts and food items through its website.

Community

Common Ground
Gold Hill House
21 High Street
Shaftesbury
Dorset SP7 8JE
Tel: 01747 850820
www.commonground.org.uk

It was set up in 1983 to offer ideas, information and inspiration to help people learn about, enjoy and take more responsibility for their local area. Common Ground encourages people to cherish and enhance local distinctiveness whether it is an apple orchard or hedgerow or a town clock. It works with artists and sculptors, and helps to organise exhibitions of creative community efforts such as drawing up parish maps. 'A greater care for local distinctiveness could help us to reinvigorate our sense of domestic attachment and to reweave the local world,' it says.

Federation of City Farms and Community Gardens
The Greenhouse
Hereford Street
Bedminster
Bristol BS3 4NA
Tel: 0117 923 1800
www.farmgarden.org.uk

These farms and gardens are community-managed projects working with people, animals and plants. Operating primarily in urban areas, they give a new lease of life to derelict pieces of land and are run by management groups drawn from the communities they serve. They attract more than 3 million visits a year, raising awareness of agriculture and food production among

273

children who might otherwise know very little about these subjects. Many city farms have shops selling their produce to local people. On a wider social level, they have acted as catalysts in reviving community spirit and activity in areas suffering varying degrees of disadvantage and dereliction. They have provided more than 2,500 training places to adults with learning difficulties.

Findhorn Community

The Park
Findhorn
Forres
Moray IV36 OTZ
Scotland
Tel: 01309 690311
www.findhorn.org

An internationally known eco-village community established in 1962. It holds workshops and conferences on personal transformation and spiritual development through the daily experiences of community life. It welcomes around 14,000 visitors a year from more than 70 countries.

National Association of Citizens Advice Bureaux

Myddelton House
115–123 Pentonville Road
London N1 9LZ
Tel: 020 7833 2181
www.nacab.org.uk

Almost every town in Britain has a citizens advice bureau staffed mainly by trained volunteers who help members of the public who can't afford expensive legal advice. Their expertise covers a huge range of areas including debt, housing and mortgage difficulties, family break-up problems, rights for the employed, the self-employed, the sick and the jobless and so on. The national association's websites (including www.adviceguide.org.uk) provide a wealth of information, and can put you in touch with your nearest CAB. Your local council office or library will also probably have these details.

National Centre for Volunteering
Regent's Wharf
8 All Saints Street
London N1 9RL
Tel: 020 7520 8900
www.volunteering.org.uk

The national centre has been promoting excellence in volunteering since 1973 and helps both individual citizens and employees to get involved in worthwhile activities. It supports the development of volunteering and carries out research on relevant issues.

National Federation of Women's Institutes
104 New King's Road
London SW6 4LY
Tel: 020 7371 9300
www.women-institute.co.uk

The largest women's organisation in the UK with some 230,000 members in England, Wales and Scotland. Established in 1915 to educate women to enable them to provide an effective role in the community, expand their horizons and develop and pass on important skills.

Time Bank
The Mezzanine
Elizabeth House
39 York Road
London SE1 7NQ
Tel: 020 7401 5420
www.timebank.org.uk

The national campaigning body for raising awareness of volunteering via the development of time banks, as described in Chapter 20.

www.renewal.net

This website is one arm of the government's neighbourhood renewal strategy, providing information about what works and what doesn't work in regeneration project work. It also features region-specific guides and pointers to events and further contacts.

Women's Royal Voluntary Service
Milton Hill House
Milton Hill
Steventon
Abingdon
Oxon OX13 6AD
Tel: 01235 442900
www.wrvs.org.uk

Some 95,000 volunteers (13,000 of them men!) help housebound and older people maintain independence and dignity in their own homes, and between them serve up around 9 million meals on wheels a year. Runs social centres and clubs for elderly, disabled and others in need. One of its prime objectives is to provide various non-medical services in hospitals. It runs playgroups in children's wards and crèches in outpatient departments; does flower arranging for patients and operates library trolleys. Helps to organise transport and other support services for people being discharged from hospital.

Environment

British Trust for Conservation Volunteers (BTCV)
163 Balby Road
Doncaster Road
South Yorkshire DN4 ORH
Tel: 01302 572 224
Fax: 01302 310 167
www.btcv.org

BTCV was founded in 1959 when 42 volunteers, including David Bellamy, went to Box Hill in Surrey to clear dogwood and encourage native chalkland plants to grow. Now the UK's biggest practical conservation organisation, with 85,000 volunteers, the trust runs courses, working holidays and volunteer groups. The Natural Break working holidays are focused on learning new skills, meeting new people and saving wildlife. Laying nature trails, clearing ponds and hedge-planting are typical activities. Conservation projects are often within national parks or nature reserves, although trust staff and volunteers also work on improving landscapes in towns and cities. For more on the Natural Break working holidays please see Chapter 19.

Centre for Alternative Technology (CAT)
Machynlleth
Powys SY20 9AZ
Wales
Tel: 01654 705 950
Fax: 01654 702 782
www.cat.org.uk

The best-known green technology public showcase in Britain, CAT offers visitors a wide variety of displays on non-polluting ways of living. These include demonstrations on the use of solar, wind and water power. The centre's office was fitted with solar panels in 1996. Also on offer to individuals or groups are short courses on renewable energy, low-energy building, organic gardening, timber frame house-building, blacksmithing, felt-making and how to reduce your personal ecological footprint.

Global Action Plan (GAP)
8 Fulwood Place
London WC1V 6HG
Tel: 020 7405 5633
Fax: 020 7831 6244
www.globalactionplan.org.uk

GAP has helped thousands of households save money and do something positive for the planet. Its detailed householder programme gives participants practical advice on how to cut down on what they spend and consume. As a result, families throw away a third less rubbish and cut home energy use by 9 per cent, water use by 13 per cent and petrol use by a tenth. Members also receive *Ergo*, a sustainable-living magazine packed with useful everyday tips. The charity also works with education authorities to do green audits of schools and with employers (including British Gas Transco, Nationwide Building Society and

London Electricity) to help employees reduce their environmental impact at work. There are a growing number of volunteer GAP groups in Britain. To find out if there is one in your area, or to start one, contact the GAP office.

Groundwork
85–87 Cornwall Street
Birmingham B3 3BY
Tel: 0121 236 8565
Fax: 0121 236 7356
www.groundwork.org.uk

Groundwork is an environmental regeneration charity which works by developing partnerships that empower local people, businesses and community organisations. Groundwork's 50 local trusts across England, Wales and Northern Ireland help to improve housing estates, parks and other public amenities. Most use volunteers who are looking for a career in environmental management or conservation. To find your local trust, visit the website or call the head office.

Willing Workers On Organic Farms (WWOOF)
19 Bradford Road
Lewes
Sussex BN7 1RB
Tel: 01273 476286
www.wwoof.org

WWOOF was set up in 1971 to help people learn organic farming methods at first hand. Volunteers receive board and lodging and a basic grounding in organic horticulture and agriculture in exchange for a weekend or week's work on a farm or smallholding. Visits are arranged through a regional organiser who puts volunteers in touch with host farms or smallholdings.

WWOOF members can also view details of host farms on-line. Transport can be arranged to and from the nearest train station. Some farms will take children, by arrangement.

Transport

CarPlus
The Studio
32 The Calls
Leeds LS2 7EW
Tel: 0113 234 9299
Fax: 0113 242 3687
www.carclubs.org.uk

Carplus is the network organisation for the UK's 30-plus commercial car clubs whose members hire cars on an hourly or daily basis as needed. Carplus works with local authorities and agencies to support development of car clubs nationwide. Its website lists all clubs nationwide to help interested motorists identify those nearest them. Its lending arm provides leases and insurance schemes for car club companies.

Environmental Transport Association (ETA)
68 High Street
Weybridge
Surrey KT13 8RS
Tel: 01932 828 882
www.eta.co.uk

The ETA is Britain's eco-friendly equivalent of the AA or RAC. Its campaign activities, aimed at generating support and funds for more sustainable forms of transport, include staging Green Transport Week and National Car Free Day once a year. The ETA offers members a full range of breakdown, vehicle inspection and home start-up services. It is also the only vehicle breakdown organisation to offer a rescue service for cyclists.

Living Streets (formerly Pedestrians' Association)
31–33 Bondway
London SW8 15J
Tel: 020 7820 1010
Fax: 020 7820 8208
www.livingstreets.org.uk

Founded in 1929, Living Streets campaigns for measures not only to make walking safer but to make roads less intimidating and more pleasant for pedestrians. It works with central and local government to discourage car dependence, and encourage more people to walk shorter journeys. It also helps communities to lobby their councils for better footpaths and town centre pedestrianisation.

Sustrans
35 King Street
Bristol BS1 4DZ
Tel: 0117 926 8893
Information line: 0845 113 0065
www.sustrans.org.uk

A national civil engineering charity, with 40,000 members, which has built 7,000 miles of traffic-free paths for cyclists and walkers, often by rivers or on disused railways. It aims to increase the National Cycle Network to 10,000 miles, with routes through most major UK towns and cities. For details of cycle routes near you or in areas where you would like to go for a cycling holiday, contact the address above or see the website. Members also receive details of fund-raising and social events and a newsletter.

Transport 2000
The Impact Centre
12–18 Hoxton Street
London N1 6NG
Tel: 020 7613 0743
Fax: 020 7613 5280
www.transport2000.org.uk

Transport 2000 campaigns for sustainable transport, promoting less car use and more use of trains and buses, cycling and walking. Its Living Streets and Home Zone campaigns and Streets for People network help communities work with local authorities to make their streets more liveable and safe with less traffic and lower speeds. It is also developing a Car Free Leisure Network with local authorities to improve non-car access to popular tourist destinations.

Media

Positive News
5 Bicton Enterprise Centre
Clun
Shropshire SY7 8NF
Tel: 01588 640022
www.positivenews.org.uk

For those who are fed up with daily servings of doom and gloom in the mainstream media, here's a quarterly newspaper that reports only good news – mainly about the local, national and international green scene, but also other influences 'that are creating a positive future'.

Resurgence Magazine
Ford House
Hartland
Bideford
Devon EX39 6EE
Tel: 01237 441293
www.resurgence.org

Inspiring bi-monthly magazine covering topics as diverse as ecology and development, culture, art and spirituality.

Holidays and Leisure

Eden Project
Bodelva
St Austell
Cornwall PL24 2SG
Visitor Centre Tel: 01726 811911
www.edenproject.com

Created out of a vast disused clay pit, this is a spectacular show-case for exploring man's relationship with plants and the wider environment. More than 100,000 plants representing 5,000 species can be seen in the two giant conservatories, or Biomes, and surrounding area. Plans for a third semi-arid Biome are in development.

Home Base Holidays
7 Park Avenue
London N13 5PG
Tel: 020 8886 8752
Fax: 020 8482 4258
www.homebase-hols.com

One of Britain's most established house-swapping agencies. Publishes a bi-monthly *House Swappers Newsletter*. Members pay an annual fee of £29 to advertise their home on-line, with photographs, and to access details of homes available for holiday exchanges in Europe, North America and Australasia.

National Trust
PO Box 39
Bromley
Kent BR1 3XL
Tel: 0870 458 4000
www.nationaltrust.org.uk

Founded in 1895 to preserve places of historic interest or natural beauty, the trust protects and opens to the public more than 200 historic houses and gardens. It owns 240,000 hectares of Britain's most beautiful countryside and 600 miles of coastline. The trust and its properties enjoy unique statutory protection. There are 3 million National Trust members and an army of volunteers helps to upkeep its properties. It also runs working holidays for 17–70-year-olds (see Chapter 19 for details).

Ramblers' Association
2nd Floor
Camelford House
87–90 Albert Embankment
London SE1 7TW
Tel: 020 7339 8500
www.ramblers.org.uk

A membership organisation and lobbying group that promotes rambling and campaigns for access to open countryside and protection of rights of way. Local groups organise regular walks and the association offers a wide range of rambling holidays in this country and abroad.

Skyros
92 Prince of Wales Road
London NW5 3NE
Tel: 020 7267 4424
www.skyros.com

A leading European alternative holiday company which focuses on personal development. It offers holidays for 'the mind, body and spirit' on the quiet, beautiful Greek island of Skyros. Guests at the Skyros Centre, in the main village, take part in writers' workshops, personal and spiritual development, painting, health and healing courses. Alternatively you can stay by the sea at Atsitsa nine miles from the village. Courses include wind-surfing, dance, yoga, t'ai chi, dreamwork, massage, theatre and music. Writers' workshops have been led by Sue Townsend, Andrew Davies and D.M. Thomas.

Futures

New Economics Foundation (NEF)
3 Jonathan Street
London SE11 5NH
Tel: 0207 820 6300
www.neweconomics.org.uk

NEF is Britain's leading think-tank on alternative economics, combining analysis with on-the-ground solutions. It introduced Local Exchange Trading Schemes to Britain in 1985 and promotes time banks. It also developed the concept of a social audit of the impact made by companies, which many leading firms now use.

The foundation campaigns for a new economic approach centred on communities and environmental protection rather than consumption and growth. It advises both organisations and individuals on all aspects of new economics. Members pay £25 a year and receive discounts on publications and events.

New Road Map Foundation
PO Box 15981
Seattle
Washington 98115
USA
Tel: 001 206 527 0437
www.newroadmap.org

The New Road Map Foundation is a non-profit-making charity at the heart of the American downshifters' network. It offers its members ways to adopt low-consumption, high-fulfilment lifestyles and produces literature on the links between such personal choices and global survival. Its founders, Vicki Robin and Joe Dominguez, co-wrote the best-selling *Your Money or Your Life* (Viking Penguin, 1992) which has helped hundreds of thousands of Americans to escape from the credit trap.

Real World
Real World
c/o Forum for the Future
227a City Road
London EC1V 1JT
www.realworld.org.uk

A coalition launched in early 1996 by 32 campaign and research groups with more than 2 million members drawn from the environmental, social justice and development fields. Set up to try and force these neglected issues on to the national political agenda, its aim is to work for environmental improvements, the eradication of poverty, community regeneration and the promotion of democracy both in Britain and internationally. Real World has challenged the three major political parties to sign up to a 12-point action programme of reforms. Details of campaigning activities in Britain are available from the above website and address.

St James's Alliance
St James's Church
197 Piccadilly
London W1V OLL
Tel: 020 7734 4511
www.st-james-piccadilly.org

The alliance seeks out new approaches to promoting social justice, economic sustainability and a way of life that can fulfill the needs of everyone in society. It believes that by bringing out the common spiritual and psychological values that motivate everyone wanting to transform the political agenda, it can attract steadily widening support from large numbers of people in all parts of the country. The alliance draws together people involved in politics, economics, ethics, religion, psychotherapy, environmentalism, education, the media and non-governmental organisations.

UK Sustainable Development Commission
5th Floor
Romney House
Tufton Street
London SW1P 3RA
Tel: 020 7944 4964
www.sd-commission.gov.uk

The commission, chaired by environmentalist Jonathon Porritt, advises government and promotes sustainable development across all sectors in the UK. It publishes reports analysing unsustainable trends in consumption and lifestyle and recommending action to reverse them. It also aims to stimulate ecologically sound practice by business and government.

And finally, visit us at www.downshifting-guide.com

Bibliography And References

Chapter 1: Our Consuming Passion

David Boyle, *Authenticity: Brands, Fakes, Spin and the Lust for Real Life*, Flamingo, 2003

Department of Food, Rural Affairs and the Environment, sustainable development website, www.sustainabledevelopment. gov.uk/indicators

Gerard Seenan, 'Pity the Poor, Struggling Middle Classes', *Guardian*, 5 September 2003

Sustainability Ltd, *Who Needs It? Market Implications of Sustainable Lifestyles*, 1995

Chapter 2: Happiness – The Missing Link

Michael Argyle, *The Psychology of Happiness*, Methuen, 1987

Michael Argyle, *The Social Psychology of Leisure*, Penguin, 1996

Mihaly Csikszentmihalyi, *Flow: The Psychology of Happiness*, Random Century Group, 1992

Richard Kinnier et al., 'What Eminent People Have Said About the Meaning of Life', *Journal of Humanistic Psychology*, winter 2003

UK Sustainable Development Commission, *Redefining Prosperity*, 2003

Chapter 3: Mission Impossible: Living Against the Clock

ICM/*Observer*, 'Precious Time Poll,' *Observer*, 29 June 2003

ONS, *Labour Force Survey*, 2003

ONS, *Volunteers, Helpers and Socialisers: Social Capital and Time Use*, February 2003

TUC, *It's About Time*, September 2003

Michael Young, *The Metronomic Society: Natural Rhythms and Human Timetables*, Thames & Hudson, 1988

Chapter 4: A New World View

Simon Caulker, 'Fair Trade and Ethical Consumer Buying Advance in UK', *Observer*, 2 May 2003

Department of Education and Employment, *Work-Life Balance 2000: Baseline Study of Work-Life Balance in Great Britain*, November 2000

European Environment Agency, *Europe's Environment: The Third Assessment*, 2003

Future Foundation, *Complicated Lives*, 2000

Future Foundation Michael Willmott and William Nelson, *Complicated Lives, Sophisticated Consumers, Intricate Lifestyles, Simple Solutions*, John Wiley, 2003

Social Market Foundation, *Consumers Need Help to Plug "Good Intentions" Gap*, 19 August 2003

UK Sustainable Development Commission, *Redefining Prosperity*, June 2003

Work-Life Balance Campaign, Department of Trade and Industry with www.reed.co.uk, *More People Want Flexible Hours than Cash, Company Car or Gym*, December 2002

Chapter 5: Simple Living Through the Ages

Robert Blatchford, *Merrie England*, London, 1894

Dennis Hardy and Colin Ward, *Arcadia for All*, Mansell Publishing, 1984

Ray Pahl, *After Success: Fin de Siècle Anxiety and Identity*, Polity Press, 1995

John Ruskin, *Unto this Last and Other Writings*, Penguin Classics, 1985

E.F. Schumacher, *Small is Beautiful*, Blond & Briggs, 1973

Chapter 6: The New American Dreamers

Duane Elgin, *Voluntary Simplicity: Towards a Life That Is Outwardly Simple, Inwardly Rich*, William Morrow, 1993

Ellen Galinsky, Stacy S. Kim and James T. Bond, *Feeling Overworked: When Work Becomes Too Much*, New York, 2001

Judy Glover, *Arkansas Democrat-Gazette*, 7 October 1986 (first US reference to 'downshifting'.)

Merck Family Fund, *Yearning for Balance: Views of Americans on Consumption, Materialism and the Environment*, 1995

Juliet Schor, *The Overspent American: Upscaling, Downshifting and the New Consumer*, Basic Books, New York, 1998

Chapter 7: The British Way of Downshifting

Australia Institute, Discussion Paper 50, *Downshifting in Australia*, 2003

Ian Christie et al., *Planning for Social Change*, Henley Centre for Forecasting, 1997

Countryside Agency, *State of the Countryside Report*, 2003

Guy King, 'Top Ten Emerging Markets', *Homes Overseas* magazine, October 2003

Dominic Nosalik, *Simplicity*, Datamonitor, 2003

Performance and Innovation Unit, *Winning the Generation Game*, April 2000

Andrew Smith, Speech to Oxford Institute of Ageing Conference, 18 September 2002

Chapter 10: The Gender Agenda

Fathers Direct, *FatherFacts newsletter*, Issue 1

Sue Harkness, 'Working 9–5?', in *The State of Working Britain*, P. Gregg and J. Wadsworth (eds.), Manchester University Press, 1999

James Levine, *Working Fathers, New Strategies for Balancing Work and Family*, Harvest Books, 1998

Article quoting Shirley Conran on motherhood and family-friendly employers. *London Evening Standard*, 7 September 2001

New Ways to Work, *Balanced Lives: Changing Work Patterns for Men*, 1995

Office of National Statistics, *Labour Force Survey*, 2000

R.E. Pahl and J.M. Pahl, *Managers and Their Wives*, 1971

Top Sante magazine, National women and work survey 2001 press release, 15 June 2001

Chapter 11: You and Your Money
Merlin Stone, *Safe as Houses*, Bristol Business School, 2003

Chapter 12: New Ways To Work
Department for Employment and Education (DfEE), *Work-Life Balance 2000 Summary Report*, November 2000

Department of Trade and Industry (DTI) and New Ways to Work, *Essential Guide to Work-Life Balance*, September 2001

Polly Ghazi, *The 24 Hour Family: A Parent's Guide to Work-Life Balance*, Women's Press, 2003

Labour Market Trends, Vol. 111, No. 9, 2003

Chapter 18: Leisure and Pleasure
Audit Commission, *Building Better Library Services*, May 2002

Department for Culture, Media and Sport, *Framework for the Future: Libraries, Learning, Information*, 2003

Chapter 20: Making a Better Community
Gill Seyfang and Karen Smith, *The Time of our Lives*, New Economics Foundation, October 2002

Index

Entries in **bold** denote entries in the Downshifter's Directory.

accountants 169
activity holidays 240–241
adjustment to downshifting:
  for men 123–129
  for women 129–134
adult literacy tutoring 249
advertising 10–11
air travel, growth 8
alcoholic drinks 196
allotments 217–218, 226–227
Amish communities 48
Andrews, Cecile 55, 57
anti-Establishment 32
'anti-politics' 32
Argyle, Prof. Michael 15;
  quoted 228
Aristotle 37
arts groups 249
assets and liabilities 139–140
Association of Independent Tour
  Operators 244

baby-sitting services 250
Bacon, Francis, quoted 173
Balanced Lives 126
BBC Radio, guidelines for writers
  233
Beauvoir, Simone de, quoted 1
Bellack, Paul, story of 97–101
bicycles *see* cycling

bird-watching 244
Blatchford, Robert 40
blood pressure 22
British Library 229
British Trust for Conservation
  Volunteers (BTCV) 315, 241,
  277
budgeting 156–157
buses 205
Butler, Daniel and Bel Crewe,
  story of 70–76

caffeine 196
camping holidays 241
cancer 22
canoeing 244
capitalism 5
car boot sales 211
caravanning holidays 241
cars 8, 29, 48, 148, 200, 201
  maintenance 202
  pooling 203
  relinquishment 206–208
  second 200–201
  see also traffic
Celente, Gerald 48
Centre for Alternative
  Technology (CAT) **278**
challenge 147
Chalmer, Sophie, story of 88–93

charities, voluntary work for 171,
230–231
charity shops 211
chemical household cleaners 215
children, provision for 128–129
China, consumerism 8
Christie, Ian 60
Citizens Advice Bureaux **274**
city versus country 178–179
city farms **273**
cleaning, greening of 215–216
cleaning materials 215
clearing up 209–211
clutter, to be cleared 209–211
coffee 196
Common Ground **273**
communes 183
community enterprises 32
community initiatives on transport 207
community organisations
273–277
Community Transport
Association 206
community work 171, 245–250
compatibility, habits and beliefs
148
composting 218–221, 223
see also information
technology
Conran, Shirley, *Superwoman* 129
conservation holidays 241, 243
consumerism 5, 7–13
reaction against 37–38
contact with people, loss of 133
control 146
Co-operative Bank **263**
Cosmopolitan 129
country versus town 178–179

countryside living 179–180
Crafts Council 266
credit cards 141
Crewe, Bel, story of 70–76
Csikszentmihalyi, Mihaly 16;
quoted 14
cycling 204–205, 206
Cyclists' Touring Club (CTC) 208

debt 141–142
decorating, home 216
Demos think tank 32
diet 28, 193–196
dioxins 29
do it yourself (DIY) 231
dog-walking 233
Dominguez, Joe and Vicki Robin
Your Money or Your Life 54
doors, and energy 214
downshifters:
characteristics 52
groups of 54
list 35
stories of 70–110
downshifter's directory **261–288**
downshifter's garden 222–225
downshifting xi, 32
authors' experience xi–xvi
checklist on 115–116
and men 123–129
origin of term 48
the process 113–122
pros and cons 118–119
psychology 120–121
sharing with partner 134
and women 129–134
draught-proofing 214
drinking alcohol 196
drinks 195–196

see also food
driving, cheaper 200
drop-outs and downshifters 52
Durning, Alan 8

Eating:
    importance 189
eco-banks 211
'ecological footprint' 29
ecology see environment
Ecology Building Society (EBS)
    264
eco-tourism 243–244
Elgin, Duane vii, 36,; quoted 47
Emerson, Ralph Waldo 48
employment:
    hours 23
    UK 3–4
energy-saving 214–216
Energy Saving Trust 215
environment:
    organisations 277–282
environmental politics 32
Environmental Transport
    Association (ETA) 200, 207,
    208, 280
ethical investment 30
Ethical Investment Research and
Information Service (EIRIS) 264
The Ethical Investor 264
European Union, working week
    24
family history 232
family life and men 128
farming, intensive 29
Farrow & Ball 216
fat, in food 194
Federation of City Farms and
    Community Gardens 273

feel-good factor 15
Financial, organisations 263–265
financial planning 156–157
Findhorn Community 153, 274
Fired Earth 216
flexible working:
    full-time 159
    job share 161–162
    part-time 160–161
    teleworking 163–165
    term time 162–163
flow theory of happiness 17
flower-power 43–44
food and drink 189, 190–191
    fast food 8
    growing 217–227
    and pollution 28
    types 192–193
    unusual arrangements 192
food and growing, organisations
    270–271
fruit and vegetables 195
fuel-saving 214
full-time flexible working 159
futures, organisations for
    285–288

Gandhi, Mahatma, quoted 185
garden clubs 226
garden cities 41
gardening 217–227
    organisations 277–280
genealogical research 232–233
Getty, John Paul, jr, quoted 137
Global Action Plan (GAP)
    278–279
global inequality 12
global warming 214, 222
'Good, Tom and Barbara' 43

Good Beach Guide 241
The Good Deal Directory **272**
The Good Life 43
granny-minding services 250
grass 221
green tourism 243–244
Greensted, Richard *Go It Alone* 167
Gregg, Richard 56
Gross Domestic Product (GDP) 28
Groundwork Foundation **279**
Groundwork Trust 230
growing your own 217–227
guidebooks for travel 238

Handy, Charles 166
happiness 14–20
Hardy, Denis and Colin Ward *Arcadia for all* 41
Hardy, Thomas, quoted 217
health 15
'health check' on finance 139–140
Health Education Authority 205
heating controls 214
Henley Centre for Forecasting vii, 59–60
on homeworking 168
on downshifting 59, 60
Henry Doubleday Research Association (HDRA) **270**
holidays 236–244
    cheap 237–238
    green 243–244
    at home 242
    organisations **283–285**
    purpose 142–143
    in UK 244
home:

alternative life-styles 174–175
    and simplification 173–183
home exchange 176–177
Home Run 90, **265**
homemaking 171–172
Horace, quoted 33
The Horse Whisperer 35
hospital visiting 249
hostility to women downshifters 132
hot water tanks 214
house swaps 233–239
household management 209–216
    greening 215–216
    organisations 271–272

immune system 22
income:
    assessment 139–140
    and happiness 14–16
    world 12
Index of Sustainable Economic Welfare (ISEW) 28
India, survey of financial well-being 17
Inferential Focus (company) 48
information technology 163, **270**
insecurity of employment 25, 128
Institute of Management, survey 131
insulation of house 214–215,
intensive farming 29
internet 61
    for holiday swaps 239
isolation of women downshifters 133

Jackson, Joe, quoted 129
James, Andrew and Sophie

Chalmers, story of 88–93
Japan, consumer society 9
job share, flexible working
 161–162
Jodha, N S 17

Kant, Immanuel, quoted 111
Keynes, John Maynard 40
Kissinger, Henry, quoted 152

lagging 214
Laidlaw, Petra, story of 77–82
leachate pollution 212
Leary, Timothy 43
Lebow, Victor 8
leisure and pleasure 228–235
 with a purpose 231
letter-writing 249
liabilities, financial 139–140
libraries, public 229
Life Style Movement 108
lightbulbs, economy 213
Living Green 108
Living Streets 281
local government, standing for 249
loft insulation 214
Lonely Planet travel books 238
lottery, national 65
low energy bulbs 213

Mabey, Richard *Food for Free* 198
McPhee, Euan and Nona Wright,
 story of 107–110
materialism, reaction to 11
media organisations 282–283
men:
 and downshifting 123
 nature, and downshifting 124
Merck survey 1995 51, 53

methane gas 212
Milne, A A, quoted 21
money:
 checking on 138
 handling 137–151
 and happiness 14
Monkcom, Charles 126
Mori polls:
 on politics 32
Morris, William 35; quoted 209
multimedia libraries 229–230
MUMPS (Mature Under-
 Motivated Professionals) 50

National Association of Citizens
 Advice Bureaux 274
National Centre for
 Volunteering UK 275
National Homelink Service 180
national parks 244
National Trust 240, 284
nature walks 240
neighbours 248
New Economics Foundation 28,
 247 285
New Road Map Foundation vii,
 54, 286
New Ways to Work 125, 126, 268
newsletters 47
see also Home Run; *Living Green*;
 Positive News

oestrogens 29
office, gardening in 225–226
organic farms, work on 242, 279
organic food 197
organic gardening 218
organisations for downshifting
 263–288

over-consumption 5
over-population 5

package holidays 237, 240
Pahl, Prof. Ray and Jan 123
paint, non-toxic 216
paper consumption 9
Parents at Work charity 268
parks, enjoyment of 234
part-time work, flexible 160–161
Peacehaven, Sussex 41
Permaculture Association 270
Pet Shop Boys, quoted 123
petrol:
    consumption 201–203
    pollution 203–204
plants 222
Plato 35
pleasure 17
    see also leisure
plotlanders 40
politics 249
    changing 32
    parties untrusted 32
pollution 42, 230
ponds 223
Popcorn, Faith, quoted 11
population 4
'portfolio' working 166
Portwood, James 50
Positive News 282
postbuses 207
poverty, international 11–12
present-giving 232–233
presenteeism 125
Priestley, J B, quoted 59
prison visiting 249
processed foods 190, 191
protest movements 32

Protestant work ethic 38
public transport 205, 206
pulses (foods) 193, 194, 197

rainwater 223
Ramblers' Association 284
reading 229
reading circles 233
Real World coalition 33, 286
recycling 209, 210–211
    see also composting
redundancy:
    authors' x–xvi
re-mortgaging the home 176
renting out accommodation
    182–183
renting property 176
repairs to cars 202
residents' associations 249
restaurants, cut down visits 198
risks, in downshifting 129
Robin, Vicki 54, 286
Robinson, Bill, story of 83–88
Rome, simple life 38
Rough Guide travel books 238
rubbish, types and amounts
    212
Ruskin, John 35, 39; quoted 16
Russell, Bertrand, quoted 239

St James's Alliance 287
Sayers, Dorothy L, quoted 189
school governors 249
Schor, Prof. Juliet 50, 51, 54
Schumacher, E F Small is
    Beautiful 42
Seattle, centre for downshifters
    53, 54
security:

financial, and women
  downsizers 133
  need for 15
self-assessment 154–155
self-employment 166–171
  from home 168–171
  in an office 171
self-help society 5
Seymour, John 71
shared jobs 161–162
sharing accommodation 182–183
sharing gardening 224
Shaw, G B, quoted 70
shopping 143–145, 189–198
  range 190–191
  time to shop 191
shopping and household, organisations 271–272
shrubs 221
simple living:
  history 37–46
  modern pioneers 51–53
Skyros 285
'small is beautiful' 42
smallholdings 226
Socrates 37
soil 221, 224
Soil Association 198, 271
spare rooms 249
spend-spend-spend culture 11
sports 240
Sports Council 205, 240
Springfield, Dusty, quoted 123
status problem for men 128
staying put, housing 175
stress 21–23
supermarkets 190, 191, 197
  own brands 193
Sustrans 281

Taoism 38
tax savings, working from home
  180–182
taxis 207
tea 196
tea tree oil 216
teleworking 163–165
television:
selling 228–229
Telework, Telecottage &
  Telecentre Association (TCA)
  268
Tenants' Association 249
term time, flexible working
  162–163
theatre 249
thermostats 214
Thoreau, Henry 48
time, pressing us 21
time versus money, decision 54
Tolstoy, Leo, quoted 26
town versus country 178–179
town-twinning 249
toxins, reduction 215
Trades Union Congress (TUC)
  269
trading homes 176–177
traffic 26
Traidcraft 272
trains 205
transport:
  organisations 280–282
  savings 199–208
Transport 2000 241
travel:
  cheap 237–238
  by Japanese 9
trees 222
Triodos Bank 265

uncertainty on downshifting, by
women 131
unemployment:
UK 4
USA 49
United Kingdom:
downshifting 66, 59–69
holidays in 244
simple life 38–39
United States of America:
consumer society 7–8
downshifting experience
57–58
groups 54–56
survey of downshifting 51–56
unpaid employment 171

values, table of 12
VAT and working from home
181
Veenhoven, Dr Ruut 16
vegetables 193
voluntary simplicity 45, 53
comparison with downshifting
56, 57
origin 56
survey of 57
'a way of life' 57
voluntary work 171–172
Voluntary Centre UK 275

walking 204–205, **281, 284**
Wall Street Journal 47
waste disposal 212
water 195–196
pollution 29
watering 224
Which Car? 208

Wiggly Wigglers 219
will-making 150–151
Willing Workers on Organic
Farms (WWOOF) 242, **279**
windows, draught-proofing 214
Winfrey, Oprah 47
women:
considerations 129–130
downshifters 54, 131–132
flexibility 131
pitfalls of downshifting 132
resignations common 131
role 128
and work 51
Women's Institute 190
Women's Royal Voluntary Service
(WRVS) **276**
work, under change 30–32
work and learning, organisations
265–270
Worker's Educational Association
(WEA) 269
working from home 180–182
working holidays 241
working patterns, possibilities
153–158
World Health Organisation 193
worms, garden 219
Wright, Nona, story of 107–110
Writers' and Artists' Yearbook,
233, 235
Writers' Handbook 233, 235
writing 233

Young, Michael 21
Youth Hostels Association 241
list of walks 240